BEHAVIORAL FINANCE AND YOUR PORTFOLIO

A NAVIGATION GUIDE FOR BUILDING WEALTH

MICHAEL M. POMPIAN

WILEY

Published by John Wiley & Sons, Inc., Hoboken, New Jersey.
Published simultaneously in Canada.

Limit of Liability/Disclaimer of Warranty: While the publisher and author have used their best efforts in preparing this book, they make no representations or warranties with respect to the accuracy or completeness of the contents of this book and specifically disclaim any implied warranties of merchantability or fitness for a particular purpose. No warranty may be created or extended by sales representatives or written sales materials. The advice and strategies contained herein may not be suitable for your situation. You should consult with a professional where appropriate. Neither the publisher nor author shall be liable for any loss of profit or any other commercial damages, including but not limited to special, incidental, consequential, or other damages.

The charts and information in this presentation are for illustrative purposes only, and are based upon sources of information that Sunpointe, LLC generally considers reliable, however we cannot guarantee, nor have we verified, the accuracy of such independent market information. The charts and information, and the sources utilized in the compilation thereof, are subjective in nature and open to interpretation.

For general information on our other products and services or for technical support, please contact our Customer Care Department within the United States at (800) 762-2974, outside the United States at (317) 572-3993, or fax (317) 572-4002.

Wiley publishes in a variety of print and electronic formats and by print-on-demand. Some material included with standard print versions of this book may not be included in e-books or in print-on-demand. If this book refers to media such as a CD or DVD that is not included in the version you purchased, you may download this material at http://booksupport.wiley.com. For more information about Wiley products, visit www.wiley.com.

Library of Congress Cataloging-in-Publication Data

Names: Pompian, Michael M., 1963- author.
Title: Behavioral finance and your portfolio : a navigation guide for building wealth / Michael M. Pompian.
Description: Hoboken, New Jersey : Wiley, [2021] | Includes index.
Identifiers: LCCN 2021008937 (print) | LCCN 2021008938 (ebook) | ISBN 9781119801610 (hardback) | ISBN 9781119802006 (adobe pdf) | ISBN 9781119801993 (epub)
Subjects: LCSH: Finance—Psychological aspects. | Investments—Psychological aspects. | Investments—Decision making.
Classification: LCC HG101 .P658 2021 (print) | LCC HG101 (ebook) | DDC 332.601/9—dc23
LC record available at https://lccn.loc.gov/2021008937
LC ebook record available at https://lccn.loc.gov/2021008938

Cover Design: Wiley
Cover Image: © sorbetto/DigitalVision Vectors/Getty Images

SKY10025920_032921

Founded in 2016, Sunpointe Investments is a wealth management firm that also creates books and articles. Sunpointe is committed to developing first class research and investing content for individuals and financial advisors. Content topics range from portfolio management to behavioral finance and much more.

For a list of article and books, please visit our Web site at www.sunpointeinvestments.com.

This book is dedicated to my three sons
Nicholas, Alexander, and Spencer.

Contents

Preface

If successful, this book will change your idea about what an optimal portfolio is. It is intended to be a guide to both understanding irrational investor behavior and creating portfolios for individual investors that account for these irrational behaviors. In this book, an optimal portfolio lies on the efficient frontier, but may move up or down it depending upon the individual needs and preferences of you as an individual investment decision-maker. When applying behavior finance to real-world investment portfolios, an optimal portfolio is one that an investor can comfortably live with, so that he or she has the ability to adhere to his or her investment program, while at the same time reach long-term financial goals.

Given the run-up in stock prices from 2009, in the wake of the global financial crisis, to 2020, and the bear market brought on by the novel coronavirus, understanding irrational investor behavior is as important as it has ever been. This is true both for the markets in general, but most especially for individual investors. The intended audience for the book is sophisticated individual investors who wish to become more introspective about their own behaviors, and to truly try to understand how to create a portfolio that works for them. The intention is that it is a guidebook, to be used and implemented in the pursuit of building better portfolios. When considering behavioral finance, investors rightly have questions. Some of these are:

- What are the most common investor biases that cause investment mistakes?
- What are the most impactful biases?
- How do I create the best allocation for me, taking into consideration my behavioral tendencies?

- How do I stick to a long-term investment plan?
- Should I buy individual stocks or stick to a diversified portfolio?

This book will answer these questions. There is difference between this book and my prior books. Most of my prior work has been written through the lens of how financial advisors advise: That is, how financial advisors can work better with their clients. This book, however, is written from the point of view of the investor. The only part of the book that has the financial advisor perspective is the case studies at the end. This is intentional. I want you, the investor, to pretend you are an advisor. This way you can implement the lessons in the book, which will drive home the learning.

In the last 25 years, the interest in behavioral finance as a discipline has not simply emerged, but rather exploded onto the scene, with many articles written by very prestigious authors in prestigious publications. We will review some of the key people who have shaped the current body of behavioral finance thinking, and review work done by them. And then the intent is to take the study of behavioral finance to another level: Developing a common understanding (definition) of behavioral biases in terms that advisors and investors can understand, and then demonstrate how they are to be used in practice through the use of case studies—a "how-to" of behavioral finance. We will also explore some of the new frontiers of behavioral finance, things not even discussed now that may be common knowledge in 25 years.

A Challenging Environment

Investors have never had more challenging times to invest in. Many investors thought they had found nirvana in the late 1990s, only to find themselves in quicksand in 2001 and 2002. And then we had the bull market of the 2000s only to get taken down by the 2008–2009 Great Recession. Today, we have had the longest bull market in history interrupted by the novel coronavirus bear market. In today's environment, as well as in the past, investors are continuously asking themselves:

- "Is asset allocation important or should I concentrate my investments?"
- "Should I invest in alternative investments?"

- "Should I have any bonds?"
- "Should I take the same approach to investing in college money as retirement money?"
- "Should I hold cash or stay fully invested?"
- "How should I modify my portfolio allocation based on my behavioral biases?"

To that end, investors need a handbook like this one that can help them deal with the behavioral and emotional side of investing, so that they can help themselves understand why they have trouble sticking to a long-term program of investing. By implementing the lessons in the book, you too can reach financial goals.

Why This Book?

When I began taking an interest in how portfolios might be adjusted for behavioral biases back in the late 1990s, when the technology bubble was in full force, I sought a book like this one, but couldn't find one. I did not set a goal of writing a book at that time, I merely took an interest in the subject, and began reading. It wasn't until my wife, who was going through a job transition and came home one night talking about the Myers-Briggs personality type test she had taken, did I begin to consider the idea of writing about behavioral finance. My thought process at the time was relatively simple: Doesn't it make sense that people of differing personality types would want to invest differently? I couldn't find any literature on this topic. Fast-forward to today and this is my fifth book, and one that brings together a "greatest hits" of my work.

As a wealth manager myself, I have found the value of understanding the behavioral biases that investors have and discovered some ways to adjust investment programs for these biases. You will learn about these methods. By writing this book, I hope to spread the knowledge that I have developed and accumulated, so that other advisors and investors can benefit from these insights. Up until now, there has not been a book available that has served as a guide for the advisor or sophisticated investor to create portfolios that account for biased investor behavior. My fervent hope is that this book changes that.

Who Should Use This Book?

For individual investors who have the ability to look introspectively and assess their behavioral biases, this book is ideal. Many individual investors who choose either to "do it yourself" or rely on a financial advisor only for peripheral advice, often find themselves unable to separate their emotions from the investment decision making process. This does not have to be a permanent condition. By reading this book and delving deep into your behaviors, individual investors can indeed learn to modify behaviors and create portfolios that help them to stick to their long-term investment programs, and thus reach their long-term financial goals. Financial Advisors can also greatly benefit from the book.

When to Use This Book

First and foremost, this book is generally intended for investors who want to apply behavioral finance to the asset allocation process and create better portfolios for themselves. Some suggestions for when to take it off the shelf are:

- *There is an opportunity to create or re-create an asset allocation from scratch.* Having a large amount of cash can be a tricky thing for any investor. When should I put the money to work? At the same time, the lack of "baggage," such as emotional ties to certain investments, tax implications, and a host of other issues that accompany an existing allocation, is ideal. The time to apply the principles learned in this book is at the moment that one has the opportunity to invest only cash or "clean house" on an existing portfolio.
- *A life "trauma" has taken place.* Sometimes investors are faced with a critical investment decision during a traumatic time, such as a divorce, a death in the family, a job loss, or other similar life event. These are the times that this book can add a significant amount of value to this type of situation by using its concepts.
- *A concentrated stock position is held.* When an investor holds a single stock or other concentrated stock position, emotions typically run high. In my practice, I find it incredibly difficult to get people "off the dime" to diversify their holdings in a single stock. The reasons are well known: "I know the company, so I feel comfortable holding the stock"; "I feel disloyal selling the stock"; "My peers will look

down on me if I sell any stock"; "My grandfather owned this stock, so I will not sell it"; the list goes on and on. This is the exact time to employ behavioral finance. Advisors must isolate what biases are being employed by the investor, and then work together with the investor to relieve the stress caused by these biases. This book is essential in these cases.

- *Retirement.* When an investor enters the retirement phase, behavioral finance becomes critically important. This is so because the portfolio structure can mean the difference between living a comfortable retirement and outliving one's assets. Retirement is typically a time of reassessment, reevaluation, and is a great opportunity for the advisor to strengthen and deepen the relationship to include behavioral finance.

- *Wealth Transfer and Legacy is being considered.* Many wealthy investors want to leave a legacy. Is there any more emotional issue than this one? Having a frank discussion about what is possible and what is not, is difficult and often fraught with emotional cross-currents that the advisor would be well advised to stand clear of. However, by bringing behavioral finance into the discussion and setting an objective outside the councilor's viewpoint, the investor may well be able to draw his or her own conclusion about what direction to take when leaving a legacy.

- *Trust Creation.* Creating a trust is also a time of emotion, that may bring psychological biases to the surface. Mental accounting comes to mind. If an investor says to him or herself "OK, I will have this pot of trust money over here to invest, and that pot of spending money over there to invest" the investor may well miss the big picture of overall portfolio management. The practical application of behavioral finance can be of great assistance at these times.

Naturally, there are many more situations not listed here that can arise where this book will be helpful.

Plan of the Book

The first part of the book is an introduction to the practical application of behavioral finance. These chapters will include an overview of what behavioral finance is at an individual investor level and an introduction to the behavioral biases that will be used when incorporating investor behavior into the asset allocation process. Parts Two, Three, and Four include a comprehensive review, complete with a general description, practical application, implications for investors, a bias diagnostic, and advice. Part Five of the book reviews four Behavioral Investor Types, or BITS, and pulls everything together in the form of case studies that will clearly demonstrate how investors can use behavioral finance in real-world portfolio settings. Part Six covers portfolio implementation: Behavioral Finance Aspects of the Active/Passive Debate, Behaviorally Aware Portfolio Construction, and Behavioral Finance and Market Corrections.

Acknowledgments

I would like to acknowledge all my colleagues and clients who have contributed to broadening my knowledge in behavioral finance and wealth management.

About the Author

Michael M. Pompian, CFA, CFP, CAIA, is the Founder and Chief Investment Officer of Sunpointe Investments, a multi-family office investment firm in St. Louis, Missouri. He was formerly a Partner at Mercer Investment Consulting for 10 years and was the National Segment Leader for the private wealth business where he consulted to the firm's largest family office clients, overseeing $8 billion. Prior to joining Mercer, Michael was a Wealth Management Advisor with Merrill Lynch and a private banker with PNC Private Bank. Prior to these positions, Michael was on the investment staff of a family office. Michael earned his MBA in Finance from Tulane University and graduated from the University of New Hampshire with a BS degree in Management. Michael has written four books: *Advising Ultra-Affluent Clients and Family Offices* (Wiley 2009), *Behavioral Finance and Wealth Management* (Wiley 2006), *Behavioral Finance and Wealth Management, 2nd Edition* (Wiley 2012) and *Behavioral Investor Types* (Wiley 2015). He writes a monthly column for *Morningstar Advisor* and has been quoted in *Money Magazine*, *The New York Times*, *Bloomberg*, and CNBC, among other media outlets. Michael holds the Chartered Financial Analyst (CFA) designation, Chartered Alternative Investment Analyst (CAIA), Certified Financial Planner (CFP®), and Certified Trust Financial Advisor (CTFA). He is a member of the CFA Institute, the New York Society of Securities Analysts (NYSSA), and the CFA Society of St. Louis. He is a regular speaker at family office conferences globally.

PART I
INTRODUCTION
TO BEHAVIORAL FINANCE

In Chapters 1 and 2, Part One of the book, readers will get an introduction to behavioral finance. This will set up Chapters 3 through 22, which review 20 behavioral biases, both cognitive and emotional. Two types of cognitive bias are reviewed in Chapters 3 through 15: Belief Perseverance cognitive biases are covered in Chapters 3 through 8, and Information Processing cognitive biases are covered in Chapters 9 through 15. Emotional biases are then covered in Chapters 16 through 22. After these chapters, the book introduces four Behavioral Investor Types (BITs) and then the BITs are applied in four case studies.

1

What Is Behavioral Finance and Why Does It Matter?

People in standard finance are rational. People in behavioral finance are normal.
—**Meir Statman, PhD, Santa Clara University**

If you are reading this book, you have decided that building the best portfolio for you, your family or your organization requires a solid understanding of human behavior. And the most important human behavior to understand is your own! After all, you need to make the best financial decisions possible and this requires understanding how you behave when money is involved. After advising individuals and families for over 25 years on their investment portfolios, and now running my own investment firm, I have found that understanding and applying behavioral finance to the investment process is the absolutely best way to manage portfolios for long term financial success. It may be counter-intuitive, but unless one has super-human capabilities to know which direction the markets are going all the time, the best strategy for managing a portfolio is to choose a comfortable level of risk and stick with that strategy. The less tinkering the better! Does this mean you don't pay attention to it? Of course not! Investors need to pay attention to the value of assets they own, the structural changes in companies or industries that occur, portfolio rebalancing points, etc.—but the core asset allocation framework should remain the same unless personal circumstances have changed. So why is it so hard for investors to stay invested during periods of market volatility? Put simply, many people don't understand how emotions and irrational behaviors creep into the investment process. This book is all about understanding and diagnosing your own behavior so that you can create the best portfolios and have long-term investment success!

At its core, behavioral finance attempts to understand and explain actual investor and market behaviors versus theories of investor behavior. This idea differs from traditional (or standard) finance, which is based on assumptions of how investors and markets should behave. Investors from around the world who want to create better portfolios have begun to realize that they cannot rely solely on theories or mathematical models to explain individual investor and market behavior. As Professor Statman's quote puts it, standard finance people are modeled as "rational," whereas behavioral finance people are modeled as "normal." This can be interpreted to mean that "normal" people may behave irrationally—but the reality is that almost no one behaves perfectly rationally when it comes to finances and dealing with normal people is what this book is all about. We will delve into the topic of the irrational market behavior; however, the focus of the book is on individual investor behavior and how to create portfolios that investors can stick with for the long haul.

Fundamentally, behavioral finance is about understanding how people make decisions, both individually and collectively. By understanding how investors and markets behave, it may be possible to modify or adapt to these behaviors in order to improve economic outcomes. In many instances, knowledge of and integration of behavioral finance may lead to superior results for investors.

We will begin this chapter with a review of the prominent researchers in the field of behavioral finance. We will then review the debate between standard finance and behavioral finance. By doing so, we can establish a common understanding of what we mean when we say *behavioral finance,* which will in turn permit us to understand the use of this term as it applies directly to the practice of creating YOUR best portfolio.

Why Behavioral Finance Matters

Market research shows that when investors try to protect their portfolios by moving in and out of the market, they limit gains and increase losses. Taking a long-term view is challenging but it is the most rewarding strategy. This is because staying invested helps fuel long-term portfolio appreciation. The primary evidence linking investor behavior to sub-par investment returns is a study done by a firm called DALBAR in Boston every year. This study compares the returns actually earned by the investor to indexed returns and inflation. Investor returns are calculated by DALBAR using the change in total mutual fund assets after excluding sales, redemptions and exchanges. This method of calculation captures realized and unrealized capital gains, dividends, interest, trading costs, sales charges, fees, expenses and any other costs. The most recently available study as of this writing is 2019.[1] That report found that the average investor took some money off the table in early 2018 as the market went up, but was poorly positioned for the second half of the year. The average investor was a net withdrawer of funds in 2018. Poor timing caused a loss of 9.42% on the year compared to an S&P 500 index that lost only 4.38%. Figure 1.1 illustrates the DALBAR data as of the 2019 report. Note the 30-year difference of 6% per annum!

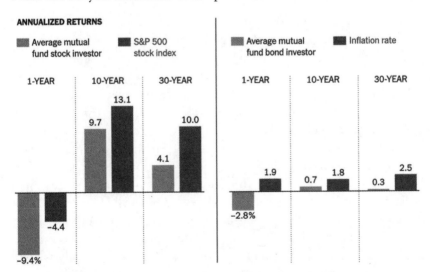

Figure 1.1 Investor Returns from the 2019 DALBAR Report
Source: DALBAR Report, 2019. ©2019, DALBAR, Inc.

---

[1] https://www.dalbar.com/Portals/dalbar/Cache/News/PressReleases/QAIB-PressRelease_2019.pdf

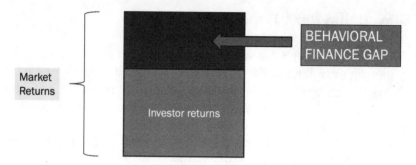

Figure 1.2 The Behavioral Finance Gap

The difference between the returns earned by investors holding a given index versus the returns earned by investors who move their money around in an emotional response to market movements is called the "Behavioral Finance Gap." Figure 1.2 demonstrates this concept. The purpose of this book is to help you minimize this gap so that you can reach your financial goals. MIND THE GAP!

Behavioral Finance: The Big Picture

Behavioral finance has become a very hot topic, generating credence with the rupture of the tech-stock bubble in March of 2000. It was pushed to the forefront of both investors' and advisors' minds with the financial market meltdown of 2008–2009. A variety of confusing terms may arise from a proliferation of topics resembling behavioral finance, at least in name, including: behavioral science, investor psychology, cognitive psychology, behavioral economics, experimental economics, and cognitive science, to name a few. Furthermore, many investor psychology books refer to various aspects of behavioral finance but fail to fully define it. In this section, we will discuss some of the acclaimed authors in the field and review their outstanding work (not an exhaustive list), which will provide a broad overview of the subject. We will then examine the two primary subtopics in behavioral finance: behavioral finance micro and behavioral finance macro. Finally, we will observe the ways in which behavioral finance applies specifically to wealth management.

Key Figures in the Field

In Chapter 2 we will review a history of behavioral finance. In this section, we will review some key figures in the field who have more recently contributed exceptionally brilliant work to the field of behavioral finance. Most of the people we will review here are active academics, but many of them have also been applying their work to the "real world," which makes them especially worthy of our attention. While this is clearly not an exhaustive list, the names of the people we will review are: Professor Robert Shiller, Professor Richard Thaler, Professor Meir Statman, Professor Daniel Kahnemann, and Professor Daniel Ariely.

The first prominent figure we will discuss is Yale University Professor Robert Shiller (Figure 1.3). He famously predicted two of the biggest bubbles of all time: the dot-com bubble and the housing bubble. Both times he published an edition of his book *Irrational Exuberance*, which described and predicted each respective bubble. Perhaps most impressive is the fact that Professor Shiller was one of three people to win the

Figure 1.3 Robert Shiller, Sterling Professor of Economics Yale University and 2013 Recipient of the Nobel Memorial Prize in Economic Sciences

Source: Bengt Nyman/Flickr

2013 Nobel Prize in Economics. The theme of the 2013 award was "Trendspotting in Asset Markets," and the Nobel Committee pointed to Shiller's work in forecasting intermediate-term moves in asset prices. The Nobel Committee was impressed with his work identifying that stock prices fluctuate much more than corporate dividends, and that the ratio of prices to dividends tends to fall when it is high, and to increase when it is low. More recently, Professor Shiller wrote *Narrative Economics: How Stories Go Viral and Drive Major Economic Events*.[2] In the book he gives a groundbreaking account of how stories help drive economic events—and why financial panics can spread like epidemic viruses.

Another high-profile behavioral finance researcher, Professor Richard Thaler, PhD (Figure 1.4), is the 2017 recipient of the Nobel Memorial Prize in Economic Sciences for his contributions to behavioral economics. Thaler studies behavioral economics and finance as well as the psychology of decision-making which lies in the gap between economics and psychology. At the University of Chicago Graduate School of Business, he investigates the implications of relaxing the standard economic assumption that everyone in the economy is rational and selfish; instead he entertains the possibility that some of the agents in the economy are human. He penned a classic commentary with Owen Lamont entitled "Can the Market Add and Subtract? Mispricing in Tech Stock Carve-Outs,"[3] on the general topic of irrational investor behavior set amid the tech bubble. The work relates to 3Com Company's 1999 spin-off of Palm, Inc. and argues that if investor behavior were indeed rational, then 3Com would have maintained a positive market value for a few months after the Palm Pilot spin-off. In actuality, after 3Com distributed shares of Palm Pilot to shareholders in March 2000, Palm Pilot traded at levels exceeding the underlying value of the shares of the original company. "This would not happen in a rational world," Thaler notes. Professor Thaler is also the author of the book *Advances in Behavioral Finance,* which was published in 1993.

More recently, Professor Thaler, is the co-author (with Cass R. Sunstein) of the global best seller *Nudge* (2008) in which the concepts of behavioral economics are used to tackle many of society's major problems. In 2015 he published *Misbehaving: The Making of Behavioral Economics.*

---

[2] Robert Shiller, *Narrative Economics: How Stories Go Viral and Drive Major Economic Events* (Princeton University Press 2019)

[3] Owen A. Lamont and Richard H. Thaler, "Can the Market Add and Subtract? Mispricing in Tech Stock Carve-Outs," *Journal of Political Economy* 111(2) (2003): 227–268.

Figure 1.4 Richard Thaler, PhD, 2017 Recipient of the Nobel Memorial Prize in Economic Sciences
Source: Anne Ryan/Chicago Booth

He has authored or edited four other books: *Quasi-Rational Economics, The Winner's Curse: Paradoxes and Anomalies of Economic Life,* and *Advances in Behavioral Finance* (editor) Volumes I and II. He has published numerous articles in prominent journals such as the *American Economics Review,* the *Journal of Finance* and the *Journal of Political Economy.*

The following is an interesting and insightful excerpt from an interview Amazon.com conducted with Thaler and Sunstein.[4] I particularly like the reference to choice architecture.

Amazon.com: What do you mean by "nudge" and why do people sometimes need to be nudged?

Thaler and Sunstein: By a nudge we mean anything that influences our choices. A school cafeteria might try to nudge kids toward good diets by putting the healthiest foods at front. We think that it's time for

---

[4] www.amazon.com

institutions, including government, to become much more user-friendly by enlisting the science of choice to make life easier for people and by gentling nudging them in directions that will make their lives better.

Amazon.com: Can you describe a nudge that is now being used successfully?

Thaler and Sunstein: One example is the *Save More Tomorrow* program. Firms offer employees who are not saving very much the option of joining a program in which their saving rates are automatically increased whenever the employee gets a raise. This plan has more than tripled saving rates in some firms and is now offered by thousands of employers.

Amazon.com: What is "choice architecture" and how does it affect the average person's daily life?

Thaler and Sunstein: Choice architecture is the context in which you make your choice. Suppose you go into a cafeteria. What do you see first, the salad bar or the burger and fries stand? Where's the chocolate cake? Where's the fruit? These features influence what you will choose to eat, so the person who decides how to display the food is the choice architect of the cafeteria. All of our choices are similarly influenced by choice architects. The architecture includes rules deciding what happens if you do nothing; what's said and what isn't said; what you see and what you don't. Doctors, employers, credit card companies, banks, and even parents are choice architects.

We show that by carefully designing the choice architecture, we can make dramatic improvements in the decisions people make, without forcing anyone to do anything. For example, we can help people save more and invest better in their retirement plans, make better choices when picking a mortgage, save on their utility bills, and improve the environment simultaneously. Good choice architecture can even improve the process of getting a divorce—or (a happier thought) getting married in the first place!

Amazon.com: You point out that most people spend more time picking out a new TV or audio device than they do choosing their health plan or retirement investment strategy. Why do most people go into what you describe as "auto-pilot mode" even when it comes to making important long-term decisions?

Thaler and Sunstein: There are three factors at work. First, people procrastinate, especially when a decision is hard. And having too many choices can create an information overload. Research shows that in many situations people will just delay making a choice altogether if they can (say by not joining their 401(k) plan), or will just take the easy way out by selecting the default option, or the one that is being suggested by a pushy salesman.

Second, our world has gotten a lot more complicated. Thirty years ago most mortgages were of the 30-year fixed-rate variety, making them easy to compare. Now mortgages come in dozens of varieties, and even finance professors can have trouble figuring out which one is best. Since the cost of figuring out which one is best is so hard, an unscrupulous mortgage broker can easily push unsophisticated borrowers into taking a bad deal.

Third, although one might think that high stakes would make people pay more attention, instead it can just make people tense. In such situations some people react by curling into a ball and thinking, well, err, I'll do something else instead, like stare at the television or think about baseball. So, much of our lives is lived on auto-pilot, because weighing complicated decisions is not so easy, and sometimes not so fun. Nudges can help ensure that even when we're on auto-pilot, or unwilling to make a hard choice, the deck is stacked in our favor.

Another prolific contributor to behavioral finance is Meir Statman, PhD, of the Leavey School of Business, Santa Clara University (Figure 1.5).

Statman is the author of many significant works in the field of behavioral finance, including an early paper entitled "Behavioral Finance: Past

Figure 1.5 Meir Statman, PhD, Glenn Klimek Professor of Finance at the Leavey School of Business, Santa Clara University
Source: www.scu.edu

Battles and Future Engagements,"[5] which is regarded as another classic in behavioral finance research. His research posed decisive questions: What are the cognitive errors and emotions that influence investors? What are investor aspirations? How can financial advisors and plan sponsors help investors? What is the nature of risk and regret? How do investors form portfolios? How important are tactical asset allocation and strategic asset allocation? What determines stock returns? What are the effects of sentiment? Statman produces insightful answers to all of these points. Professor Statman has won the William F. Sharpe Best Paper Award, a Bernstein Fabozzi/Jacobs Levy Outstanding Article Award, and two Graham and Dodd Awards of Excellence.

More recently, Professor Statman has written a book entitled *What Investors Really Want.*[6] According to Statman, what investors really want is three kinds of benefits from our investments: utilitarian, expressive, and emotional. Utilitarian benefits are those investment benefits that drop to the bottom line: what money can buy. Expressive benefits convey to us and to others an investor's values, tastes, and status. For example, Statman contends that hedge funds express status, and socially responsible funds express virtue. Emotional benefits of investments express how people feel. His examples are: insurance policies make people feel safe, lottery tickets and speculative stocks give hope, and stock trading gives people excitement.

Perhaps the greatest realization of behavioral finance as a unique academic and professional discipline is found in the work of Daniel Kahneman and Vernon Smith, who shared the very first behavioral finance–related Nobel Prize in Economic Sciences in 2002. The Nobel Prize organization honored Kahneman for "having integrated insights from psychological research into economic science, especially concerning human judgment and decision-making under uncertainty." Smith similarly "established laboratory experiments as a tool in empirical economic analysis, especially in the study of alternative market mechanisms," garnering the recognition of the committee.[7]

---

[5] This paper can be found on Meir Statman's home page at http://lsb.scu.edu/finance/faculty/Statman/Default.htm

[6] Meir Statman, *What Investors Really Want: Discover What Drives Investor Behavior and Make Smarter Financial Decisions* (New York: McGraw Hill, 2011).

[7] Nobel Prize web site: http://nobelprize.org/economics/laureates/2002/

Figure 1.6 Daniel Kahneman, 2002 Nobel Prize Winner in Economic Sciences
Source: The White House

Professor Kahneman (Figure 1.6) found that under conditions of uncertainty, human decisions systematically depart from those predicted by standard economic theory. Kahneman, together with Amos Tversky (deceased in 1996), formulated prospect theory. An alternative to standard models, prospect theory provides a better account for observed behavior and is discussed at length in later chapters. Kahneman also discovered that human judgment may take heuristic shortcuts that systematically diverge from basic principles of probability. His work has inspired a new generation of research employing insights from cognitive psychology to enrich financial and economic models.

Another notable figure is Professor Dan Ariely (Figure 1.7). Professor Ariely is the James B. Duke Professor of Psychology and Behavioral Economics at Duke University and a founding member of the Center for Advanced Hindsight. He does research in behavioral economics on the irrational ways people behave. His immersive introduction to irrationality took place as he overcame injuries sustained in an explosion. He began researching ways to better deliver painful and unavoidable treatments to patients. Ariely became engrossed with the idea that we repeatedly and predictably make the wrong decisions in many aspects of our lives, and that research could help change some of these patterns.

Figure 1.7 Professor Dan Ariely, James B. Duke Professor of Marketing
Source: Yael Zur, for Tel Aviv University Alumni Organization, https://commons.wikimedia
.org/wiki/File:Dan_Ariely_January_2019.jpg. CC BY-SA 4.0.

His works include *Irrationally Yours, Predictably Irrational, The Upside of
Irrationality, The (Honest) Truth About Dishonesty*, the movie *Dishonesty* and
the card game *Irrational Game*. These works describe his research findings in
non-academic terms, so that more people will discover the excitement of
behavioral economics and use some of the insights to enrich their own lives.

Behavioral Finance Micro versus Behavioral Finance Macro

As we have observed, behavioral finance models and interprets phenomena ranging from individual investor conduct to market-level outcomes.
Therefore, it is a difficult subject to define. For practitioners and investors reading this book, this is a major problem, because our goal is to
develop a common vocabulary so that we can apply behavioral finance.
For purposes of this book, we adopt an approach favored by traditional
economics textbooks; we break our topic down into two subtopics:
behavioral finance micro and behavioral finance macro.

1. Behavioral finance micro (BFMI) examines behaviors or biases of
   individual investors that distinguish them from the rational actors
   envisioned in classical economic theory.

2. Behavioral finance macro (BFMA) detects and describe anomalies in the efficient market hypothesis that behavioral models may explain.

Each of the two subtopics of behavioral finance corresponds to a distinct set of issues within the standard finance versus behavioral finance discussion. With regard to BFMA, the debate asks: Are markets "efficient," or are they subject to behavioral effects? With regard to BFMI, the debate asks: Are individual investors perfectly rational, or can cognitive and emotional errors impact their financial decisions? These questions are examined in the next section of this chapter; but to set the stage for the discussion, it is critical to understand that much of economic and financial theory is based on the notion that individuals act rationally and consider all available information in the decision-making process. In academic studies, researchers have documented abundant evidence of irrational behavior and repeated errors in judgment by adult human subjects.

Finally, one last thought before moving on. It should be noted that there is an entire body of information available on what the popular press has termed the *psychology of money*. This subject involves individuals' relationship with money—how they spend it, how they feel about it, and how they use it. There are many useful books in this area; however, this book will not focus on these topics, it will focus on building better portfolios.

Standard Finance versus Behavioral Finance

This section reviews two basic concepts in standard finance that behavioral finance disputes: rational markets and the rational economic man. It also covers the basis on which behavioral finance proponents challenge each tenet and discusses some evidence that has emerged in favor of the behavioral approach.

Overview

On Monday, October 18, 2004, a significant but mostly unnoticed article appeared in the *Wall Street Journal*. Eugene Fama, one of the leading scholars of the efficient market school of financial thought, was cited admitting that stock prices could become "somewhat irrational."[8] Imagine a renowned and rabid Boston Red Sox fan proposing that Fenway Park be renamed Mariano Rivera Stadium (after the outstanding New York Yankees pitcher), and you may begin to grasp the gravity of Fama's concession. The development raised eyebrows and pleased many behavioralists. (Fama's paper "Market Efficiency, Long-Term Returns, and Behavioral Finance" noting this concession at the Social Science Research Network is one of the most popular investment downloads on the web site.) The *Journal* article also featured remarks by Roger Ibbotson, founder of Ibbotson Associates: "There is a shift taking place," Ibbotson observed. "People are recognizing that markets are less efficient than we thought."[9]

As Meir Statman eloquently put it, "Standard finance is the body of knowledge built on the pillars of the arbitrage principles of Miller and Modigliani, the portfolio principles of Markowitz, the capital asset pricing theory of Sharpe, Lintner, and Black, and the option-pricing theory of Black, Scholes, and Merton."[10] Standard finance theory is designed to provide mathematically elegant explanations for financial questions that, when posed in real life, are often complicated by imprecise, inelegant conditions. The standard finance approach relies on a set of assumptions that oversimplify reality. For example, embedded within standard finance is the notion of *Homo economicus,* or rational economic man. It prescribes that humans make perfectly rational economic decisions at all times. Standard finance, basically, is built on rules about how investors "should" behave, rather than on principles describing how they actually behave. Behavioral finance attempts to identify and learn from the human psychological phenomena at work in financial markets and within individual investors. Standard finance grounds its assumptions in idealized financial behavior; behavioral finance grounds its assumptions in observed financial behavior.

---

[8] Jon E. Hilsenrath, "Belief in Efficient Valuation Yields Ground to Role of Irrational Investors: Mr. Thaler Takes on Mr. Fama," *Wall Street Journal,* October 18, 2004.

[9] Jon E. Hilsenrath, "Belief in Efficient Valuation Yields Ground to Role of Irrational Investors: Mr. Thaler Takes on Mr. Fama," *Wall Street Journal,* October 18, 2004.

[10] Meir Statman, "Behavioral Finance: Past Battles and Future Engagements," *Financial Analysts Journal* 55(6) (November/December 1999): 18–27.

Efficient Markets versus Irrational Markets

During the 1970s, the standard finance theory of market efficiency became the model of market behavior accepted by the majority of academics and a good number of professionals. The efficient market hypothesis had matured in the previous decade, stemming from the doctoral dissertation of Eugene Fama. Fama persuasively demonstrated that in a securities market populated by many well-informed investors, investments will be appropriately priced and will reflect all available information. There are three forms of the efficient market hypothesis:

1. The "Weak" form contends that all past market prices and data are fully reflected in securities prices; that is, technical analysis is of little or no value.
2. The "Semi-strong" form contends that all publicly available information is fully reflected in securities prices; that is, fundamental analysis is of no value.
3. The "Strong" form contends that all information is fully reflected in securities prices; that is, insider information is of no value.

If a market is efficient, then no amount of information or rigorous analysis can be expected to result in outperformance of a selected benchmark. An efficient market can basically be defined as a market wherein large numbers of rational investors act to maximize profits in the direction of individual securities. A key assumption is that relevant information is freely available to all participants. This competition among market participants results in a market wherein, at any given time, prices of individual investments reflect the total effects of all information, including information about events that have already happened, and events that the market expects to take place in the future. In sum, at any given time in an efficient market, the price of a security will match that security's intrinsic value.

At the center of this market efficiency debate are the actual portfolio managers who manage investments. Some of these managers are fervently passive, believing that the market is too efficient to "beat"; some are active managers, believing that the right strategies can consistently generate alpha (alpha is performance above a selected benchmark). In reality, active managers have a hard time beating their benchmarks. This may explain why the popularity of exchange-traded funds (ETFs) has exploded and why venture capitalists are now supporting new ETF companies, many of which are offering a variation on the basic ETF theme.

The implications of the efficient market hypothesis are far-reaching. Most individuals who trade stocks and bonds do so under the assumption that the securities they are buying (selling) are worth more (less) than the prices that they are paying. If markets are truly efficient and current prices fully reflect all pertinent information, then trading securities in an attempt to surpass a benchmark is a game of luck, not skill.

The market efficiency debate has inspired literally thousands of studies attempting to determine whether specific markets are in fact "efficient." Many studies do indeed point to evidence that supports the efficient market hypothesis. Researchers have documented numerous, persistent anomalies, however, that contradict the efficient market hypothesis. There are three main types of market anomalies: Fundamental Anomalies, Technical Anomalies, and Calendar Anomalies.

Fundamental Anomalies

Irregularities that emerge when a stock's performance is considered in light of a fundamental assessment of the stock's value are known as fundamental anomalies. Many people, for example, are unaware that value investing—one of the most popular and effective investment methods—is based on fundamental anomalies in the efficient market hypothesis. There is a large body of evidence documenting that investors consistently overestimate the prospects of growth companies and underestimate the value of out-of-favor companies.

One example concerns stocks with low price-to-book-value (P/B) ratios. Eugene Fama and Kenneth French performed a study of low price-to-book-value ratios that covered the period between 1963 and 1990.[11] The study considered all equities listed on the New York Stock Exchange (NYSE), the American Stock Exchange (AMEX), and the Nasdaq. The stocks were divided into 10 groups by book/market and were reranked annually. The lowest book/market stocks outperformed the highest book/market stocks 21.4 percent to 8 percent, with each decile performing more poorly than the previously ranked, higher-ratio decile. Fama and French also ranked the deciles by beta and found that the value stocks posed lower risk and that the growth stocks had the highest risk. Another famous value investor, David Dreman, found that

---

[11] Eugene Fama and Kenneth French, "The Cross-Section of Expected Stock Returns," *Journal of Finance* 47(2) (1992): 427–465.

for the 25-year period ending in 1994, the lowest 20 percent P/B stocks (quarterly adjustments) significantly outperformed the market; the market, in turn, outperformed the 20 percent highest P/B of the largest 1,500 stocks on Compustat.[12]

Securities with low price-to-sales ratios also often exhibit performance that is fundamentally anomalous. Numerous studies have shown that low P/B is a consistent predictor of future value. In *What Works on Wall Street,* however, James P. O'Shaughnessy demonstrated that stocks with low price-to-sales ratios outperform markets in general and also outperform stocks with high price-to-sales ratios. He believes that the price/sales ratio is the strongest single determinant of excess return.[13]

Low price-to-earnings ratio (P/E) is another attribute that tends to anomalously correlate with outperformance. Numerous studies, including David Dreman's work, have shown that low P/E stocks tend to outperform both high P/E stocks and the market in general.[14]

Ample evidence also indicates that stocks with high dividend yields tend to outperform others. The Dow Dividend Strategy counsels purchasing the 10 highest-yielding Dow stocks.

Technical Anomalies

Another major debate in the investing world revolves around whether past securities prices can be used to predict future securities prices. "Technical analysis" encompasses a number of techniques that attempt to forecast securities prices by studying past prices. Sometimes, technical analysis reveals inconsistencies with respect to the efficient market hypothesis; these are technical anomalies. Common technical analysis strategies are based on relative strength and moving averages, as well as on support and resistance. While a full discussion of these strategies would prove too intricate for our purposes, there are many excellent books on the subject of technical analysis. In general, the majority of research-focused technical analysis trading methods (and, therefore, by extension, the weak-form efficient market hypothesis) finds that prices adjust rapidly in response to new stock market information and that technical analysis techniques are not likely to provide any advantage to

---

[12] Dream Value Management web site: www.dreman.com/

[13] James O'Shaughnessy, *What Works on Wall Street* (New York: McGraw-Hill Professional, 2005).

[14] Dream Value Management web site: www.dreman.com/

investors who use them. However, proponents continue to argue the validity of certain technical strategies.

Calendar Anomalies

One calendar anomaly is known as "The January Effect." Historically, stocks in general and small stocks in particular have delivered abnormally high returns during the month of January. Robert Haugen and Philippe Jorion, two researchers on the subject, note that "the January Effect is, perhaps, the best-known example of anomalous behavior in security markets throughout the world."[15] The January Effect is particularly illuminating because it hasn't disappeared, despite being well known for 25 years (according to arbitrage theory, anomalies should disappear as traders attempt to exploit them in advance).

The January Effect is attributed to stocks rebounding following year-end tax selling. Individual stocks depressed near year-end are more likely to be sold for tax-loss harvesting. Some researchers have also begun to identify a "December Effect," which stems both from the requirement that many mutual funds report holdings as well as from investors buying in advance of potential January increases.

Additionally, there is a Turn-of-the-Month Effect. Studies have shown that stocks show higher returns on the last and on the first four days of each month relative to the other days. Frank Russell Company examined returns of the Standard & Poor's (S&P) 500 over a 65-year period and found that U.S. large-cap stocks consistently generate higher returns at the turn of the month.[16] Some believe that this effect is due to end-of-month cash flows (salaries, mortgages, credit cards, etc.). Chris Hensel and William Ziemba found that returns for the turn of the month consistently and significantly exceeded averages during the interval from 1928 through 1993 and "that the total return from the S&P 500 over this sixty-five-year period was received mostly during the turn of the month."[17] The study implies that investors making regular purchases may benefit by scheduling those purchases prior to the turn of the month.

---

[15] Robert Haugen and Philippe Jorion, "The January Effect: Still There after All These Years," *Financial Analysts Journal* 52(1) (January–February 1996): 27–31.

[16] Russell Investment Group web site: www.russell.com/us/education_center/

[17] Chris R. Hensel and William T. Ziemba, "Investment Results from Exploiting Turn-of-the-Month Effects," *Journal of Portfolio Management* 22(3) (Spring 1996): 17–23.

Validity exists in both the efficient market and the anomalous market theories. In reality, markets are neither perfectly efficient nor completely anomalous. Market efficiency is not black or white but rather, varies by degrees of gray, depending on the market in question. In markets exhibiting substantial inefficiency, savvy investors can strive to outperform less savvy investors. Many believe that large-capitalization stocks, such as GE and Microsoft, tend to be very informative and efficient stocks but that small-capitalization stocks and international stocks are less efficient, creating opportunities for outperformance. Real estate, while traditionally an inefficient market, has become more transparent and, there are REIT index products for gaining direct market exposure. Finally, the venture capital market, lacking fluid and continuous prices, is considered to be less efficient due to information asymmetries between players.

Rational Economic Man versus Behaviorally Biased Man

Stemming from neoclassical economics, Homo economicus is a simple model of human economic behavior, which assumes that principles of perfect self-interest, perfect rationality, and perfect information govern economic decisions by individuals. Like the efficient market hypothesis, Homo economicus is a tenet that economists uphold with varying degrees of stringency. Some have adopted it in a semi-strong form; this version does not see rational economic behavior as perfectly predominant but still assumes an abnormally high occurrence of rational economic traits. Other economists support a weak form of Homo economicus, in which the corresponding traits exist but are not strong. All of these versions share the core assumption that humans are "rational maximizers" who are purely self-interested and make perfectly rational economic decisions. Economists like to use the concept of the rational economic man for two primary reasons:

1. Homo economicus makes economic analysis relatively simple. Naturally, one might question how useful such a simple model can be.
2. Homo economicus allows economists to quantify their findings, making their work more elegant and easier to digest. If humans are perfectly rational, possessing perfect information and perfect self-interest, then perhaps their behavior can be quantified.

Most criticisms of Homo economicus proceed by challenging the bases for these three underlying assumptions—perfect rationality, perfect self-interest, and perfect information.

1. Perfect rationality. When humans are rational, they have the ability to reason and to make beneficial judgments. However, rationality is not the sole driver of human behavior. In fact, it may not even be the primary driver, as many psychologists believe that the human intellect is actually subservient to human emotion. They contend, therefore, that human behavior is less the product of logic than of subjective impulses, such as fear, love, hate, pleasure, and pain. Humans use their intellect only to achieve or to avoid these emotional outcomes.

2. Perfect self-interest. Many studies have shown that people are not perfectly self-interested. If they were, philanthropy would not exist. Religions prizing selflessness, sacrifice, and kindness to strangers would also be unlikely to prevail as they have over centuries. Perfect self-interest would preclude people from performing such unselfish deeds as volunteering, helping the needy, or serving in the military. It would also rule out self-destructive behavior, such as suicide, alcoholism, and substance abuse.

3. Perfect information. Some people may possess perfect or near-perfect information on certain subjects; a doctor or a dentist, one would hope, is impeccably versed in his or her field. It is impossible, however, for every person to enjoy perfect knowledge of every subject. In the world of investing, there is nearly an infinite amount to know and learn; and even the most successful investors don't master all disciplines.

Many economic decisions are made in the absence of perfect information. For instance, some economic theories assume that people adjust their buying habits based on the Federal Reserve's monetary policy. Naturally, some people know exactly where to find the Fed data, how to interpret it, and how to apply it; but many people don't know or care who or what the Federal Reserve is. Considering that this inefficiency affects millions of people, the idea that all financial actors possess perfect information becomes implausible.

Again, as with market efficiency, human rationality rarely manifests in black or white absolutes. It is better modeled across a spectrum of gray. People are neither perfectly rational nor perfectly irrational; they possess diverse combinations of rational and irrational characteristics, and benefit from different degrees of enlightenment with respect to different issues.

2

Introduction
to Behavioral Biases

Nothing in life is quite as important as you think it is while you're thinking about it.
—Daniel Kahneman

Introduction

In order to create your best portfolio, it is essential that you obtain an understanding of the irrational behaviors that you have—or be able to recognize the biases of others that may be involved in your investment decision-making process. Numerous research studies have shown that when people are faced with complex decision-making problems that demand substantial time and cognitive decision-making requirements, they have difficulty devising a rational approach to developing and analyzing a proper course of action. This problem is exacerbated by the fact that many consumers need to contend with a potential overload of information to process. Have you walked down the shampoo aisle lately? Way too many choices—how do you pick? And this is one of the easier decisions we face! When it comes to our money, it becomes even more complicated. For more meaningful decisions, people don't systematically describe problems, record necessary data, and/or synthesize information to create rules for making decisions, which is really the best way to make complex decisions. Instead, people usually follow a more subjective path of reasoning to determine a course of action consistent with their desired outcome or general preferences.

Individuals make decisions, although typically suboptimal ones, by simplifying the choices presented to them, typically using a subset of the information available, and discarding some (usually complicated but potentially good) alternatives to get down to a more manageable number. They are content to find a solution that is "good enough" rather than arriving at the optimal decision. In doing so, they may (unintentionally) bias the decision-making process. These biases may lead to irrational behaviors and flawed decisions. In the investment realm, this happens a lot; many researchers have documented numerous biases that investors have. This chapter will introduce these biases, which we will review in the coming chapters, and highlight the importance of understanding them and dealing with them before they have a chance to negatively impact the investment decision-making process.

Behavioral Biases Defined

The dictionary defines a "bias" in several different ways, including: (a) a statistical sampling or testing error caused by systematically favoring some outcomes over others; (b) a preference or an inclination, especially one that inhibits impartial judgment; (c) an inclination or prejudice in favor of a particular viewpoint; and (d) an inclination of temperament or outlook, especially, a personal and sometimes unreasoned judgment. In this book, we are naturally concerned with biases that cause irrational financial decisions due to either: (1) faulty cognitive reasoning or (2) reasoning influenced by emotions, which can also be considered feelings, or, unfortunately, due to both. The first dictionary definition (a) of bias is consistent with faulty *cognitive* reasoning or thinking, while (b), (c), and (d) are more consistent with impaired reasoning influenced by feelings or *emotion*.

Behavioral biases are defined, essentially, the same way as systematic errors in judgment. Researchers distinguish a long list of specific biases and have applied over 100 of these to individual investor behaviors in recent studies. When one considers the derivative and the undiscovered biases awaiting application in personal finance, the list of systematic investor errors seems very long indeed. More brilliant research seeks to categorize these biases according to a meaningful framework. Some authors refer to biases as heuristics (rules of thumb), while others call them beliefs, judgments, or preferences. Psychologists' factors include cognitive information processing shortcuts or heuristics, memory errors, emotional and/or motivational factors, and social influences such as family upbringing or societal culture. Some biases identified by psychologists are understood in relation to human needs such as those identified by Maslow—physiological, safety, social, esteem, and self-actualizing. In satisfying these needs, people will generally attempt to avoid pain and seek pleasure. The avoidance of pain can be as subtle as refusing to acknowledge mistakes in order to maintain a positive self-image. The biases that help to avoid pain and instead produce pleasure may be classified as emotional. Other biases are attributed by psychologists to the particular way the brain perceives, forms memories, and makes judgments; the inability to do complex mathematical calculations, such as updating probabilities; and the processing and filtering of information.

This sort of bias taxonomy is helpful as an underlying theory about why and how people operate under bias, but no universal theory has been developed (yet). Instead of a universal theory of investment behavior, behavioral finance research relies on a broad collection of evidence pointing to the ineffectiveness of human decision making in various economic decision-making circumstances.

Why Understanding and Identifying Behavioral Biases Is Crucial

By understanding the effects that behavioral biases have on the investment process, investors may be able to significantly improve their economic outcomes and attain stated financial objectives. As noted in Chapter 1, during my 30+ year career advising clients, I have found that recognizing and managing the most frequently occurring behavioral biases is crucial to obtaining financial success. For many years I have had my "Top 3" most common behavioral biases—Loss Aversion, Confirmation and Recency biases. Coincidentally, a recent study by Charles Schwab confirms my Top 3, albeit in a slightly different order as can be seen in Figure 2.1 which illustrates how often financial advisors see each bias in the clients they serve. If you are short on time, and you want to only review the most common biases, skip ahead to the chapters containing Loss Aversion, Confirmation, and Recency biases.

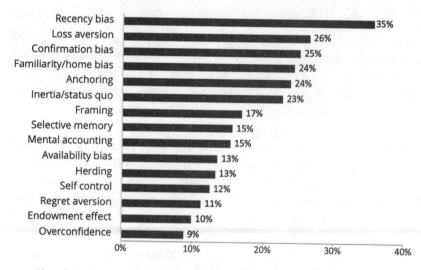

Figure 2.1 Most Significant Behavioral Biases Affecting Client Investment Decisions 2019

Source: Charles Schwab

In my experience, simply identifying a behavioral bias at the right time can save investors from potential financial disaster. During my 30+, spanning numerous economic meltdowns, including but not limited to 1987 (my first year in the business), 1998, 2001, 2008–2009, 2018, and 2020, I've talked many of my clients "down from the ledge" and out of selling their risky assets at the wrong time due to irrational panic behavior. In fact, many of my long-time clients are now used to volatility and do not panic. They look at market drops as buying opportunities. This behavior-modifying advice has helped investors to reach their financial goals. In other cases, I was able to identify a behavioral bias or a group of biases and decided to adapt to the biased behavior so that overall financial decisions improved and the most appropriate portfolios were built—that is, one the investors could stick to over time. It is crucial for you to understand how you make decision to build the best portfolio for you. For example, some investors have a gambling instinct, or want to take risks with some of their capital. My advice in many of these cases is to carve out a small percentage of the portfolio for risky bets, leaving the vast majority of wealth in a prudent, well-organized portfolio. In short, knowledge of the biases reviewed in this book and the modification of or adaption to irrational behavior may lead to superior results.

How to Identify Behavioral Biases

Biases can be diagnosed by means of a specific series of questions. In this book, Chapters 3 through 22 contain a list of diagnostic questions to determine susceptibility to each bias. In addition, a case-study approach is used to illustrate susceptibility to biases is given with advice on how to build portfolios. In either case, investors who wish to incorporate behavioral analysis into their portfolio management practices will need to administer diagnostic "tests" with utmost discretion, especially at the outset of a relationship. When one becomes very good at diagnosing irrational behavior, it can be done without fanfare or much notice. As one gets to know their biases, better portfolio outcomes are the result.

Categorization of Behavioral Biases

In its simplest form, cognitive biases are those biases based on faulty cognitive reasoning (cognitive errors), while emotional biases are those based on reasoning influenced by feelings or emotions. Cognitive errors stem from basic statistical, information processing, or memory errors; cognitive errors may be considered to be the result of faulty reasoning. Emotional biases stem from impulse or intuition; emotional biases may be considered to result from reasoning influenced by feelings. Behavioral biases, regardless of source, may cause decisions to deviate from the assumed rational decisions of traditional finance. A more elaborate distinction between cognitive and emotional biases is made in the next section.

Differences between Cognitive and Emotional Biases

In this book, behavioral biases are classified as either cognitive or emotional biases, not only because the distinction is straightforward but also because the cognitive-emotional breakdown provides a useful framework for understanding how to effectively deal with them in practice. I recommend thinking about investment decision making as occurring along a (somewhat unrealistic) spectrum from the completely rational decision making of traditional finance to purely emotional decision making. In that context, cognitive biases are basic statistical, information processing, or memory errors that cause the decision to deviate from rationality. Emotional biases are those that arise spontaneously as a result of attitudes and feelings and that cause the decision to deviate from the rational decisions of traditional finance.

Cognitive errors, which stem from basic statistical, information processing, or memory errors, are more easily corrected for than are emotional biases. Why? Investors are better able to adapt their behaviors or modify their processes if the source of the bias is illogical reasoning, even if the investor does not fully understand the investment issues under consideration. For example, an individual may not understand the complex mathematical process used to create a correlation table of asset classes, but he can understand that the process he is using to create a portfolio of uncorrelated investments is best. In other situations, cognitive biases can be thought of as "blind spots" or distortions in the human mind. Cognitive biases do not result from emotional or intellectual predispositions toward certain judgments, but rather from subconscious mental procedures for processing information. In general, because cognitive errors stem from faulty reasoning, better information, education, and advice can often correct for them.

Difference among Cognitive Biases

In this book, we review 13 cognitive biases, their implications for financial decision making, and suggestions for correcting for the biases. As previously mentioned, cognitive errors are statistical, information processing, or memory errors—a somewhat broad description. An individual may be attempting to follow a rational decision-making process but fails to do so because of cognitive errors. For example, they may fail to update probabilities correctly, to properly weigh and consider information, or to gather information. If corrected by supplemental or educational information, an individual attempting to follow a rational decision-making process may be receptive to correcting the errors.

To make things simpler, I have identified and classified cognitive biases into two categories. The first category contains "belief perseverance" biases. In general, belief perseverance may be thought of as the tendency to cling to one's previously held beliefs irrationally or illogically. The belief continues to be held and justified by committing statistical, information processing, or memory errors.

Belief Perseverance Biases

Belief perseverance biases are closely related to the psychological concept of cognitive dissonance, a bias I will review in the next chapter. Cognitive dissonance is the mental discomfort that one feels when new information conflicts with previously held beliefs or cognitions. To resolve this discomfort, people tend to notice only information of interest to them (called selective exposure), ignore or modify information that conflicts with existing beliefs (called selective perception), and/or remember and consider only information that confirms existing beliefs (called selective retention). Aspects of these behaviors are contained in the biases categorized as belief perseverance. The six belief perseverance biases covered in this book are: cognitive dissonance, conservatism, confirmation, representativeness, illusion of control, and hindsight.

Information-Processing Biases

The second category of cognitive biases has to do with "processing errors," and describes how information may be processed and used illogically or irrationally in financial decision making. As opposed to belief perseverance biases, these are less related to errors of memory or in assigning and updating probabilities and instead have more to do with how information is processed. The seven processing errors discussed are: anchoring and adjustment, mental accounting, framing, availability, self-attribution bias, outcome bias, and recency bias.

Individuals are less likely to make cognitive errors if they remain vigilant to the possibility that they may occur. A systematic process to describe problems and objectives; to gather, record, and synthesize information; to document decisions and the reasoning behind them; and to compare the actual outcomes with expected results will help reduce cognitive errors.

Emotional Biases

Although *emotion* has no single universally accepted definition, it is generally agreed upon that an emotion is a mental state that arises spontaneously rather than through conscious effort. Emotions are related to feelings, perceptions, or beliefs about elements, objects, or relations between them; these can be a function of reality or the imagination. Emotions may result in physical manifestations, often involuntary. Emotions can cause investors to make suboptimal decisions. Emotions may be unwanted by the individuals feeling them, and while they may wish to control the emotion and their response to it, they often cannot.

Emotional biases are harder to correct for than cognitive errors because they originate from impulse or intuition rather than conscious calculations. In other words, a bias that is an inclination of temperament or outlook, especially a personal and sometimes unreasonable judgment, is harder to correct. When investors adapt to a bias, they accept it and make decisions that recognize and adjust for it rather than making an attempt to reduce it. To moderate the impact of a bias is to recognize it and to attempt to reduce or even eliminate it within the individual rather than to accept the bias. In the case of emotional biases, it may be possible to only recognize the bias and adapt to it rather than correct for it.

Emotional biases stem from impulse, intuition, and feelings and may result in personal and unreasoned decisions. When possible, focusing on cognitive aspects of the biases may be more effective than trying to alter an emotional response. Also, educating the investors about the investment decision-making process and portfolio theory can be helpful in moving the decision making from an emotional basis to a cognitive basis. When biases are emotional in nature, drawing them to the attention of the individual making the decision is unlikely to lead to positive outcomes. The individual is likely to become defensive rather than receptive to considering alternatives. Thinking of the appropriate questions to ask and to focus on as well as potentially altering the decision-making process are likely to be the most effective options.

Emotional biases can cause investors to make suboptimal decisions. The emotional biases are rarely identified and recorded in the decision-making process because they have to do with how people feel rather than what and how they think. The six emotional biases discussed are: loss aversion, overconfidence, self-control, status quo, endowment, and regret aversion. In the discussion of each of these biases, some related biases may be discussed.

Emotional Biases	Cognitive Biases: Belief Perseverance	Cognitive Biases: Information Processing
Endowment	Cognitive Dissonance	Anchoring
Loss Aversion	Conservatism	Mental Accounting
Regret Aversion	Confirmation	Framing
Status Quo	Representativeness	Availability
Overconfidence	Illusion of Control	Self Attribution
Self-Control	Hindsight	Outcome
Affinity		Recency

Figure 2.2 Categorization of Twenty Behavioral Biases

Figure 2.2 below is a roadmap for the 20 biases that you will be seeing in the upcoming chapters.

A Final Word on Biases

The cognitive-emotional distinction will help us determine when and how to adjust for behavioral biases in financial decision making. However, it should be noted that specific biases may have some common aspects and that a specific bias may seem to have both cognitive and emotional aspects. Researchers in financial decision making have identified numerous and specific behavioral biases. This book will not attempt to discuss all identified biases but rather will discuss what I consider to be the most important biases within the cognitive-emotional framework for considering potential biases. This framework will be useful in developing an awareness of biases, their implications, and ways of moderating their impact or adapting to them. The intent is to help investors and their advisors to have a heightened awareness of biases so that financial decisions and resulting economic outcomes are potentially improved.

PART II
BELIEF PERSEVERANCE
BIASES DEFINED
AND ILLUSTRATED

In Chapters 3 through 22, 20 behavioral biases, both cognitive and emotional, will be discussed. There are two types of cognitive bias reviewed in Chapters 3 through 15. The first type, belief perseverance biases, the focus of Part Two of the book, are covered now in Chapters 3 through 8. The second type, information processing cognitive biases, will be covered in Chapters 9 through 15. Emotional biases are then covered in Chapters 16 through 22.

In these chapters, the same basic format is used to discuss each bias, in order to promote greater accessibility. First, each bias is named, categorized as emotional or cognitive, including subtype (belief perseverance or information processing), and then generally described. This is followed by the all-important concrete practical application, in which it is demonstrated how each bias has been used, or can be used, in a practical situation. The practical application portion varies in content, consisting of either an intensive review of applied research or a case study. Implications for investors are then delineated. A diagnostic test and test-result analysis follow, providing a tool to indicate potential susceptibility to certain biases. Finally, advice on managing the effects of each bias, in order to minimize its effects, is offered.

3

Belief Perseverance Bias #1: Cognitive Dissonance Bias

This above all: to thine own self be true, And it must follow, as the night the day, Thou canst not then be false to any man.

—Polonius to Laertes, in Shakespeare's *Hamlet*

Bias Description

Bias Name: Cognitive dissonance
Bias Type: Cognitive
Subtype: Belief perseverance

General Description

When newly acquired information conflicts with preexisting understandings, people often experience mental discomfort—a psychological phenomenon known as cognitive dissonance. *Cognitions,* in psychology, represent attitudes, emotions, beliefs, or values; *cognitive dissonance* is a state of imbalance that occurs when contradictory cognitions intersect.

The term *cognitive dissonance* encompasses the response that arises as people struggle to harmonize cognitions and thereby relieve their mental discomfort. For example, a consumer might purchase a certain brand of mobile phone, initially believing that it is the best mobile phone available. However, when a new cognition that favors a substitute mobile phone is introduced, representing an imbalance, cognitive dissonance occurs in an attempt to relieve the discomfort that comes with the notion that perhaps the buyer did not purchase the right mobile phone. People will go to great lengths to convince themselves that the mobile phone they actually bought is better than the one they just learned about, to avoid mental discomfort associated with their initial purchase. In essence, they persist in their belief that they are correct. In that sense, cognitive dissonance bias is the basis for all of the belief perseverance biases in this section with different variations on the same theme.

Example of Cognitive Dissonance

Smoking is a classic example of cognitive dissonance. Although it is widely accepted by the general public that cigarettes cause lung cancer and heart disease, virtually everyone who smokes wants to live a long and healthy life. In terms of cognitive dissonance theory, the desire to live a long life is dissonant with the activity of doing something that will most likely shorten one's life. The tension produced by these contradictory ideas can be reduced by denying the evidence of lung cancer and heart disease or justifying one's smoking because it reduces stress or similar benefit. A smoker might rationalize his or her behavior by believing that only a few smokers become ill (it won't be me), that it only happens to two-pack-a-day smokers, or that if smoking does not kill them, something else will. While chemical addiction may operate in addition to cognitive dissonance for existing smokers, new smokers may exhibit a simpler case of the latter.

This case of dissonance could also be interpreted in terms of a threat to the self-concept.[1] The thought, "I am increasing my risk of lung cancer," is dissonant with the self-related belief, "I am a smart, reasonable person who makes good decisions." Because it is often easier to make excuses than it is to change behavior, dissonance theory leads to the conclusion that humans are sometimes rationalizing, and not always rational beings.

---

[1] James Montier, *Behavioural Finance: Insights into Irrational Minds and Markets* (West Sussex, England: John Wiley & Sons, 2002).

Implications for Investors

Investors, like everyone else, sometimes have trouble living with their decisions and they often go to great lengths to rationalize decisions on prior investments, especially failed investments. Moreover, people displaying this tendency might also irrationally delay unloading assets that are not generating adequate returns. In both cases, the effects of cognitive dissonance are preventing investors from acting rationally and, in certain cases, preventing them from realizing losses for tax purposes and reallocating at the earliest opportunity. Furthermore, and perhaps even more important, the need to maintain self-esteem may prevent investors from learning from their mistakes. To ameliorate dissonance arising from the pursuit of what they perceive to be two incompatible goals—self-validation and acknowledgment of past mistakes—investors will often attribute their failures to chance rather than to poor decision making. Of course, people who miss opportunities to learn from past miscalculations are likely to miscalculate again, renewing a cycle of anxiety, discomfort, dissonance, and denial.

Both selective perception (information distortion to meet a need, which gives rise to subsequent decision-making errors) and selective decision making (an irrational drive to achieve some specified result for the purpose of vindicating a previous decision) can have significant effects on investors. Box 3.1 illustrates four behaviors that result from cognitive dissonance and that cause investment losses.

BOX 3.1 Cognitive Dissonance Bias: Behaviors That Can Cause Investment Mistakes

1. Cognitive dissonance can cause investors to hold losing securities positions that they otherwise would sell because they want to avoid the mental pain associated with admitting that they made a bad decision.
2. Cognitive dissonance can cause investors to continue to invest in a security that they already own after it has gone down (average down) to confirm an earlier decision to invest in that security without judging the new investment with objectivity and rationality. A common phrase for this concept is "throwing good money after bad."

3. Cognitive dissonance can cause investors to get caught up in herds of behavior; that is, people avoid information that counters an earlier decision (cognitive dissonance) until so much counter information is released that investors herd together and cause a deluge of behavior that is counter to that decision.

4. Cognitive dissonance can cause investors to believe "it's different this time." People who purchased high-flying, hugely overvalued growth stocks in the late 1990s ignored evidence that there were no excess returns from purchasing the most expensive stocks available. In fact, many of the most high-flying companies are now far below their peaks in price.

Am I Subject to Cognitive Dissonance Bias?

This test begins with a scenario that illustrates some criteria that can determine susceptibility to cognitive dissonance.

Cognitive Dissonance Bias Test

Scenario: Suppose that you recently bought a new car, Brand A, Model B. You are very pleased with your purchase. One day, your neighbor finds you in your driveway washing your new car and comments on your new purchase: "Wow, love the new car. I know this model. Did you know that Brand Y, Model Z (Model Z is nearly identical to Model B), was giving away a free navigation system when you bought the car?"

You are initially confused. You were unaware, until now, that Model Z was including a navigation system with purchase of the car. You would have liked to have it. Perhaps, you wonder, was getting Model B a bad decision? You begin to second-guess yourself. After your neighbor leaves, you return to your house.

Question: Your next action is, most likely, which of the following?

a. You immediately head to your home office and page through the various consumer magazines to determine whether you should have purchased Model B.

b. You proceed with washing the car and think, "If I had it to do all over again, I may have purchased Model Z. Even though mine doesn't have a navigation system, I'm still pleased with Model B."

c. You contemplate doing some additional research on Model Z. However, you decide not to follow through on the idea. The car was a big, important purchase, and you've been so happy with it—the prospect of discovering an error in your purchase leaves you feeling uneasy. Better to just put this thought to rest and continue to enjoy the car.

Test Results Analysis

Answering "c" may indicate a propensity for cognitive dissonance. The next section gives advice on coping with this bias. Does this make sense?

Investment Advice

The investment advice presented here is primarily preventative. People who can recognize cognitive dissonance in action and prevent it from causing mistakes become much better investors. Specifically, there are three common responses to cognitive dissonance that have potentially negative implications for personal finance and, consequently, should be avoided:

1. modifying beliefs,
2. modifying actions, and
3. modifying perceptions of relevant action(s).

1. Modifying beliefs. Perhaps the easiest way to resolve dissonance between actions and beliefs is simply to alter the relevant beliefs. When the principle in question is important to you, however, such a course of action becomes unlikely. People's most basic beliefs tend to remain stable; they don't just go around modifying their fundamental moral matrices on a day-to-day basis.

Investors, however, do sometimes opt for this path of least resistance when attempting to eliminate dissonance (although the belief-modification mechanism is the least common, in finance, of the three coping tactics discussed here). For example, if the behavior in question was "selling a losing investment" that has little chance of recovering one might concoct a rationale along the lines of "it is okay not to sell a losing investment" in order to resolve cognitive dissonance and permit yourself to hold onto a stock. This behavior, obviously, may pose hazards to your wealth. Taking a tax loss and moving on is typically the best course of action in this scenario.

2. Modifying actions. On realizing that you have engaged in behavior contradictory to some preexisting belief, you might attempt to instill fear and anxiety into your decision in order to averse-condition yourself against committing the same act in the future. However, averse conditioning is often a poor mechanism for learning, especially if you can train yourself, over time, to simply tolerate the distressful consequences associated with a "forbidden" behavior.

   Investors may successfully leverage averse conditioning. For example, in the instance wherein a losing investment must be sold, an individual could summon such anxiety at the prospect of actually losing money. Again, taking a tax loss and moving on is a good solution. Even the best investors take losses and move on.

3. Modifying perceptions of relevant action(s). A more difficult approach to reconciling cognitive dissonance is to rationalize whatever action has brought you into conflict with your beliefs. For example, you may decide that while hitting a dog is generally a bad idea, the dog whom you hit was not behaving well; therefore, you haven't done anything wrong. People relying on this technique try to recontextualize whatever action has generated the current state of mental discomfort so that the action no longer appears to be inconsistent with any particular belief.

   An investor might rationalize retaining a losing investment: "I don't really need the money right now, so I won't sell" is a justification that might resolve cognitive dissonance. This type of rationalization often leads to sub-optimal investment results.

4

Belief Perseverance Bias #2: Conservatism Bias

To invest successfully over a lifetime does not require a stratospheric IQ, unusual business insight, or inside information. What's needed is a sound intellectual framework for decisions and the ability to keep emotions from corroding that framework.
— **Warren Buffett**

Bias Description

Bias Name: Conservatism
Bias Type: Cognitive
Subtype: Belief perseverance

General Description

Conservatism bias is a mental process in which people cling to their prior views or forecasts at the expense of acknowledging new information. For example, suppose that an investor receives some bad news regarding a company's earnings and that this news negatively contradicts another earnings estimate issued the previous month. Conservatism bias may cause the investor to *underreact* to the new information, maintaining impressions derived from the previous estimate rather than acting on the updated information investors persevere in a previously held belief rather than acknowledging new information; this is again a variation on the cognitive dissonance theme described in the last section.

Example of Conservatism Bias

James Montier is author of the book *Behavioural Finance: Insights into Irrational Minds and Markets*[1] and an analyst for DKW in London. Montier has done some exceptional work in the behavioral finance field. Although Montier primarily studied the stock market in general, concentrating on the behavior of securities analysts in particular, the concepts presented here can and will be applied to individual investors later on.

Commenting on conservatism as it relates to the securities markets in general, Montier noted: "The stock market has a tendency to underreact to fundamental information—be it dividend omissions, initiations, or an earnings report. For instance, in the United States, in the 60 days following an earnings announcement, stocks with the biggest positive earnings surprise tend to outperform the market by 2 percent, even after a 4 to 5 percent outperformance in the 60 days prior to the announcement."

In relating conservatism to securities analysts, Montier wrote:

> People tend to cling tenaciously to a view or a forecast. Once a position has been stated, most people find it very hard to move away from that view. When movement does occur, it does so only very slowly. Psychologists call this conservatism bias. The chart below [Figure 4.1] shows conservatism in analysts' forecasts. We have taken a linear time trend out of both the operating earnings numbers and the analysts' forecasts. A cursory glance at the chart reveals that analysts are exceptionally good at telling you what has just happened. They have invested too heavily in their view and hence will only change it when presented with indisputable evidence of its falsehood.[2]

This is clear evidence of conservatism bias in action. Montier's research documents the behavior of securities analysts, but the trends observed can easily be applied to individual investors, who also forecast securities prices, and will cling to these forecasts even when presented with new information.

---

[1] James Montier, *Behavioural Finance: Insights into Irrational Minds and Markets* (West Sussex, England: John Wiley & Sons, 2002).

[2] James Montier, "Equity Research" (research report, Dresdner Kleinwort Wasserstein, 2002).

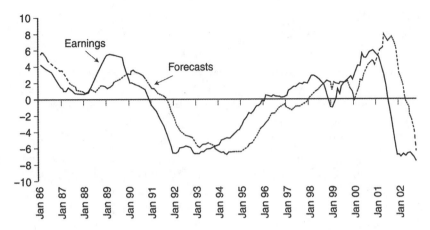

Figure 4.1 Montier Observes That Analysts Cling to Their Forecasts
Source: Dresdner Kleinwort Wasserstein, 2012

Implications for Investors

Investors too often give more attention to forecast outcomes than to new data that actually describes emerging outcomes. Investors are sometimes unable to rationally act on updated information regarding their investments because they are "stuck" on prior beliefs. Box 4.1 lists three behaviors stemming from conservatism bias that can cause investment mistakes.

BOX 4.1 Conservatism Bias: Behaviors That Can Cause Investment Mistakes

1. Conservatism bias can cause investors to cling to a view or a forecast, behaving too inflexibly when presented with new information. For example, assume an investor purchases a security based on the knowledge that the company is planning a forthcoming announcement regarding a new product. The company then announces that it has experienced problems bringing the product to market. The investor may cling to the initial, optimistic impression of some imminent, positive development by the company and may fail to take action on the negative announcement.
2. When conservatism-biased investors do react to new information, they often do so too slowly. For example, if an earnings

announcement depresses a stock that an investor holds, the conservative investor may be too slow to sell. The pre-existing view that, for example, the company has good prospects, may linger too long and exert too much influence, causing an investor exhibiting conservatism to unload the stock only after losing more money than necessary.

3. Conservatism can relate to an underlying difficulty in processing new information. Because people experience mental stress when presented with complex data, an easy option is to simply stick to a prior belief. For example, if an investor purchases a security on the belief that the company is poised to grow and then the company announces that a series of difficult-to-interpret accounting changes may affect its growth, the investor might discount the announcement rather than attempt to decipher it. More clear-cut and, therefore, easier to maintain is the prior belief that the company is poised to grow.

Am I Subject to Conservatism Bias?

The following diagnostic quiz can help to detect elements of conservatism bias.

Conservatism Bias Test

Question 1: Suppose that you live in Baltimore, Maryland, and you make a forecast such as, "I think it will be a snowy winter this year." Furthermore, suppose that, by mid-February, you realize that no snow has fallen. What is your natural reaction to this information?

a. There's still time to get a lot of snow, so my forecast is probably correct.

b. There still may be time for some snow, but I may have erred in my forecast.

c. My experience tells me that my forecast was probably incorrect. Most of the winter has elapsed; therefore, the cumulative amount of snow is not likely to be significant.

Question 2: When you recently hear news that has potentially negative implications for the price of an investment you own, what is your natural reaction to this information?

a. I tend to ignore the information. Because I have already made the investment, I've already determined that the company will be successful.

b. I will reevaluate my reasons for buying the stock, but I will probably stick with it because I usually stick with my original determination that a company will be successful.

c. I will reevaluate my reasoning for buying the stock and will decide, based on an objective consideration of all the facts, what to do next.

Question 3: When news comes out that has potentially negative implications for the price of a security that you own, how quickly do you react to this information?

a. I usually wait for the market to communicate the significance of the information and then I decide what to do.

b. Sometimes, I wait for the market to communicate the significance of the information, but other times, I respond without delay.

c. I respond without delay.

Test Results Analysis

People answering "a" or "b" to any of the preceding questions may indicate susceptibility to conservatism bias.

Investment Advice

Because conservatism is a cognitive bias, advice and information can often correct or lessen its effect. Specifically, investors must first avoid clinging to forecasts; they must also be sure to react, decisively, to new information. This does not mean that investors should respond to events without careful analysis. However, when the wisest course of action becomes clear, it should be implemented resolutely and without hesitation. Additionally, investors should seek professional advice when trying to interpret information that they have difficulty understanding. Otherwise, investors may not take action when they should.

When new information is presented, ask yourself: How does this impact my portfolio? Does it actually jeopardize my forecast about how my portfolio will perform? If investors can answer these questions honestly, then they have achieved a very good handle on conservatism bias. Recognizing conservatism can prevent bad decisions from being made, and investors need to remain mindful of any propensities they might exhibit that make them cling to old views and react slowly toward promising, emerging developments.

5

Belief Perseverance Bias #3: Confirmation Bias

It is the peculiar and perpetual error of the human understanding to be more moved and excited by affirmatives than by negatives.

—Francis Bacon

Bias Description

Bias Name: Confirmation Bias
Bias Type: Cognitive
Sub Type: Belief Perseverance

General Description

Confirmation bias refers to a type of selective perception that emphasizes ideas that confirm our beliefs, while devaluing whatever contradicts our beliefs. For example, it is quite typical for someone to decide, after having bought a much-desired item such as a television, to look for the same television at a store that is known to have higher prices in order to confirm that he or she made a good purchase decision. This behavior, going back to cognitive dissonance in the last chapter, is caused by our attempt to resolve the post-decisional dissonance between the decision made and the possibility of being wrong.

To describe this phenomenon another way, we might say that confirmation bias refers to our all-too-natural ability to convince ourselves of whatever it is that we want to believe. We attach undue emphasis to events that corroborate the outcomes we desire and downplay whatever contrary evidence arises. Political television channels are a concrete example. Certain channels promote republican ideals and others promote democratic ideas. Rarely do viewers want to "see the other side" point of view by watching the "other party's" channel. We are inclined to "hear what we want to hear."

Example of Confirmation Bias

To demonstrate confirmation bias, we discuss employees' penchant for overconcentrating in company stock. Employees may rationalize their disproportionate holdings by citing the promising "big things" that are developing at their companies. Numerous shareholders in Enron and WorldCom, and Lehman Brothers and Bear Stearns (during the great financial crisis of 2008–2009) probably speculated that great growth was under way—if only these investors had had some clue as to the nature of the "big things" that would soon befall their employers!). When employees load up on company stock en masse and bullish commentary on employer stock prices dominates water cooler conversation, inauspicious details can be easily overlooked. For a more elaborate example, we are going "retro" back to the early 1990's. A strong cautionary tale emerged during that time at a well-established tech firm: IBM.

In the early 1990s, many IBM employees were convinced that their company's OS/2 operating system would achieve industry standard status. They frequently ignored unfavorable signs, including evidence of competition from Microsoft Windows. These employees loaded up on IBM stock, anticipating that OS/2's performance would drive the company forward. In 1991, IBM stock reached a split-adjusted peak of $35 per share. Over the course of the next two years, however, IBM slid to a low of $10. It would not reach $35 again until the end of 1996. During this five-year slump, IBM employees rallied around seemingly positive developments that "confirmed" that IBM was making a comeback. Some even delayed retirement. Unfortunately, in an effort to engineer a turnaround, IBM laid off a number of its employees. In the end, OS/2 caused many people to become less wealthy. For some, the failed operating system even led to unemployment. This is a classic case of confirmation bias in action.

Investors sometimes ignore downside risks of, for example, employer stock and focus only on the upside potential. Why? In this case, confirmation bias played a significant role in the behavior of the IBM employees. It led them to accept information that supported their rosy predictions regarding IBM while discounting evidence of increased competition from Microsoft. Consequently, these employees lost money as IBM's stock price fell. Only those few who were able to hang on, over the course of five years of uncertainty—history, remember, shows us that most investors "panic" in such a situation—had the opportunity to profit in the end.

Implications for Investors

Anyone who has played a hand or two of poker knows well the downside of confirmation bias. Suppose you are entrenched in a game, and you get three kings on the flop. Your opponent raises the pot, and you are only happy to raise him back. You aren't really paying attention as the turn card comes out. Your cards are telling you "I can't lose." You are oblivious to the fact that a series of hearts are showing up. A two comes up on the river and you pretty much are guaranteed to win. You bet big. You get called. Oops, someone had a flush, and you lose.

In the context of the poker analogy, what's important to note is that, by "listening" only to information that confirms your belief that you have the best hand, you ignore the other players' cards. Focusing on the payoff of the present hand might eventually earn a profit; however, you don't analyze the implications of a loss—even if some indication has cropped up during the game that another player might be collecting hearts. While the poker metaphor isn't flawless, it gets the point across: People believe what they want to believe and ignore evidence to the contrary. This is the essence of confirmation bias.

In finance, the effects of confirmation bias can be observed almost daily. Investors often fail to acknowledge anything negative about investments they've just made, even when substantial evidence begins to argue against these investments. A classic example took place on the Internet message boards during the technology stock boom of the late 1990s. Many of these chat-roomers would harass anyone who voiced a negative opinion of the company they invested in.

Rather than try to glean some useful insight into their company through other investors, they only sought confirmations of their own beliefs.

Box 5.1 summarizes investment mistakes that can be caused by confirmation bias.

BOX 5.1 Confirmation Bias: Behaviors That Can Cause Investment Mistakes

1. Confirmation bias can cause investors to seek out only information that confirms their beliefs about an investment that they have made and to not seek out information that may contradict their beliefs. This behavior can leave investors in the dark regarding, for example, the imminent decline of a stock.

2. When investors believe strongly in predetermined "screens," such as stocks breaking through a 52-week price high, confirmation bias is usually at work. These investors use only information that confirms their beliefs. They may blind themselves to information that demonstrates that a stock breaking through its 52-week high may not make a good investment.

3. Confirmation bias can cause employees to overconcentrate in company stock. As IBM and other examples demonstrate, intraoffice buzz about a company's prospects does not justify indiscriminate reliance by employees on company stock. People naturally tend to unduly emphasize evidence suggesting that the companies they work for will do well.

4. Confirmation bias can cause investors to continue to hold underdiversified portfolios. Investors sometimes become infatuated with certain stocks—not always the stocks of employer corporations. Over the course of years, such an investor might accrue a large position that ultimately produces a lopsided portfolio. These investors do not want to hear anything negative about favored investments but rather seek, single-mindedly, confirmation that the position will pay off.

Am I Subject to Confirmation Bias?

These questions are designed to detect cognitive errors stemming from confirmation bias. To complete the test, select the answer choice that best characterizes your response to each item.

Confirmation Bias Test

Question 1: Suppose you have invested in a security after some careful research. Now, you come on a press release that states that the company you've invested in may have a problem with its main product line. The second paragraph, however, describes a completely new product that the company might debut later this year. What is your natural course of action?

a. I will typically take notice of the new product announcement and research that item further.

b. I will typically take notice of the problem with the company's product line and research that item further.

Question 2: Suppose you have invested in a security after some careful research. The investment appreciates in value but not for the reason you predicted (e.g., you were enticed by some buzz surrounding a new product, but resurgence by an older product line ultimately buoyed the stock). What is your natural course of action?

a. Since the company did well, I am not concerned. The shares I've selected have generated a profit. This confirms that the stock was a good investment.

b. Although I am pleased, I am concerned about the investment. I will do further research to confirm the logic behind my position.

Question 3: Suppose you decide to invest in a global emerging markets bond fund. You performed careful research to determine that this investment is a good way to hedge the dollar. Three months after you invest, you realize that the dollar hasn't depreciated much against the currencies of the bonds in the fund, but the investment seems to be doing well. This is not what you expected. How do you react?

a. I will just "go with it." The reason that an investment performs well is not important. What's important is that I made a good investment.

b. I will do research to try and determine why the fund is doing well. This will help me determine if I should remain invested in the fund.

Test Results Analysis

Question 1: People who select answer choice "a," indicating they would more readily research the new product line than the potential complications in the old product line, are likely to be susceptible to confirmation bias. They are avoiding information that might confirm—but, crucially, might also overrule—the previous decision to invest in the company.

Question 2: People who select "a" are more likely to exhibit confirmation bias than people who select "b." Rationalizing that only the company's recent performance is relevant, answer choice "a" implies that the respondent will avoid seeking out information that might contradict previously held beliefs regarding the quality of the (hypothetical) investment. "b" is the more economically rational choice.

Questions 3: Again, "a" is the response that signals susceptibility to confirmation bias. To "just go with it," in this instance, means adopting some arbitrary rationale just because it happens to confirm a previous conviction ("I made a good investment decision"). Answer choice "b," which entails further research, is unattractive to people suffering from confirmation bias. This is because further research might unearth information that contradicts a previous conviction ("I made a good investment decision").

Investment Advice

The following advice corresponds to each of the four problem areas listed in Box 5.1.

General Confirmation Bias Behavior. The first step toward overcoming confirmation bias is to recognize that the bias exists. Then people can mindfully compensate by making sure to seek out information that could contradict—not just confirm—their investment decisions. It is important to remember that the mere existence of contradictory evidence does not necessarily mean an investment was unwise. Rather, uncovering all available data simply facilitates informed decisions. Even the most precisely calculated judgments can go awry; however, when investors make sure to consider all available contingencies and perspectives, they are less likely to make mistakes.

Selection Bias. When an investment decision is based on some preexisting criterion—such as a trend regarding stocks that break through 52-week highs—it is advisable to cross verify the decision from additional angles. Fundamental research on a company, industry, or sector, for example, can often provide another informative dimension. This will help to ensure that investment selections don't blindly adhere to preconceived principles while ignoring practical considerations.

Company Stock. Overconcentrating in company stock is inadvisable for numerous reasons. In guarding against confirmation bias, employees should monitor any negative press regarding their own companies and conduct research on any competing firms. While it is easy to become desensitized toward bad news regarding one's own company, remember: "Where there's smoke, there's (too often) fire." Employee investors should heed the warning signs—or risk getting burned.

Overconcentration. Company stock isn't the only investment with which people can become unduly enamored. People who demonstrate a disproportionate degree of commitment to any stock whatsoever should remember to seek out unfavorable data regarding that stock. This is especially true for investors whose portfolios concentrate discernibly in a favored investment.

6

Belief Perseverance Bias #4: Representativeness Bias

Fit no stereotypes. Don't chase the latest management fads. The situation dictates which approach best accomplishes the team's mission.

—Colin Powell

Bias Description

Bias Name: Representativeness
Bias Type: Cognitive
Subtype: Belief perseverance

General Description

In order to derive meaning from life experiences, people have developed an innate propensity for classifying objects and thoughts. When they confront a new phenomenon that is inconsistent with any of their pre-constructed classifications, they subject it to those classifications anyway, relying on a rough best-fit approximation to determine which category should house and, thereafter, form the basis for their understanding of the new element. This perceptual framework provides an expedient tool for processing new information by simultaneously incorporating insights gained from (usually) relevant/analogous past experiences. It endows people with a quick response reflex that helps them to survive. Sometimes, however, new stimuli resemble—are *representative* of—familiar elements that have already been classified. In reality, these are drastically different analogues. In such an instance, the classification reflex leads to deception, producing an incorrect understanding of the new element that often persists and biases all our future interactions with that element.

Similarly, people tend to perceive probabilities and odds that resonate with their own preexisting ideas—even when the resulting conclusions drawn are statistically invalid. For example, the "gambler's fallacy" refers to the commonly held impression that gambling luck runs in streaks. However, subjective psychological dynamics, not mathematical realities, inspire this perception. Statistically, the streak concept is nonsense. Humans also tend to subscribe to something researchers call "the law of small numbers," which is the assumption that small samples faithfully represent entire populations. No scientific principle, however, underlies or enforces this "law."

Examples of Representativeness Bias

This section presents and analyzes two miniature case studies that demonstrate potential investor susceptibility to each variety of representativeness bias.

Miniature Case Study 1: Base-Rate Neglect

Case Presentation

Suppose George, an investor, is looking to add to his portfolio and hears about a potential investment through a friend, Peter, at a local coffee shop. The conversation goes something like this:

GEORGE: Hi, Peter. My portfolio is really suffering right now. I could use a good long-term investment. Any ideas?

PETER: Well, George, did you hear about the new IPO [initial public offering] pharmaceutical company called PharmaGrowth (PG) that came out last week? PG is a hot new company that should be a great investment. Its president and CEO was a "mover and shaker" at an Internet company that did great during the tech boom, and she has PharmaGrowth growing by leaps and bounds.

GEORGE: No, I didn't hear about it. Tell me more.

PETER: Well, the company markets a generic drug sold over the Internet for people with a stomach condition that millions of people have. PG offers online advice on digestion and stomach health, and several Wall Street firms have issued "buy" ratings on the stock.

GEORGE: Wow, sounds like a great investment!

PETER: Well, I bought some. I think it could do great.

GEORGE: I'll buy some, too.

George proceeds to pull out his cell phone, call his broker, and place an order for 100 shares of PG.

Analysis

In this example, George displays base-rate neglect representativeness bias by considering this hot IPO is, necessarily, representative of a good long-term investment. Many investors like George believe that IPOs make good long-term investments due to all the up-front hype that surrounds them. In fact, numerous studies have shown that a very low percentage of IPOs actually turn out to be good long-term investments. This common investor misperception is likely due to the fact that investors in hot IPOs usually make money in the first few days after the offering. Over time, however, these stocks tend to trail their IPO prices, often never returning to their original levels.

George ignores the statistics and probabilities by not considering that, in the long run, the PG stock will most likely incur losses rather than gains. This concept can be applied to many investment situations. There is a relatively easy way to analyze how an investor might fall prey to base-rate neglect. For example, what is the probability that person A (Simon, a shy, introverted man) belongs to Group B (stamp collectors) rather than Group C (BMW drivers)? In answering this question, most people typically evaluate the degree to which A (Simon) "represents" B or C; they might conclude that Simon's shyness seems to be more representative of stamp collectors than BMW drivers. This approach neglects base rates, however: statistically, far more people drive BMWs than collect stamps.

Similarly, George, our hypothetical investor, has effectively been asked: what is the probability that Company A (PharmaGrowth, the hot IPO) belongs to Group B (stocks constituting successful long-term investments) rather than Group C (stocks that will fail as long-term investments)? Again, most individuals approach this problem by attempting to ascertain the extent to which A appears characteristically representative of B or C. In George's judgment, PG possesses the properties of a successful long-term investment rather than a failed one. Investors arriving at this conclusion, however, ignore the base-rate fact that IPOs are more likely to fail than to succeed.

Miniature Case Study 2: Sample–Size Neglect

Case Presentation

Suppose George revisits his favorite coffee shop the following week and this time encounters bowling buddy Jack. Jack raves about his stockbroker, whose firm employs an analyst who appears to have made many recent successful stock picks. The conversation goes something like this:

GEORGE: Hi, Jack, how are you?
JACK: Hi, George. I'm doing great! I've been doing superbly in the market recently.
GEORGE: Really? What's your secret?
JACK: Well, my broker has passed along some great picks made by an analyst at her firm.
GEORGE: Wow, how many of these tips have you gotten?
JACK: My broker gave me three great stock picks over the past month or so. Each stock is up now, by over 10 percent.
GEORGE: That's a great record. My broker seems to give me one bad pick for every good one. It sounds like I need to talk to your broker; she has a much better record!

Analysis

As we'll see in a moment, this conversation exemplifies sample-size neglect representativeness bias. Jack's description has prompted George to arrive at a faulty judgment regarding the success rate of

Jack's broker/analyst. George is impressed, but his assessment is based on a very small sample size; the recent, successful picks Jack cites are inevitably only part of the story. George concluded that Jack's broker is successful because Jack's account of the broker's and analyst's performances seems *representative* of the record of a successful team. However, George disproportionately weighs Jack's testimony, and if he were to ask more questions, he might discover that his conclusion draws on too small a sample size. In reality, the analyst that Jack is relying on happens to be one who covers an industry that is popular at the moment, and *every* stock that this analyst covers has enjoyed recent success. Additionally, Jack neglected to mention that last year, this same broker/analyst team made a string of three *losing* recommendations. Therefore, both Jack's and George's brokers are batting 50 percent. George's reasoning demonstrates the pitfalls of sample-size neglect representativeness bias.

Implications for Investors

Both types of representativeness bias can lead to substantial investment mistakes. Box 6.1 lists examples of behaviors, attributable to base-rate neglect and sample-size neglect, respectively, that can cause harm to an investor's portfolio. Advice on these four areas will come later.

BOX 6.1 Harmful Effects of Representativeness Bias

Examples of the Harmful Effects of Sample-Size Neglect for Investors

1. Investors can make significant financial errors when they examine a money manager's track record. They peruse the past few quarters or even years and conclude, based on inadequate statistical data, that the fund's performance is the result of skilled allocation and/or security selection.
2. Investors also make similar mistakes when investigating track records of stock analysts. For example, they look at the success of an analyst's past few recommendations, erroneously assessing the analyst's aptitude based on this limited data sample.

Examples of the Harmful Effects of Base-Rate Neglect for Investors

1. What is the probability that Company A (ABC, a 75-year-old steel manufacturer that is having some business difficulties) belongs to group B (value stocks that will likely recover) rather than to Group C (companies that will go out of business)? In answering this question, most investors will try to judge the degree to which A is representative of B or C. In this case, some headlines featuring recent bankruptcies by steel companies make ABC Steel appear more representative of the latter categorization, and some investors conclude that they had best unload the stock. They are ignoring, however, the base-rate reality that far more steel companies survive or get acquired than go out of business.

2. What is the probability that AAA-rated Municipal Bond A (issued by an "inner city" and racially divided county) belongs to Group B (risky municipal bonds) rather than to Group C (safe municipal bonds)? In answering this question, most investors will again try to evaluate the extent to which A seems representative of B or C. In this case, Bond A's characteristics may seem representative of Group A (risky bonds) because of the county's "unsafe" reputation; however, this conclusion ignores the base-rate fact that, historically, the default rate of AAA bonds is virtually zero.

Am I Subject to Representativeness Bias?

This test will help to determine your susceptibility to both base-rate bias and sample-size neglect bias.

Base-Rate Neglect Representativeness Bias Test

Question 1: Jack is an ex-college-baseball player. After he graduated from college, Jack became a physical education teacher. Jack has two sons, both of whom are excellent athletes. Which is more likely?

a. Jack coaches a local Little League team.

b. Jack coaches a local Little League team and plays softball with the local softball team.

Sequence 1

Sequence 2

Figure 6.1 Sample-Size Neglect Diagnostic: Which Sequence of Coin Toss Results Appears Likelier?

Sample-Size Neglect Representativeness Bias Test

Question 2: Consider the two sequences of coin-toss results shown (Figure 6.1). Assume that an unbiased coin has been used. Which of the sequences pictured do you think is more likely: A or B?

Test Results Analysis

Question 1: Respondents who chose "b," which is the predictable answer, are likely to suffer from base-rate neglect representativeness bias. It is *possible* that Jack both coaches and plays softball, but it is *more likely* that he only coaches Little League.

Question 2: Most people ascertain Sequence A to be more likely, simply because it appears more "random." In fact, both sequences are equally likely because a coin toss generates a 50:50 probability ratio of heads to tails. Therefore, respondents who chose Sequence B may be subject to sample-size neglect representativeness bias (also known in this case as gambler's fallacy, or the law of small numbers). If six tosses of a fair coin all turn out to be heads, the probability that the next toss will turn up heads is still one-half. However, many people still harbor the notion that in coin tossing, a roughly even ratio of heads to tails should result and that a sequence of consecutive heads signals that a tails is overdue. Again, this is a case of representativeness bias. The law of large numbers when applied to a small sample will produce such biased estimates.

Investment Advice

In both sample-size neglect and base-rate neglect, investors ignore the statistically dominant result in order to satisfy their need for patterns. Due to the fact that many examples of representativeness bias exist, this advice tries to address two especially prevalent errors that representativeness-biased investors often commit. One of these mistakes falls in the base-rate neglect category, while the other exemplifies sample-size neglect.

Advice for Base-Rate Neglect

Earlier in the chapter, a very effective method for dealing with base-rate neglect was presented. When you sense that base-rate neglect might be a problem, stop and perform the following analysis: "What is the probability that Person A (Simon, a shy, introverted man) belongs to Group B (stamp collectors) rather than Group C (BMW drivers)?"

Recalling this example will help you to think through whether you are erroneously assessing a particular situation. It will likely be necessary to go back and do some more research to determine if you have indeed committed an error (i.e., "Are there really more BMW drivers than stamp collectors?"). In the end, however, this process should prove conducive to better investment decisions.

Advice for Sample-Size Neglect

In the earlier example of sample-size neglect (George and Jack), an investor might conclude that a mutual fund manager possesses remarkable skill, based on the fund's performance over just the past three years. Viewed in the context of the thousands of investment managers, a given manager's three-year track record is just as likely an indication that the manager has benefited from luck as it is an indication of skill, right? Consider the following study. In 2016, Morningstar published the results of a study on the performance persistence among U.S. mutual funds.[1] This study differs from many others by measuring fund performance relative to peers within several Morningstar Categories over several lookback and holding periods. It also digs into the drivers behind these

---

[1] See Morningstar web site: www.morningstar.com

return differences. The study found: There is some evidence that relative fund performance persists in the short term. In the equity categories, this appears to be attributable to differences in exposure to momentum stocks, rather than differences in manager skill. Over the long term, there is no meaningful relationship between past and future fund performance. In most cases, the odds of picking a future long-term winner from the best-performing quintile in each category aren't materially different than selecting from the bottom quintile. Survivorship rates are higher among previous winners than they are among previous losers. This difference increases with the length of the prior performance window and subsequent holding period. Overall, the results strongly indicate that long-term investors should not select funds based on past performance alone. Rather, they should combine performance analysis with an assessment of other quantitative and qualitative factors, such as the fund's fees, the quality of its investment process and management team, and the stewardship practices of the asset management firm. This more holistic approach should improve investors' odds of success.

7

Belief Perseverance Bias #5: Illusion-of-Control Bias

I claim not to have controlled events, but confess plainly that events have controlled me.
—**Abraham Lincoln**

Bias Description

Bias Name: Illusion of control
Bias Type: Cognitive
Subtype: Belief perseverance

General Description

The *Illusion-of-control bias,* another form of dissonant behavior, describes the tendency of human beings to believe that they can control or at least influence outcomes when, in fact, they cannot. This bias can be observed in Las Vegas, where casinos play host to many forms of this psychological fallacy. Some casino patrons swear that they are able to impact random outcomes such as the product of a pair of tossed dice. In the casino game "craps," for example, various research has demonstrated that people actually cast the dice more vigorously when they are trying to attain a higher number or when an "important" roll is happening. Some people, when successful at trying to predict the outcome of a series of coin tosses, actually believe that they are "better guessers," and some claim that distractions might diminish their performance at this statistically arbitrary task.

Example of Illusion of Control Bias

When subject to Illusion-of-control bias, people feel as if they can exert more control over their environment than they actually can. An excellent application of this concept was devised by Andrea Breinholt and Lynnette Dalrymple, two researchers at Westminster College in Salt Lake City, Utah. Their study entitled "The Illusion of Control: What's Luck Got to Do with It?"[1] illustrates that people often harbor unfounded illusions of control.

Breinholt and Dalrymple sought to examine subjects' susceptibility to illusions of control as determined by the intersection of two common impulses: the desire for control and the belief in good luck as a controllable attribute. Two hundred eighty-one undergraduate students participated in the study, and all rated themselves based on a "Desirability of Control Scale" and a "Belief in Luck Scale" immediately prior to the experiment. The subjects then participated in an online, simulated gambling task. Participants were randomly assigned either a high-involvement or a low-involvement condition and, also randomly, were rewarded with either a descending or a random sequence of outcomes.

All participants played 14 hands of "Red & Black," using four cards from a standard poker deck. Each card was presented face down on the screen, and subjects were asked to wager as to whether a chosen card matched a selected, target color. Each player began with 50 chips. In each hand, participants could wager between zero and five chips; winning increased the participant's total stock of chips by the wagered amount. Likewise, following a lost hand, a player's supply of chips automatically decreased by the wagered amount. The odds of winning each hand were calibrated at 50:50.

---

[1] Andrea Breinholt and Lynnette A. Dalrymple, "The Illusion of Control: What's Luck Got to Do with It?" *The Myriad: Westminster College Undergraduate Academic Journal* (Summer 2004).

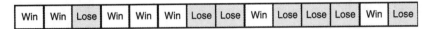

Figure 7.1 A Sample Distribution of the Descending Outcome Sequence in "The Illusion of Control: What's Luck Got to Do with It?"
Source: Andrea Breinholt and Lynnette A. Dalrymple, "The Illusion of Control: What's Luck Got to Do with It?" The Myriad: Westminster College Undergraduate Academic Journal (Summer 2004).

Participants randomly assigned to the high-involvement condition were allowed to "shuffle" and "deal" the cards themselves. They could also choose, in each hand, the target color and the amount wagered. After the high-involvement participants chose their cards, the computer revealed each result accordingly. This sequence repeated over the course of 14 trials. The high-involvement condition was designed to maximize the participants' perception that they were controlling the game.

In the low-involvement condition, the computer shuffled and dealt the cards. The participants chose the amounts wagered, but the computer randomly selected the card on which the outcome of each hand would rest.

The descending outcome sequence was designed to maximize the illusion of control, letting the majority of successful outcomes occur during the first seven trials.[2] The descending sequence, for example, consisted of the outcomes depicted in Figure 7.1.

The random outcome sequence was designed to minimize the illusion of control by spacing the successful outcomes more evenly over the course of the 14 trials.

Ultimately, participants in the high-involvement condition tended to wager more chips on each hand than did participants in the low-involvement condition. Moreover, in the low-involvement condition, wagers did not differ reliably as a function of distributed feature composition (DFC)—in other words, participants receiving the descending sequence of outcomes did not wager more or less, on average, than did participants allotted the random outcome sequence. In contrast, in the high-involvement condition, high-DFC participants wagered more than did low-DFC participants. These findings support the presence of an illusion of control phenomenon in the traditional sense.

---

[2] Andrea Breinholt and Lynnette A. Dalrymple, "The Illusion of Control: What's Luck Got to Do with It?" *The Myriad: Westminster College Undergraduate Academic Journal* (Summer 2004).

This study clearly demonstrates the illusion-of-control bias in practice. Investors are very much susceptible to this bias.

Implications for Investors

Box 7.1 lists four primary behaviors that can lead to investment mistakes by investors who are susceptible to illusion-of-control bias.

BOX 7.1 Illusion-of-Control Bias: Behaviors That Can Cause Investment Mistakes

1. Illusion-of-control bias can lead investors to trade more than is prudent. Researchers have found that traders, especially online traders, believe themselves to possess more control over the outcomes of their investments than they actually do. An excess of trading results, in the end, in decreased returns.[3]

2. Illusions of control can lead investors to maintain under-diversified portfolios. Researchers have found that investors hold concentrated positions because they gravitate toward companies over whose fate they feel some amount of control. That control proves illusory, however, and the lack of diversification hurts the investors' portfolios.

3. Illusion-of-control bias can cause investors to use limit orders and other such techniques in order to experience a false sense of control over their investments. In fact, the use of these mechanisms can often lead to an overlooked opportunity or, worse, a detrimental, unnecessary purchase based on the occurrence of an arbitrary price.

4. Illusion-of-control bias contributes, in general, to investor overconfidence. (Please see Chapter 18 for a detailed discussion of related pitfalls and compensation techniques.) In particular, investors who have been successful in business or other professional pursuits believe that they should also be successful in the investment realm. What they find is that they may have had the ability to shape outcomes in their vocation, but investments are a different matter altogether.

---

[3] Terrance Odean, "Do Investors Trade Too Much?" *American Economic Review*, 89(5) (1999): 1279–1298.

Am I Subject to Illusion of Control Bias?

This diagnostic test helps to determine whether people taking the test harbor illusions of control.

Illusion of Control Bias Test

Question 1: When you participate in games of chance that involve dice—such as backgammon, Monopoly, or craps—do you feel most in control when you roll the dice yourself?

a. I feel more in control when I roll the dice.

b. I am indifferent as to who rolls the dice.

Question 2: When returns to your portfolio increase, to what do you mainly attribute this turn of events?

a. The control that I've exercised over the outcome of my investments.

b. Some combination of investment control and random chance.

c. Completely random chance.

Question 3: When you are playing cards, are you usually most optimistic with respect to the outcome of a hand that you've dealt yourself?

a. A better outcome will occur when I am controlling the dealing of the cards.

b. It makes no difference to me who deals the cards.

Question 4: When and if you purchase a lottery ticket, do you feel more encouraged, regarding your odds of winning, if you choose the number yourself rather than using a computer-generated number?

a. I'm more likely to win if I control the numbers picked.

b. It makes no difference to me how the numbers are chosen.

Test Results Analysis

Question 1: People who feel more confident rolling the dice themselves, rather than allowing someone else to roll, are more likely to be susceptible to illusion-of-control bias.

Question 2: People who feel that they are able to exert control over their investments are likely to be susceptible to illusion-of-control bias.

Question 3: Question 3 parallels Question 1. People who perceive that they have more control over the outcome of a hand of cards when dealing the cards themselves are likely to be susceptible to illusion-of-control bias.

Question 4: Respondents selecting "a," indicating that they feel more optimistic when choosing their own lottery numbers instead of accepting randomized numbers, are likely to be susceptible to illusion-of-control bias.

Investment Advice

Following are four advisories that investors can implement to stem the detrimental financial effects of illusions of control.

1. Recognize that successful investing is a probabilistic activity. The first step on the road to recovery from illusion-of-control bias is to take a step back and realize how complex U.S. and global capitalism actually is. Even the wisest investors have absolutely no control over the outcomes of the investments that they make.
2. Recognize and avoid circumstances that trigger susceptibility illusions of control. A villager blows his trumpet every day at 6 p.m., and no stampede of elephants ensues. Does the trumpet really keep the elephants away? Applying the same concept to investing, just because you have deliberately determined to purchase a stock, do you really control the fate of that stock or the outcome of that purchase? Rationally, it becomes clear that some correlations are arbitrary rather than causal. Don't permit yourself to make financial decisions on what you can logically discern is an arbitrary basis.
3. Seek contrary viewpoints. As you contemplate a new investment, take a moment to ponder whatever considerations might weigh against the trade. Ask yourself: Why am I making this investment? What are the downside risks? When will I sell? What might go wrong? These important questions can help you to screen the logic behind a decision before implementing that decision.

4. Keep records. Once you have decided to move forward with an investment, one of the best ways to keep illusions of control at bay is to maintain records of your transactions, including reminders spelling out the rationales that underlie each trade. Write down some of the important features of each investment that you make, and emphasize those attributes that you have determined to be in favor of the investment's success.

If you want proof that this fourth habit, in particular, pays off, look no further than renowned former Fidelity Magellan Fund manager Peter Lynch. Lynch was a meticulous record keeper, documenting his opinions on different companies at every opportunity. When I was a young analyst in Boston right out of college, I had the occasion to visit some colleagues at Fidelity and met Mr. Lynch in his office. What I saw was astounding. Lynch maintained an archive of notebooks filled with information. His office was literally wall-to-wall research papers. He expected his subordinates to be equally thorough. When analysts made a recommendation, Lynch would require a written presentation outlining the details and the basis of each recommendation. Average investors should strive to reach this standard.

8

Belief Perseverance Bias #6: Hindsight Bias

Hindsight is a wonderful thing.

—**David Beckham**

Bias Description

Bias Name: Hindsight bias
Bias Type: Cognitive
Subtype: Belief perseverance

General Description

Described in simple terms, *hindsight bias* is the impulse that insists: "I knew it all along!" This is perhaps the most pronounced version of belief perseverance biases. Once an event has elapsed, people afflicted with hindsight bias tend to perceive that the event was predictable— even if it wasn't. This behavior is precipitated by the fact that *actual* outcomes are more readily grasped by people's minds than the infinite array of outcomes that could have but didn't materialize. Therefore, people tend to overestimate the accuracy of their own predictions. This is not to say, obviously, that people cannot make accurate predictions, but merely that people may believe that they made an accurate prediction in hindsight. Hindsight bias has been demonstrated in experiments involving investing—a few of which will be examined shortly—as well as in other diverse settings, ranging from politics to medicine. Unpredictable developments bother people, since it's always embarrassing to be caught off guard. Also, people tend to remember their own predictions of the future as more accurate than they actually were because they are biased by having knowledge of what actually happened. To alleviate the discomfort associated with the unexpected, people tend to view things that have already happened as being relatively inevitable and predictable. This view is often caused by the reconstructive nature of memory. When people look back, they do not have perfect memory; they tend to "fill in the gaps" with what they prefer to believe. In doing so, people may prevent themselves from learning from the past.

Example of Hindsight Bias

Many people have observed hindsight bias in the investment realm. They watch people fool themselves into thinking that they could have predicted the outcome of some financial gamble, but they achieve such crystal-clear insight only after the fact. Perhaps the most obvious example recalls the prevailing response by investors to the behavior of the U.S. stock market between 1998 and 2003. In 1998 and 1999, virtually nobody viewed the soaring market indexes as symptomatic of a short-lived "bubble" (or if they did harbor such misgivings, investors did not act on them). Above-average returns were the norm, though even a casual glance at historical business-cycle trends should have foretold that, eventually, the 1990s bull market had to recede. Still, sadly, even some of the most sophisticated investors succumbed to the fantasy: "It's different this time!" Similarly, in 2006, when the first edition of this book was published, it was inconceivable to most people that housing could be an unsafe "investment" and that a financial crisis of epic proportions was in the making. Now, in 2021, most people concede the reality of the housing and credit bubbles, the Internet stock bubble, and the subsequent meltdown in a distant memory or have forgotten altogether. In fact, chatting with most investors today, you'll get the impression that they expected the collapse of housing prices. The collapse of late 2000s prosperity was "clearly in the cards," or they comment: "Wasn't it obvious that we were in a bubble?" Giving in to hindsight bias can be very destructive because it leads investors to believe that they have better predictive powers than they actually do. Relying on these "powers" can invite poor decision making in the future.

Implications for Investors

Perhaps the hindsight bias's biggest implication for investors is that it gives investors a false sense of security when making investment decisions. This can manifest itself in excessive risk-taking behavior and place people's portfolios at risk. Box 8.1 reviews some common behaviors, rooted in hindsight bias that can cause investment mistakes.

BOX 8.1 Hindsight Bias: Behaviors That Can Cause Investment Mistakes

1. When an investment appreciates, hindsight-biased investors tend to rewrite their own memories to portray the positive developments as if they were predictable. Over time, this rationale can inspire excessive risk taking because hindsight-biased investors begin to believe that they have superior predictive powers, when, in fact, they do not. The bursting of the technology bubble is an example of this bias in action.

2. Hindsight-biased investors also "rewrite history" when they fare poorly and block out recollections of prior, incorrect forecasts in order to alleviate embarrassment. This form of self-deception, in some ways similar to cognitive dissonance, prevents investors from learning from their mistakes. A clear example of this bias took place in the early 1980s, when energy stocks generated over 20 percent of S&P 500 returns, and lots of investors were caught up in the boom. By the 1990s, though, the energy bubble subsided, and many stockholders lost money. Most now prefer, in hindsight, to not recognize that the speculative frenzy clouded their judgments.

3. Hindsight-biased investors can unduly fault their money managers when funds perform poorly. Looking back at what has occurred in securities markets, these investors perceive every development as inevitable. How, then, could a worthwhile manager be caught by surprise? In fact, even top-quartile managers who implement their strategies correctly may not succeed in every market cycle.

Managers of small-cap value funds in the late 1990s, for example, drew a lot of criticism. However, these people weren't poor managers; their style was simply out of favor at the time.

4. Conversely, hindsight bias can cause investors to unduly praise their money managers when funds perform well. The clarity of hindsight obscures the possibility that a manager's strategy might simply have benefited from good timing or good fortune. Consider the wisdom attributed to managers of aggressive-growth tech funds in the late 1990s.

Am I Subject to Hindsight Bias?

These questions are designed to detect cognitive errors caused by hindsight bias. To complete the test, select the answer choice that best characterizes your response to each item.

Hindsight Bias Test

Question 1: Suppose you make an investment, and it increases in value. Further suppose, though, that your reasons for purchasing the investment did not rely on the forces underlying its growth. How might you naturally react?

a. I do not concern myself with the reasons an investment does well. If it performs well, it means I did a good job as an investor, and doing well makes me more confident about the next investment I make.

b. Even though the stock went up, I'm concerned that the factors I thought were important didn't end up impacting its performance. In cases like this, I usually try to revisit the reasons that I bought the stock, and I also try to understand why it succeeded. Overall, I think I'd be more cautious the next time around.

Question 2: Suppose you make an investment and it goes down. What is your natural reaction to this situation?

a. Generally, I don't fault myself—if an investment doesn't work out, this may simply be due to bad luck. I'll sell the stock and move on, rather than pursuing the details of what went wrong.

b. I would want to investigate and determine why my investment failed. In fact, I'm very interested in finding out what went wrong. I put a lot of emphasis on the reasons behind my investment decisions, so I need to be aware of the reasons behind my investment's performance.

Question 3: Suppose you are investigating a money manager for inclusion in your portfolio. Your advisor suggests a large-cap value manager for you. What is your natural approach to examining the manager's performance?

a. I tend to look primarily at a manager's track record, comparing his or her performance to some relevant benchmark. I don't concern myself with the strategy that the manager employs. The results that a manager achieves are most important. If returns impress me, then I will select that manager; if I see a mediocre history, I'll pass.

b. I look at the returns, which are important, but I also look at the manager's strategy and try to determine what the manager was doing during the time frame I'm examining. In the case of the value manager, I will look, for example, at 2002—the manager was probably down, but by how much? Which companies did the manager invest in at the time? Evidence of a sound strategy makes me more likely to select this money manager.

Test Results Analysis

Questions 1, 2, and 3: Hindsight bias is a difficult bias to measure because people are rarely aware that they harbor it. So, few are likely to take a test like this and effectively respond: "Yes, I am susceptible to 'I-knew-it-all-along' behavior." Even people with reason to believe, objectively, that they might suffer from hindsight bias are unlikely to admit it to themselves. So, this diagnostic test looks for clues that might indicate *symptoms* of potential hindsight bias. For each item, respondents identifying with the rationale in "a" should be aware that they exhibit such symptoms and that they may suffer from hindsight bias.

Investment Advice

In order to overcome hindsight bias, it is necessary, as with most biases, for the investors to understand and admit their susceptibility. Here are some thoughts to help you better deal with hindsight bias:

"Rewriting history"—predicting gains. When an investor overestimates the degree to which some positive investment outcome was foreseeable, this may be due to hindsight bias. Consider the collapse of the credit bubble in the 2008–2009 period, when risks fueled by excessive credit cost stockholders billions. Many investors used rationales like "I knew that stock was going to go up! I told you so," which is a cautionary tale that can highlight the pitfalls of overestimating one's own predictive powers.

"Rewriting history"—predicting losses. Investors need to recognize that many people prefer to block recollections of poor investment decisions. Understanding why investments go awry, however, is critical to obtaining insight into markets and, ultimately, to finding investment success. Investors need to carefully examine their investment decisions, both good and bad. Encourage self-examination. This will help eliminate repeats of past investment mistakes.

Unduly criticizing money managers for poor performance. Investors need to understand that markets move in cycles and that, at certain times, an investment manager will underperform in his or her class, relative to other asset classes. Investors should understand that a good manager adheres to a consistent, valid style, through good times and bad. A manager is hired to do a job, and that job is to implement a defined investment strategy. Education is critical here. Just because many growth managers underperformed in the early 2000's, when values of many stocks were in a downward cycle, does not mean that growth managers are categorically unskilled. A similar case can be made for managers of "quality" stocks (safe, large-capitalization companies).

Unduly praising a money manager for good performance. Using the same line of reasoning, investors should guard against becoming too giddy over the prospects offered by managers who happen to be in the right asset class at the right time. There are plenty of investment managers who benefit circumstantially from market cycles and still do not meet benchmarks. These are the managers to avoid. Again, education is critical; once investors understand the role that a manager plays in determining fund performance, hindsight bias can be curtailed.

PART III
INFORMATION PROCESSING
BIASES DEFINED
AND ILLUSTRATED

I n Chapters 3 through 22, 20 behavioral biases, both cognitive and emotional, will be discussed. There are two types of cognitive bias that are reviewed in Chapters 3 through 15. The first type of cognitive biases, belief perseverance biases were covered in Chapters 3 through 8. The second type, information processing cognitive biases, the focus of Part Three of the book, will be covered now in Chapters 9 through 15. Emotional biases are then covered in Chapters 16 through 22.

In these chapters, the same basic format is used to discuss each bias, in order to promote greater accessibility. First, each bias is named, categorized as emotional or cognitive, including subtype (belief perseverance or information processing), and then generally described. This is followed by the all-important concrete practical application, in which it is demonstrated how each bias has been used, or can be used, in a practical situation. The practical application portion varies in content, consisting of either an intensive review of applied research or a case study. Implications for investors are then delineated. A diagnostic test and test-result analysis follow, providing a tool to indicate the potential susceptibility to certain biases. Finally, advice on managing the effects of each bias in order to minimize its effects, is offered.

9

Information Processing Bias #1: Mental Accounting Bias

There's no business like show business, but there are several businesses like accounting.
—**David Letterman, Television Personality**

Bias Description

Bias Name: Mental accounting
Bias Type: Cognitive
Subtype: Information processing

General Description

First coined by University of Chicago professor Richard Thaler, *mental accounting* describes people's tendency to code, categorize, and evaluate economic outcomes by grouping their assets into any number of non-fungible (noninterchangeable) mental accounts.[1] A completely rational

---

[1] Richard H. Thaler, "Towards a Positive Theory of Consumer Choice," *Journal of Economic Behavior and Organization* 1 (1980): 39–60.

person would never succumb to this sort of psychological process because mental accounting causes subjects to take the irrational step of treating various sums of money differently based on where these sums are mentally categorized, for example, the way that a certain sum has been obtained (work, inheritance, gambling, bonus, etc.) or the nature of the money's intended use (leisure, necessities, etc.). Money is money, regardless of the source or intended use.

The concept of framing is important in mental accounting analysis. In framing, people alter their perspectives on money and investments according to the surrounding circumstances that they face. Thaler[2] performed an experiment in which he offered one group of people $30 and an accompanying choice: either pocket the money, no strings attached, or gamble on a coin toss, wherein a win would add $9 and a loss would subtract $9 from the initial $30 endowment. Seventy percent of the people offered this choice elected to gamble, because they considered the $30 to be "found" money—a little fortuitous windfall, not the sum of pennies meticulously saved and not the wages of hours spent slaving at some arduous task. So, why not have a little fun with this money? After all, what did these subjects really stand to lose?

A second group of people confronted a slightly different choice. Outright, they were asked: Would you rather gamble on a coin toss, in which you will receive $39 for a win and $21 for a loss? Or, would you rather simply pocket $30 and forgo the coin toss? The key distinction is that these people were not awarded $30, seemingly out of the blue, in the initial phase, as was the first group. Rather, at the outset of the exercise, the options were presented in terms of their ultimate payoffs. As you might expect, the second group reacted differently from the first. Only 34 percent of them chose to gamble, even though the economic prospects they faced were identical to those offered to group one. Sometimes people create mental accounts in order to justify actions that seem enticing but that are, in fact, unwise. Other times, people derive benefits from mental accounting; for example, earmarking money for retirement may prevent some households from spending that money prematurely. Such concepts will be explored at greater length later in this chapter.

---

[2] Richard H. Thaler, "Towards a Positive Theory of Consumer Choice," *Journal of Economic Behavior and Organization* 1 (1980): 39–60.

Practical Application

Marketing professors Drazen Prelec and Duncan Simester of Massachusetts Institute of Technology (MIT) brought mental accounting to life through an ingenious experiment.[3] Prelec and Simester organized a sealed-bid auction for tickets to a Boston Celtics game during the team's victorious Larry Bird era in the 1980s. Half the participants in the auction were told that whoever won the bidding would need to pay for the tickets in cash within 24 hours. The other half was informed that the winning bidder would pay by credit card. Prelec and Simester then compared the average bids put forth within each group. As predicted, bidders who thought that they were relying on their credit cards wagered, on average, nearly twice the average cash bid.

This experiment illustrated that people put money in separate "accounts" when presented with a financial decision. In this case, the auction participants value cash more highly than credit card remittances, even though both forms of payment draw, ultimately, from the participant's own money. People may allocate money to a "cash" (expenditures only paid in cash) account, while simultaneously placing additional funds in a "credit card" (expenditures paid only by credit card) account. Viewed in light of the life-cycle theory mentioned in the previous section, the cash might be more likely to represent a "current asset," and the credit card might represent "future income," which are two separate accounts. It probably goes without saying that this behavior touches on another bias previously reviewed: self-control.

Implications for Investors

Mental accounting is a deep-seated bias with many manifestations, and it can cause a variety of problems for investors. The most basic of these problems is the placement of investment assets into discrete "buckets" according to asset type, without regard for potential correlations connecting investments across categories. Tversky and Kahneman contended that the difficulty individuals have in addressing interactions between investments leads investors to construct portfolios in a layered, pyramid format. Each tier addresses a particular investment goal independently of

---

[3] Drazen Prelec and Duncan Simester, "Always Leave Home without It: A Further Investigation of the Credit Card Effect on Willingness to Pay," *Marketing Letters* 12(1): 5–12.

any additional investment goals. For example, when the objective is to preserve wealth, investors tend to target low-risk investments, like cash and money market funds. For income, they rely mostly on bonds and dividend-paying stocks. For a chance at a more drastic reward, investors turn to riskier instruments, like emerging market stocks and initial public offerings (IPOs). Combining different assets whose performances do *not* correlate with one another is an important consideration for risk reduction, but it is often neglected in this "pyramid" approach. As a result, investment positions held without regard to correlations might offset one another in a portfolio context, creating suboptimal inefficiencies. People quite often fail to evaluate a potential investment based on its contribution to overall portfolio return and aggregate portfolio risk; rather, they look only at the recent performance of the relevant asset layer. This common, detrimental oversight stems from mental accounting.

Box 9.1 reviews five investment mistakes that mental accounting can cause. Please note that this list is not exhaustive, as mental accounting bias is a vast, varied topic. Advice on each of the five potential pitfalls will follow in subsequent portions of this chapter.

BOX 9.1 Mental Accounting Bias: Behaviors That Can Cause Investment Mistakes

1. Mental accounting bias can cause people to imagine that their investments occupy separate "buckets," or accounts. These categories might include, for example, college fund or money for retirement. Envisioning distinct accounts to correspond with financial goals, however, can cause investors to neglect positions that offset or correlate across accounts. This can lead to suboptimal aggregate portfolio performance.

2. Mental accounting bias can cause investors to irrationally distinguish between returns derived from income and those derived from capital appreciation. Many people feel the need to preserve capital (i.e., principal) sums and prefer to spend interest. As a result, some investors chase income streams and can unwittingly erode principal in the process. Consider, for example, a high-income bond fund or a preferred stock that pays a high dividend yet, at times, can suffer a loss of principal due to interest rate fluctuations. Mental accounting can make instruments like these appealing, but they may not benefit the investor in the long run.

3. Mental accounting bias can cause investors to allocate assets differently when employer stock is involved. Studies have shown that participants in company retirement plans that offer no company stock as an option tend to invest in a balanced way between equities and fixed-income instruments. However, when employer stock is an option, employees usually allocate a portion of contributions to company stock, with the remainder disbursed evenly over equity and fixed-income investments. Total equity allocation, then, could be too high when company stock was offered, causing these investors' portfolios to potentially be under-diversified. This can be a sub-optimal condition because these investors do not fully comprehend the risk that exists in their portfolio.

4. In the same vein as anchoring bias, mental accounting bias can cause investors to succumb to the "house money" effect, wherein risk-taking behavior escalates as wealth grows. Investors exhibiting this rational behave irrationally because they fail to treat all money as fungible. Biased financial decision making can, of course, endanger a portfolio. (In the Research Review of this chapter, we will review some excellent research on the house money effect.)

5. Mental accounting bias can cause investors to hesitate to sell investments that once generated significant gains but, over time, have fallen in price. During the bull market of the 1990s, investors became accustomed to healthy, unrealized gains. When most investors had their net worth deflated by the market correction, they hesitated to sell their positions at the then-smaller profit margin. Many today still regret not reaping gains when they could; a number of investments to which people clung following the 1990s boom have become nearly worthless.

Am I Subject to Mental Accounting Bias?

These questions are designed to detect signs of cognitive bias stemming from mental accounting. To complete the test, select the answer choice that best characterizes your response to each item.

Mental Accounting Bias Test

Question 1—Part A: Suppose that you are at a warehouse store, where you intend to purchase a flat-screen television. The model you've selected is priced at $750, and you are about to pay. However, at the last minute, you notice a discarded advertising flier featuring the same television—at a price of $720. You retrieve the ad, examine it more closely, and discover that the offer is still valid. To receive the discount, you'll need to drive to a competing electronics outlet about 10 minutes away. Will you get into your car and travel to the other store to take advantage of the lower price?

a. Yes.

b. No.

Question 1—Part B: Now suppose that you are in the same warehouse store, this time to buy a mahogany table. The table that you want costs $4,000, and you are willing to pay. While you are waiting, you strike up a conversation with another store patron, who reveals that she's seen the same table available for $3,970 at a competing local furniture store about 10 minutes away. Will you get into your car and drive to the other store to obtain the lower price?

a. Yes.

b. No.

Question 2—Part A: Suppose that you have purchased a ticket to a concert by your favorite music artist. You arrive at the venue excited, but quickly panic as you realize that you have misplaced your ticket! You paid $100 for the ticket initially and discover that some similar seats are still available at the same price. What is the probability that you will purchase another $100 ticket in order to see the show?

a. 100 percent.

b. 50 percent.

c. 0 percent.

Question 2—Part B: Suppose that you have not purchased any concert tickets in advance but planned to buy one for $100 at the door. When you arrive at the box office to buy your ticket, you panic because you realize you've lost $100 on the subway en route to the show. There is an ATM close by, so you can still get cash and purchase a ticket. What is the probability that you will make a cash withdrawal and then purchase a ticket for $100 to see the show?

a. 100 percent.

b. 50 percent.

c. 0 percent.

Question 3—Part A: Suppose that you've taken half a day off work to shop for a new, ride-on lawnmower. You have a big yard, and trimming it with your current, push-propelled mower simply takes too long. You have been eyeing the Model A300, which offers all the features you require at a cost of $2,000. As luck would have it, you won $500 the previous evening playing bingo at your local Rotary Club. When you arrive at the lawnmower shop, you notice that they also stock Model A305, which has some fancy, desirable new options. This premium model costs $2,250. Considering the previous night's winnings, what is the probability that you will indulge yourself by purchasing the A305?

a. 100 percent.

b. 50 percent.

c. 0 percent.

Question 3—Part B: Suppose that your budget and your needs regarding the lawnmower are exactly as described in Question 3A and that again you've taken half a day off work to go buy the simpler-but-sufficient A300. However, imagine that while you've not been especially lucky at bingo, you do discover a $500 check in your jacket pocket. You recall that the money was a gift from your mother last year, something to be "put away for a rainy day." You apparently forgot that you put it in your jacket and have just come upon it. When you arrive at the lawnmower shop, you again notice the pricier A305 for $2,250, with its coveted, innovative mowing features. Considering the check you just found, what is the probability that you will go ahead and purchase the A305?

a. 100 percent.

b. 50 percent.

c. 0 percent.

Test Results Analysis

Question 1—Parts A and B: Most people would probably drive an extra 10 minutes to save $30 on the television but wouldn't go to the same trouble to save the same amount of money on the table. While both scenarios net a savings of $30, a typical mental accounting scheme doesn't envision things this way. So people who are more likely to go out of their way to receive a discount in Part A than in Part B are likely susceptible to mental accounting bias.

Question 2—Parts A and B: If the respondent is like most people, he or she answered "no" to the first question and "yes" to the second, even though both scenarios present the same prospect: an initial loss of $100, an additional $100 outlay for the ticket. Mental accounting causes people to perceive in the first scenario an aggregate cost of $200 for the show—two tickets, each costing $100. Conversely, for most people the loss of $100 cash and the additional $100 ticket price are somehow separate in the second scenario. Mentally, these sums are debited from two independent categories or accounts, meaning that no single, larger loss of $200 ever registers. In both cases, of course, the concert costs $200. If the respondent indicated a greater willingness to pay for a ticket in Part B than in Part A, then mental accounting bias is likely present.

Question 3—Parts A and B: Most people would answer "yes" in Part A and "no" in Part B. They would be willing to allocate the bingo winnings but not the check from Mom toward the purchase of the premium lawnmower. This is because most people engage in mental accounting. In this instance, mental accounting values dollars obtained from different sources differently. However, money is indeed fungible. Responses demonstrate that this all-too-typical inconsistency between Parts A and B probably indicates mental accounting bias.

Investment Advice

The following advice has been incremented to correspond to each of the five investment errors discussed in Box 9.1. It is important to note that mental accounting is very common and that nearly everyone is susceptible to this bias in some way or another. Remember, moreover, that mental accounting can sometimes serve as a beneficial rather than as a harmful cognitive mechanism for investors. This section concludes with a special "bonus" discussion of the helpful aspects of mental accounting.

Correlations between investment "buckets." The most effective method to prevent investors from viewing their money in terms of discrete investment buckets is demonstrating how investments identified with separate mental accounts can actually correlate with one another, impacting portfolio performance. A straightforward discussion of the harms of excessive correlation and the benefits of sufficient diversification ought to effectively refute the bucket rationale. Since mental accounting is a cognitive bias, education can often defeat it.

Total returns as priority. The best way to prevent mental accounting from weakening total returns is to remind yourself that total returns are, after all, the number one priority of any allocation. A renewed focus on global portfolio performance—not simply piecemeal aspects, such as principal or income—is often achievable. As investors become more conscious of total returns, they will likely recognize the pitfalls of excessive mental accounting, and the problem will remedy itself.

Company stock and diversification. Investors should diversify away from company stock is indeed a theme that emerges again and again in contending with various behavioral biases. This problem arises once more with mental accounting. As in previous instances involving portfolios overly dominated by company stock, investors need to recognize the benefits of a balanced, diversified portfolio. Excessive concentration in any stock is not good, but a variety of behavioral biases can crop up and cause investors to feel irrationally comfortable with their own companies' stocks.

House money effect. As the research review demonstrates, the house money effect is a manifestation of mental accounting that can cause people to take on more risk as their wealth increases. This specific bias is perhaps the most pernicious of any reviewed in this chapter; however, education can help investors overcome it. Gentle but straightforward reminders regarding the risk of a chosen investment or the fungibility of money in general can diminish the house money effect. The house money effect causes investors to devalue a dollar as aggregate dollars accumulate. Recall that this rationale causes investors to devalue individual dollars. They sense that they are now playing with the "house's" money, not their own. Remember, dollars won or found seem, for many people, irrationally expendable. When investors appear subject to the house money effect, it is crucial to stress the underlying truth that *a dollar equals a dollar*—no matter which mental account each dollar occupies.

Clinging to formerly gainful investments. Mental accounting bias prevailed during the collapse of the tech boom in 2000 and 2001. Any investor who recalls those years should be somewhat inoculated against this behavior. Unfortunately, however, many people have short memories. If a company's prospects today do not look good and if it is still possible to divest from that company and capture a gain, then the investors should evacuate the position immediately. The investment may have generated great profits in the past, but most investors should rationally grasp that the present-day outlook matters most. A convenient reminder is: "No one ever got hurt taking a profit."

10

Information Processing Bias #2: Anchoring Bias

To reach a port we must sail, sometimes with the wind, and sometimes against it. But we must not drift or lie at anchor.

—Oliver Wendell Holmes

Bias Description

Bias Name: Anchoring
Bias Type: Cognitive
Subtype: Information processing

General Description

When required to estimate a value with unknown magnitude, people generally begin by envisioning some initial, default number—an "anchor"—which they then adjust up or down to reflect subsequent information and analysis. The anchor, once fine-tuned and reassessed, matures into a final estimate. Numerous studies demonstrate that regardless of how the initial anchors were chosen, people tend to adjust their anchors insufficiently and produce end approximations that are, consequently, biased. People are generally better at estimating relative comparisons rather than absolute figures, which this example illustrates.

Suppose you are asked whether the population of Canada is greater than or less than 20 million. Obviously, you will answer either above 20 million or below 20 million. If you were then asked to guess an absolute population value, your estimate would probably fall somewhere near 20 million, because you are likely subject to anchoring by your previous response.

Example of Anchoring and Bias

This chapter reviews one miniature case study and provides an accompanying analysis and interpretation that will demonstrate investor potential for Anchoring Bias.

Miniature Case Study: Anchoring Bias

Case Presentation

Suppose Alice owns stock in Corporation ABC. She is a fairly astute investor and has recently discovered some new information about ABC. Her task is to evaluate this information for the purpose of deciding whether she should increase, decrease, or simply maintain her holdings in ABC. Alice bought ABC two years ago at $12, and the stock is now at $15. Several months ago, ABC reached $20 after a surprise announcement of higher-than-expected earnings, at which time Alice contemplated selling the stock but did not. Unfortunately, ABC then dropped to $15 after executives were accused of faulty accounting practices. Today, Alice feels as though she has "lost" 25 percent of the stock's value, and she would prefer to wait and sell her shares in ABC once it returns to its recent $20 high.

Alice has a background in accounting, and she does some research that leads her to conclude that ABC's methods are indeed faulty, but not extremely so. However, Alice cannot entirely gauge the depth of the problem and realizes that holding ABC contains risk, but ABC is also a viable corporate entity with good prospects. Alice must make a decision. On one hand, she has confirmed that ABC does have an accounting problem, and she is unsure of how severe the problem might become. On the other hand, the company has a solid business, and Alice wants to recoup the 25 percent that she feels she lost. What should Alice do?

Analysis

Most investors have been confronted with situations similar to this one. They decide to invest in a stock; the stock goes up and then declines. Investors become conflicted and must evaluate the situation to determine whether to hold on to the stock. A rational investor would examine the company's financial situation; make an objective assessment of its business fundamentals; and then decide to buy, hold, or sell the shares. Conversely, some irrational investors—even after going through the trouble of performing the aforementioned rational analysis—permit cognitive errors to cloud their judgment. Alice, for example, may irrationally disregard the results of her research and "anchor" herself to the $20 figure, refusing to sell unless ABC once again achieves that price. This type of response reflects an irrational behavioral bias and should be avoided.

Implications for Investors

A wide variety of investor behaviors can indicate susceptibility to Anchoring Bias. Box 10.1 highlights some important examples of which investors and advisors should be aware.

BOX 10.1 Anchoring Bias: Behaviors That Can Cause Investor Mistakes

1. Investors tend to make general market forecasts that are too close to current levels. For example, if the Dow Jones Industrial Average (DJIA) is at 10,500, investors are likely to forecast the index in a way narrower than what might be suggested by historical fluctuation. For example, an investor subject to anchoring might forecast the DJIA to fall between 10,000 and 11,000 at year-end, versus making an absolute estimate based on historical standard deviation (rational) analysis.

2. Investors (and securities analysts) tend to stick too closely to their original estimates when new information is learned about a company. For example, if an investor determines that next year's earnings estimate is $2 per share and the company subsequently falters, the investor may not readjust the $2 figure enough to reflect the change because he or she is "anchored" to the $2 figure. This is not

---

limited to downside adjustments—the same phenomenon occurs when companies have upside surprises. (At the end of the chapter, we will review a behaviorally based investment strategy leveraging this concept that has proven to be effective at selecting investments.)

3. Investors tend to make a forecast of the percentage that a particular asset class might rise or fall based on the current level of returns. For example, if the DJIA returned 10 percent last year, investors will be anchored on this number when making a forecast about next year.

4. Investors can become anchored on the economic states of certain countries or companies. For example, in the 1980s, Japan was an economic powerhouse, and many investors believed that they would remain so for decades. Unfortunately for some, Japan stagnated for years after the late 1980s. Similarly, IBM was a bellwether stock for decades. Some investors became anchored to the idea that IBM would always be a bellwether. Unfortunately for some, IBM did not last as a bellwether stock.

Am I Subject to Anchoring Bias?

In this section, we outline a hypothetical decision-making problem and discuss how and why various reactions to this problem may or may not indicate susceptibility to Anchoring Bias.

Anchoring Bias Test

Scenario: Suppose you have decided to sell your house and downsize by acquiring a townhouse that you have been eyeing for several years. You do not feel extreme urgency in selling your house, but the associated taxes are eating into your monthly cash flow, and you want to unload the property as soon as possible. Your real estate agent, whom you have known for many years, prices your home at $900,000—you are shocked. You paid $250,000 for the home only 15 years ago, and the $900,000 figure is almost too thrilling to believe. You place the house on the market and wait a few months, but you don't receive any nibbles. One day, your real estate agent calls, suggesting that the two of you meet right away. When he arrives, he tells you that TechGrowth, a company that moved into town eight years ago in conjunction with its much-publicized initial public offering (IPO), has just declared Chapter 11 bankruptcy. Now, 7,500 people are out of work. Your agent has been in meetings all week with his colleagues, and together they estimate that local real estate prices have taken a hit of about 10 percent across the board. Your agent tells you that you must decide the price at which you want to list your home, based on this new information. You tell him that you will think it over and get back to him shortly.

Question: Assume your house is at the mean in terms of quality and salability. What is your likeliest course of action?

1. You decide to keep your home on the market for $900,000.
2. You decide to lower your price by 5 percent, and ask $855,000.
3. You decide to lower your price by 10 percent, and ask $810,000.
4. You decide to lower your price to $800,000 because you want to be sure that you will get a bid on the house.

Test Results Analysis

A tendency toward either of the first two responses probably indicates susceptibility of the subject to Anchoring Bias. Remember that real estate prices here have declined 10 percent. If the subject wants to sell his or her home, he or she clearly must lower the price by 10 percent. Resistance to an adequate adjustment in price can stem, however, from being anchored to the $900,000 figure. Anchoring Bias impairs the subject's ability to incorporate updated information. This behavior can have significant impact in the investment arena and should be counseled extensively.

Investment Advice

Before delving into specific strategies for dealing with Anchoring, it's important and, perhaps, uplifting to note that you can actually exploit this bias to your advantage. Understanding Anchoring can, for example, be a powerful asset when negotiating. Many negotiation experts suggest that the participants communicate radically strict initial positions, arguing that an opponent subject to anchoring can be influenced even when the anchor values are extreme. If one party begins a negotiation by offering a given price or condition, then the other party's subsequent counteroffer will likely reflect that anchor. So, when negotiating, it is wise to start with an offer much less generous than reflects your actual position (beware, however, of overdoing this). When presenting someone with a set of options, state first the options that you would most prefer that the other party select. Conversely, if a rival negotiator makes a first bid, do not assume that this number closely approximates a potential final price.

From the investment perspective, awareness is the best countermeasure to Anchoring Bias. Investors should ask themselves: "Am I analyzing the situation rationally, or am I holding out to attain an anchored price?" When making forecasts about the direction or magnitude of markets or individual securities, ask yourself: "Is my estimate rational, or am I anchored to last year's performance figures?" Taking these sorts of actions will undoubtedly root out any Anchoring Bias that might take hold during asset sales or asset reallocation.

Finally, when considering a recommendation by a securities analyst, delve further into the research and ask yourself: "Is this analyst anchored to some previous estimate, or is the analyst putting forth an objective rational response to a change in a company's business fundamentals?" Investment professionals are not immune to the effects of Anchoring Bias. In fact, there is an investment strategy that can leverage this behavior, which will be discussed in the "bonus discussion."

Bonus Discussion: Investment Strategies That Leverage Anchoring Bias

An awareness of the mechanics of anchoring can actually serve as a fundamental tenet of a successful investment strategy. Some finance professionals leverage Anchoring Bias by observing patterns in securities analyst earnings upgrades (downgrades) on various stocks and then purchasing (selling) the stocks in response. The behavioral aspect of this strategy is that it takes advantage of the tendency exhibited by securities analysts to underestimate, both positively and negatively, the magnitudes of earnings fluctuations due to Anchoring Bias.

As previously noted, when issuing upgrades and downgrades, analysts anchor on their initial estimates, which can be exploited. If an analyst is anchored to an earnings estimate and earnings are rising, this is an opportunity for investors to win, as it is likely that the analyst is underestimating the magnitude of the earnings upgrades. Conversely, if the analyst is anchored to an earnings estimate and earnings are falling, this is an opportunity to lose, so it's best to sell immediately on the first earnings downgrade, as it is likely that the analyst is underestimating the magnitude of the earnings downgrades.

In sum, we have learned that we need to be aware of the tendency toward Anchoring Bias and the ill effects it can have on our portfolios. At the same time, we can leverage it to our advantage in certain cases, such as in negotiation and in the investment strategy just reviewed.

11

Information Processing Bias #3: Framing Bias

You better cut the pizza in four pieces, because I'm not hungry enough to eat six.
— **Yogi Berra**

Bias Description

Bias Name: Framing bias
Bias Type: Cognitive
Subtype: Information processing

General Description

Framing bias notes the tendency of decision makers to respond to various situations differently based on the context in which a choice is presented (framed). This can happen in a number of contexts, including how word problems are described, how data is presented in tables and charts, and how figures are illustrated. For example, take a look at Figure 11.1. Which line is longer?

People subject to visual framing bias experience an optical illusion, which leads them to insist that the line on the bottom is longer. The graphic is reproduced, however, in Figure 11.2, this time with vertical marks added in as a guide. Which line is longer?

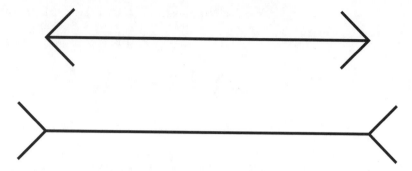

Figure 11.1 Which Line Is Longer?

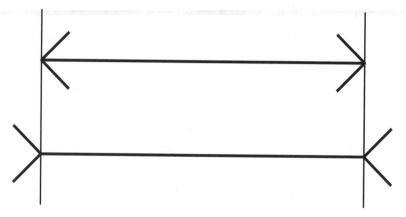

Figure 11.2 Which Line Is Longer?

With the framing effect of the "arrow" detail neutralized, it becomes clear that the line on the top and the line on the bottom are equal in length.

In the context of everyday evidence of framing bias, we can look at how retailers price their products. Many grocers, for example, will price items in multiples: "2 for $2" or "3 for $7."

This doesn't necessarily imply, however, that any kind of bulk discount is being offered. Have you ever found an item priced at "3 for $7" also available at a unit price of $2.33? This isn't unusual. Shopping represents a rudimentary rational choice problem ("How many oranges should I buy?"), and good salespeople try to frame a solution for a buyer that benefits the store. "Don't buy oranges in units of one," suggests the price policy. "Buy them in multiples of three." This takes advantage of people's susceptibility to framing. Applications to investing will follow later in the chapter.

Example of Framing Bias

Decision frames are quite prevalent in the context of investor behavior. Building on the definitions outlined in the preceding section, we can now use our newly acquired insights into framing bias as we consider a typical investor risk tolerance questionnaire. This will demonstrate how framing bias is applied in practice and how advisors should be aware of its effects.

Suppose that an investor completes a risk tolerance questionnaire for the purpose of determining the "risk category" into which he or she falls. The responses the investor selects are highly relevant because the risk category outcome will determine the types of investments that are selected for this individual's portfolio. Ideally, question phrasing and framing—elements uncorrelated with the investor's actual level of risk tolerance—should not be factors that affect the questionnaire's results. Let's examine some of the material that might appear on a typical risk tolerance questionnaire.

First, suppose that the items on the questionnaire refer to a hypothetical securities portfolio, Portfolio ABC. Over a 10-year period, ABC has historically returned an annual average of 10 percent, with a standard deviation of 15 percent. (Recall that standard deviation quantifies the amount of expected variation in an investment's performance from year to year.) Basic statistics dictate that 67 percent of ABC's returns will fall within one standard deviation of the mean, or annual average, return that ABC generates. Similarly, 95 percent of returns will fall within two standard deviations, and 99.7 percent within three standard deviations of the mean. So, if ABC's mean return was 10 percent and its standard deviation was 15 percent, then two-thirds of all returns produced by ABC would equal 10 percent plus-or-minus no more than 15 percent; that is, 67 percent of the time, ABC's return will likely be somewhere between –5 percent and 25 percent. It follows that 95 percent of ABC's returns will fall between –20 percent and 40 percent and that 99.7 percent will fall somewhere between –35 percent and 55 percent.

Now, imagine that one, but not both, of the following questions is to appear on an investor's risk tolerance questionnaire. Both concern

Portfolio ABC, and both try to measure an investor's comfort level with ABC, given its average returns, volatility, and so on. However, the two questions frame the situation very differently. As you compare Questions 1 and 2, try to imagine how an average investor, probably subject to a few common behavioral biases, might respond to each respective frame. Do you think most investors' answers would be identical in each instance?

1. Based on Table 11.1, which investment portfolio seems like the best fit, bearing in mind your own risk tolerance as well as your desire for long-term return?
   a. Portfolio XYZ
   b. Portfolio DEF
   c. Portfolio ABC

2. Assume that you own Portfolio ABC and that it lost 15 percent of its value over the past year, despite previous years of good performance. This loss is consistent with the performance of similar funds during the past year. What is your reaction to this situation?

   a. Sell all Portfolio ABC shares.
   b. Sell some, but not all, Portfolio ABC shares.
   c. Continue to hold Portfolio ABC shares.
   d. Increase investment in Portfolio ABC.

There is a chance that a person will select similar answers for both questions. However, there is also a significant probability that inconsistent framing will generate inconsistent responses from many investors. Specifically, respondents might reject Portfolio ABC in Question 1, yet decide to proceed with ABC in Question 2.

Table 11.1 Portfolio Selection: Which Portfolio Seems Best?

Portfolio Number	95% Probability Gain/ Loss Range	Long-Term Return
XYZ	2% to 4%	3%
DEF	−6% to 18%	6%
ABC	−20% to 40%	10%

In Question 1, "95% Probable Gain/Loss Range" refers (in Table 11.1) to an interval of two standard deviations above and below the mean. In 95 percent of all cases, ABC returned 10 percent plus-or-minus 30 percent; its standard deviation is 15 percent.

In Question 2, ABC produced a return that, in two-thirds of all cases, would have been the worst return imaginable: It returned one standard deviation below the mean. However, because Question 2 employs one standard deviation rather than two, readers are less likely to consider the one-third of all cases in which ABC could lose more than 5 percent of its value (entering into the 95 percent, rather than the 67 percent, probable gain/loss range).

Like the method employed by grocers (pricing produce in multiples), which subtly suggests some arbitrary, benchmark quantity of oranges for purchase, Question 1 similarly invites people to more intuitively consider the rarer, heavier losses Portfolio ABC could incur if returns breached the 67 percent confidence interval. Here, the implications of framing are important: Inconsistent responses to Questions 1 and 2 could make the questionnaire inconsistent and an inaccurate measure of investor risk tolerance (the questionnaire's outcome would be, accordingly, a flawed basis for structuring an allocation). Practitioners need to be acutely aware of how framing can affect the outcome of various investment choices.

Implications for Investors

An individual's willingness to accept risk can be influenced by how questions/scenarios are framed—positively or negatively. Recall, for example, the subjective difference between "25 percent of crops will be saved" and "75 percent of crops will die." The same optimism or pessimism in framing can affect investment decision making. For example, suppose that Mrs. Smith chooses to invest in either Portfolio A or Portfolio B. Further suppose that Portfolios A and B are identical in every respect. Mrs. Smith learns that Portfolio A will offer her a 70 percent chance of attaining her financial goals, whereas Portfolio B offers Mrs. Smith a 30 percent chance of not attaining her financial goals. If Mrs. Smith is like most people, she will choose Portfolio A, because its performance prospects were more attractively framed.

Another key point to keep in mind is that framing bias and loss aversion bias can and do work together. When people have suffered losses, they may view losses as the right time to embark on risk-taking behavior; when people have gained, they may feel threatened by options that entail additional risk. For example, an investor who has just suffered a net loss is likely to seek risk with his or her investments. Someone who has gained, however, is more likely to opt for a sure thing.

Box 11.1 reviews four investor mistakes caused by framing bias.

BOX 11.1 Framing Bias: Behaviors That Can Cause Investment Mistakes

1. Depending on how questions are asked, framing bias can cause investors to communicate responses to questions about risk tolerance that are either unduly conservative or unduly aggressive. For example, when questions are worded in the "gain" frame, a risk-averse response is more likely. When questions are worded in the "loss" frame, risk-seeking behavior is the likely response.

2. The optimistic or pessimistic manner in which an investment or asset allocation recommendation is framed can affect people's willingness or lack of willingness to invest. Optimistically worded questions are more likely to garner affirmative responses, and optimistically worded answer choices are more likely to be selected than pessimistically phrased alternatives. Framing contexts are often arbitrary and uncorrelated and therefore shouldn't impact investors' judgments . . . but, they do.

3. *Narrow framing,* a subset of framing bias, can cause even long-term investors to obsess over short-term price fluctuations in a single industry or stock. This behavior works in concert with myopic loss aversion (see Chapter 17): the risk here is that by focusing only on short-term market fluctuations, excessive trading may be the result. This trading behavior has proven to be less than optimal for investors.

4. Framing and loss aversion can work together to explain excessive risk aversion. An investor who has incurred a net loss becomes likelier to select a riskier investment, whereas a net gainer feels predisposed toward less risky alternatives.

Am I Subject to Framing Bias?

These questions are designed to detect signs of cognitive bias stemming from framing. Instead of one test, however, this section contains two shorter tests designed to be taken in tandem. Would you respond differently to the same dilemma if its framing were altered? Answer the following items and find out.

Framing Bias Mini–Test 1

Question 1: Suppose that you have the opportunity to invest in a mutual fund called MicroTrend. Over the past 10 years, MicroTrend has had an average annual return of 6 percent, with a standard deviation of 10 percent. So if MicroTrend continues to perform consistently, you can expect two-thirds of all returns to fall between −4 percent and 16 percent. How comfortable would you feel about investing in MicroTrend?

a. Comfortable

b. Somewhat comfortable

c. Uncomfortable

Question 2: Suppose that you have the opportunity to invest in a fund called MicroTrend. Over the past 10 years, MicroTrend has had an average annual return of 6 percent, with a standard deviation of 10 percent. So if MicroTrend continues to perform consistently, you can expect 95 percent of all returns to fall between −14 percent and 26 percent. How comfortable would you feel about investing in MicroTrend?

a. Comfortable

b. Somewhat comfortable

c. Uncomfortable

Framing Bias Mini–Test 2

Question 1: Suppose you are preparing for retirement. You need $50,000 annually to live comfortably, but you could take care of basic needs at about $40,000 and could even survive on a minimum of $30,000 if necessary. Further assume that there is no inflation. Now, imagine that you are choosing between two hypothetical investment options. Option 1 guarantees you an income of $40,000 per year—offering you a chance at a risk-free lifestyle. Option 2 offers you a 50 percent chance at $50,000 and a 50 percent chance at receiving $30,000 each year. Which option would you choose?

a. Option 1

b. Option 2

Question 2: Suppose you are preparing for retirement. You need $50,000 to live comfortably, but could take care of basic needs at about $40,000, and could even survive on a minimum of $30,000 if necessary. Further assume that there is no inflation. Now, imagine that you are choosing between two hypothetical investment options. Option 1 guarantees you enough income to cover your needs, but it will never provide you a comfortable lifestyle. With Option 2, you have the opportunity for a better lifestyle. With a probability of 50 percent, you might be limited to your bare minimum acceptable income. But with a corresponding probability of 50 percent, you would enjoy the comfortable lifestyle you desire and an income of $50,000. Which option do you choose?

a. Option 1

b. Option 2

Test Results Analysis

Mini–Test 1: People who answer the second question differently from the first are likely subject to framing bias. Typically, investors susceptible to framing bias choose the riskier strategy in Question 2.

Mini–Test 2: This test can't be interpreted too rigidly because lifestyle preferences are not black and white. However, people subject to framing bias will probably prefer an assured income in Question 1 and a riskier strategy in Question 2. This is because Question 1 is framed in a relatively positive fashion, focusing on the attribute "safe" lifestyle offered from the guarantee in Option 1. The framing in Question 2, however, is less upbeat; it reminds you that neither investment option offers you a reliably pleasurable standard of living. When framing intersects with loss aversion, this type of response pattern is especially likely to result.

Investment Advice

Financial markets don't just reflect financial realities. Investors' beliefs, perceptions, and desires exert a tremendous influence on most instruments and indexes. Sometimes, the formulation of the question itself also matters because framing determines reference points and defines expectations. Each investor has the right to express his or her personal financial objectives and should expect investment plans to be created relative to these desires. Assessing investor risk tolerance is a process wherein framing can be particularly influential. Ultimately, question framing can and does determine appropriate information elicitation.

This section offers advice on each of the specific investor errors outlined in Box 11.1.

Narrow framing. Investors engaging in narrow framing may become preoccupied with short-term price oscillations in an isolated stock or industry, or they may favor certain asset classes while remaining oblivious to others. Investors should keep the big picture in mind: overall wealth accumulation and long-term financial goals. Investors should work on building balanced asset allocations and focus on ensuring that those allocations are helping them meet their financial goals.

Framing and loss aversion. Investors who feel that they've been faring poorly will seek out risks, while those pleased with their recent returns tend to play it safe. Investors should isolate from their ongoing decision making any references to gains or losses incurred in a prior period. Advisors should also try to ask questions that are less likely to elicit biased answers. Finally, an emphasis on education, diversification, and proper portfolio management can help to neutralize these biases.

Unintended investment choices based on incorrectly framed questions. Risk tolerance questionnaires are critical in assessing investor goals and selecting appropriate investments. Investors, therefore, need to be thoroughly familiar with question wording and need to understand—and remain alert for—biases that can be awakened when options are formulated in certain ways. Remember, clear communication ensures the success of the advisory relationship.

Positive and negative frames. We've observed the considerable influence that positive and negative framing can exert. The lesson for investors is to interpret facts and choices as neutrally and uniformly as possible. This reduces the likelihood of a biased response and should help you to help investors achieve their financial goals.

12

Information Processing Bias #4: Availability Bias

It is ironic that the greatest stock bubble coincided with the greatest amount of information available. I always thought this would be a good thing, but maybe it was not so good.
—James J. Cramer, financial news analyst for CNBC

Bias Description

Bias Name: Availability bias
Bias Type: Cognitive
Subtype: Information processing

General Description

The *availability bias* is a rule of thumb, or mental shortcut, that causes people to estimate the probability of an outcome based on how prevalent or familiar that outcome appears in their lives. People exhibiting this bias perceive easily recalled possibilities as being more likely than those prospects that are harder to imagine or difficult to comprehend.

One classic example cites the tendency of most people to guess that shark attacks more frequently cause fatalities than airplane parts falling from the sky do. However, as difficult as it may be to comprehend, the latter is actually 30 times more likely to occur. Shark attacks are probably assumed to be more prevalent because sharks invoke greater fear or because shark attacks receive a disproportionate degree of media attention. Consequently, dying from a shark attack is, for most respondents, easier to imagine than death by falling airplane parts. In sum, the availability rule of thumb underlies judgments about the likelihood or frequency of an occurrence based on readily available information, not necessarily based on complete, objective, or factual information.

Example of Availability Bias

Availability bias has four variations, which each have unique implications in personal finance. Let's explore these now.

1. Retrievability. Most investors, if asked to identify the "best" mutual fund company, are likely to select a firm that engages in heavy advertising, such as Fidelity or Schwab. In addition to maintaining a high public relations profile, these firms also "cherry pick" the funds with the best results in their advertising, which makes this belief more "available" to be recalled. In reality, the companies that manage some of today's highest-performing mutual funds undertake little to no advertising. Consumers who overlook these funds in favor of more widely publicized alternatives may exemplify retrievability/availability bias.
2. Categorization. Although this is changing, most Americans, if asked to pinpoint one country, worldwide, that offers the best investment prospects, would designate their own: the United States. Why? When conducting an inventory of memories and stored knowledge regarding "good investment opportunities" in general, the country category that most Americans most easily recall is the United States. However, to dismiss the wealth of investment prospects abroad as a result of this phenomenon is irrational. In reality, over 50 percent of equity market capitalization exists outside the United States. People who are unduly "patriotic" when looking for somewhere to invest often suffer from availability bias.
3. Narrow range of experience. Assume that an employee of a fast-growing, high-tech company is asked: "Which industry generates the most successful investments?" Such an individual, who probably

comes into contact with other triumphant tech profiteers each and every day, will likely overestimate the relative proportion of corporate successes stemming from technologically intensive industries. Like the NBA star who got his start in college and, therefore, too optimistically estimates the professional athletic prospects of college basketball players, this hypothetical high-tech employee demonstrates narrow range of experience availability bias.

4. Resonance. People often favor investments that they feel match their personality. A thrifty individual who frequents discount shops, clips coupons, and otherwise seeks out bargains, may demonstrate a natural inclination toward value investing. At the same time, such an investor might not heed the wisdom of balancing value assets with more growth-oriented ventures, owing to a reluctance to front the money and acquire a quality growth stock. The concept of value is easily available in such an investor's mind, but the notion of growth is less so. This person's portfolio could perform sub-optimally as a result of resonance availability bias.

Special Topic: Which Political Party Is Best for the Stock Market?

Economic theory, and the political leanings of much of Wall Street, suggests that stock markets do better under Republican presidents than Democrats. Agree? This is classic Availability Bias in action. A longer-term analysis shows, however, that in fact investors are not as well rewarded under Republican leaders as Democrats. Many investors think the Republicans' pro-business credentials boost growth and capital markets. In fact, on average, in the postwar period, Republican presidents oversaw sub-par growth and equity market returns. Natixis Investment Managers found that since 1976 the average annualized return under Democratic presidents has been 14.3 percent, against 10.8 percent under Republicans. A compounding of the parties' market performance shows that a continuously held Democratic portfolio outperforms a continuously held Republican portfolio by even more: The Carter-Clinton-Obama Democratic presidencies produced an average annualized return of 14.9 percent, against 4.9 percent for the Republican Reagan–Bush Senior–Bush Junior–Trump presidencies.[1]

---

[1] https://www.ft.com/content/38829e98-5180-11ea-a1ef-da1721a0541e

Implications for Investors

Box 12.1 summarizes the primary implications for investors of susceptibility to availability bias in each of the four forms we've reviewed.
In all such instances, investors ignore potentially beneficial investments
because information on those investments is not readily available, or they
make investment decisions based on readily available information, avoiding diligent research.

BOX 12.1 Availability Bias: Behaviors That Can Cause Investment Mistakes

1. *Retrievability.* Investors will choose investments based on information that is available to them (advertising, suggestions from advisors,
   friends, etc.) and will not engage in disciplined research or due
   diligence to verify that the investment selected is a good one.
2. *Categorization.* Investors will choose investments based on categori-
   cal lists that they have available in their memory. In their minds,
   other categories will not be easily recalled and, thus, will be ignored.
   For example, U.S. investors may ignore countries where potentially
   rewarding investment opportunities may exist because these countries may not be an easily recalled category in their memory.
3. *Narrow range of experience.* Investors will choose investments that fit
   their narrow range of life experiences, such as the industry they
   work in, the region they live in, and the people they associate with.
   For example, investors who work in the technology industry may
   believe that only technology investments will be profitable.
4. *Resonance.* Investors will choose investments that resonate with their
   own personality or that have characteristics that investors can relate
   to their own behavior. Taking the opposite view, investors ignore
   potentially good investments because they can't relate to, or do not
   come in contact with, the characteristics of those investments. For
   example, thrifty people may not relate to expensive stocks (high
   price/earnings multiples) and potentially miss out on the benefits
   of owning these stocks.

Am I Subject to Availability Bias?

This brief test helps detect investor availability bias.

Availability Bias Test

Question 1: Suppose you have some money to invest and you hear about a great stock tip from your neighbor who is known to have a good stock market sense. He recommends you purchase shares in Mycrolite, a company that makes a new kind of lighter fluid for charcoal grills. What is your response to this situation?

a. I will likely buy some shares because my neighbor is usually right about these things.

b. I will likely take it under advisement and go back to my house and do further research before making a decision.

Question 2: Suppose that you are planning to buy stock in a generic drug maker called "Generics Plus." Your friend Marian sent you a report on the company and you like the story, so you plan to purchase 100 shares. Right before you do, you hear on a popular financial news show that "GN Pharmaceuticals," another generic drug maker, just reported great earnings and the stock is up 10 percent on the news. What is your response to this situation?

a. I will likely take this information as confirmation that generics are a good area to be in and proceed with my purchase of Generics Plus.

b. I will pause before buying Generics Plus and request research on GN prior to proceeding with the purchase of Generics Plus.

c. I will purchase GN rather than Generics Plus because GN appears to be a hot stock and I want to get in on a good thing.

Question 3: Which claims more lives in the United States?

a. Lightning.

b. Tornadoes.

Test Results Analysis

Question 1: Respondents choosing "a" are likely to be susceptible to availability bias.

Question 2: Respondents choosing "c" are likely to be susceptible to availability bias.

Question 3: Respondents choosing "b" are likely to be susceptible to availability bias. More Americans are killed annually by lightning than by tornadoes. Media attention, drills, and other publicity, however, make tornado fatalities memorable and therefore more "available" for people.[2]

Investment Advice

Generally speaking, in order to overcome availability bias, investors need to carefully research and contemplate investment decisions before executing them. Focusing on long-term results, while resisting chasing trends, are the best objectives on which to focus if availability bias appears to be an issue. Be aware that everyone possesses a human tendency to mentally overemphasize recent, newsworthy events; refuse to let this tendency compromise you. The old axiom that "nothing is as good or as bad as it seems" offers a safe, reasonable recourse against the impulses associated with availability bias.

When selecting investments, it is crucial to consider the effects of the availability rule of thumb. For example, stop and consider how you decide which investments to research before making an investment. Do you frequently focus on companies you've read about in the *Wall Street Journal* or on investments that have been mentioned on popular financial news programs such as *Mad Money*? Jonathan S. Hartley and Matthew Olson of the Wharton School, University of Pennsylvania analyzed Jim Cramer's stock picks in their paper entitled *Jim Cramer's "Mad Money"*

---

[2] See Paul Slovic, Baruch Fischoff, and Sarah Lichtenstein, "Facts versus Fiction: Understanding Public Fears," in Daniel Kahneman, Paul Slovic, and Amos Tversky, eds., *Judgment under Uncertainty: Heuristics and Biases* (New York: Cambridge University Press, 1982), 463–491.

Charitable Trust Performance and Factor Attribution.[3] They found the following after studying the complete historical performance of Jim Cramer's Action Alerts PLUS portfolio from 2001 to 2016, which includes many of the stock recommendations made on Cramer's TV show "Mad Money." Both since inception of the portfolio and since the start of "Mad Money" in 2005 (when it was converted into a charitable trust), Cramer's portfolio has underperformed the S&P 500 total return index and a basket of S&P 500 stocks that does not reinvest dividends (both on an overall returns basis and in Sharpe ratio).

It is also important to keep in mind that people tend to view things that occur more than a few years ago as past history. For example, if you got a speeding ticket last week, you will probably reduce your speed over the course of the next month or so. However, as time passes, you are likely to revert to your old driving habits. Likewise, availability bias causes investors to overreact to present-day market conditions, whether they are positive or negative. The housing bubble of the late 2000s provided a superb illustration of this phenomenon. Investors, swept up in the euphoria of the day, disregarded elementary risks. When the market corrected itself, these same investors lost confidence and over-focused on the short-term, negative results that they were experiencing.

Another significant problem is that much of the information investors receive is inaccurate and is based on insufficient information and multiple opinions. Furthermore, the information can be outdated or confusingly presented. Availability bias causes people to attribute disproportionate degrees of credibility to such information when it arrives amid a flurry of media attention. Many investors, suffering from information overload, overlook the fact that they often lack the training, experience, and objectivity to filter or interpret this deluge of data. As a result, investors often believe themselves to be more accurately informed than is, ultimately, the case. Because availability bias is a cognitive bias, often it can be corrected with updated information.

---

[3] https://static1.squarespace.com/static/568f03c8841abaff89043b9d/t/5734f6e2c
2ea51b32cf53885/1463088868550/HartleyOlson2016+Jim+Cramer+
Charitable+Trust+Performance+and+Factor+Attribution.pdf

13

Information Processing Bias #5: Self-Attribution Bias

Heads I win, tails it's chance.

—Ellen Langer and Jane Roth, 1975

Bias Description

Bias Name: Self-Attribution Bias
Bias Type: Cognitive
Subtype: Information Processing

General Description

Self-attribution bias (or self-serving attribution bias) refers to the tendency of individuals to ascribe their successes to innate aspects, such as talent or foresight, while more often blaming failures on outside influences, such as bad luck. Students faring well on an exam, for example, might credit their own intelligence or work ethic, while those failing might cite unfair grading. Similarly, athletes often reason that they have simply performed to reflect their own superior athletic skills if they win a game, but they might allege unfair calls by a referee when they lose a game.

Example of Self-Attribution Bias

Dr. Dana Dunn, a professor of psychology at Moravian College in Bethlehem, Pennsylvania, has done some excellent work regarding self-attribution bias. She observed that her students often have trouble recognizing self-attribution bias in their own behaviors. To illustrate this phenomenon, she performs an experiment in which she asks students to take out a sheet of paper and draw a line down the middle of the page. She then tells them to label one column "strengths" and the other "weaknesses" and to list their personal strengths and weaknesses in the two columns. She finds that students consistently list more strengths than weaknesses.[1]

Dunn's result suggests that her students tend to suffer from self-attribution bias. Investors are not immune from this behavior. The old Wall Street adage "Don't confuse brains with a bull market" is relevant here. When an investor who is susceptible to self-attribution bias purchases an investment and it goes up, then it was due, naturally, to their business and investment savvy. In contrast, when an investor who is susceptible to self-attribution bias purchases an investment and it goes down, then it was due, naturally, to bad luck or some other factor that was not the fault of the investor. People's strengths, generally, consist of personal qualities that they believe empower them to succeed, whereas weaknesses are traits they possess that predispose them to fail. Investors subject to self-attribution bias perceive that investment successes are more often attributable to innate characteristics and that investment failures are due to exogenous factors.

Implications for Investors

Irrationally attributing successes and failures can impair investors in two primary ways. First, people who aren't able to perceive mistakes they've made are, consequently, unable to learn from those mistakes. Second, investors who disproportionately credit themselves when desirable outcomes do arise can become detrimentally overconfident in their own

---

[1] Dana S. Dunn, "Demonstrating a Self-Serving Bias," *Teaching of Psychology* 16 (1989): 21–22.

market savvy. Box 13.1 describes the pitfalls of self-serving behavior that often lead to financial mistakes.

BOX 13.1 Self-Attribution Bias: Behaviors That Can Cause Investment Mistakes

1. Self-attribution investors can, after a period of successful investing (such as one quarter or one year), believe that their success is due to their acumen as investors rather than to factors out of their control. This behavior can lead to taking on too much risk, as the investors become too confident in their behavior.
2. Self-attribution bias often leads investors to trade too much than is prudent. As investors believe that successful investing (trading) is attributed to skill versus luck, they begin to trade too much, which has been shown to be "hazardous to your wealth."
3. Self-attribution bias leads investors to "hear what they want to hear." That is, when investors are presented with information that confirms a decision that they made to make an investment, they will ascribe "brilliance" to themselves. This may lead to investors that make a purchase or hold an investment that they should not.
4. Self-attribution bias can cause investors to hold under-diversified portfolios, especially among investors that attribute the success of a company's performance to their own contribution, such as corporate executives, board members, and so on. Often, the performance of a stock is not attributed to the skill of an individual person, but rather to many factors, including chance; thus, holding a concentrated stock position can be associated with self-attribution and should be avoided.

Am I Subject to Self-Attribution Bias?

This diagnostic quiz can help to detect susceptibility to self-attribution bias.

Self-Attribution Test

Question 1: Suppose you make an investment and it does well, but not for the reason you thought it would. You are feeling good about yourself for making the investment. Which of the following would most accurately describe your feelings?

a. Your keen eye for a good investment is alive and well.

b. Even though the investment did well for the wrong reason, it was still a great investment.

c. Actually, I'm not feeling that great even though I made money because the reason I thought the investment would go up did not occur; I got lucky.

Question 2: When returns to your portfolio increase, to what do you believe the change in performance is mainly due?

a. Your investment skill.

b. A combination of investment skill and luck.

c. Luck.

Question 3: After you make a successful trade, how likely are you to put your profits to work in a quick, subsequent trade, rather than letting the money idle until you're sure you've located another good investment?

a. When I sell a profitable investment, I usually invest the money again right away because I might be on a hot streak.

b. I will usually wait until I find something I really like before making a new investment.

c. Some combination of choices A and B.

Question 4: Relative to other investors, how good an investor are you?

a. Below average

b. Average

c. Above average

d. Well above average

Test Results Analysis

Question 1: People whose response indicates that their keen eye for investments is alive and well are likely to suffer from self-attribution bias. This is so because an investment success, in this case, was not due to good, but to good luck.

Question 2: Attributing financial success to skill tends to indicate susceptibility to self-attribution bias.

Question 3: Investors who roll over their money immediately without carefully plotting their next move are, often, disproportionately attributing their successes to their own market savvy. Therefore, they are likely to suffer from self-attribution bias.

Question 4: Investors who rate themselves as "above average" or "well above average" in skill are likely to suffer from self-attribution bias.

Investment Advice

Recall again the old Wall Street adage that perhaps provides the best warning against the pitfalls of self-attribution bias: "Don't confuse brains with a bull market."

Often, when financial decisions pan out well, investors like to congratulate themselves on their shrewdness. When things don't turn out so profitably, however, they can console themselves by concluding that someone or something else is at fault. In many cases, neither explanation is entirely correct. Winning investment outcomes are typically due to any number of factors, a bull market being the most prominent; stocks' decline in value, meanwhile, can be equally random and complex. Sometimes, the fault does lie in arenas well beyond an investor's control, such as fraud or mismanagement.

One of the best things investors can do is view both winning and losing investments as objectively as possible. However, most people don't take the time to analyze the complex confluence of factors that helped them realize profit or to confront the potential mistakes that aggravated a loss. Post-analysis is one of the best learning tools at any investor's disposal. It's understandable but, ultimately, irrational to fear an examination of one's past mistakes. The only real, grievous error is to continue to succumb to overconfidence and, as a result, to repeat the same mistakes!

Advisors and individual investors should perform a post-analysis of each investment: Where did you make money? Where did you lose money? Mentally separate your good, money-making decisions from your bad ones. Then, review the beneficial decisions and try to discern what, exactly, you did correctly: Did you purchase the stock at a particularly advantageous time? Was the market, in general, on an upswing?

Similarly, you should review the decisions that you've categorized as poor: What went wrong? Did you buy stocks with poor earnings? Were those stocks trading at or near their recent price highs when you purchased them, or did you pick up the stocks as they were beginning to decline? Did you purchase a stock aptly and simply make an error when it came time to sell? Was the market, in general, undergoing a correction phase?

When reviewing unprofitable decisions, look for patterns or common mistakes that perhaps you were unaware of making. Note any such tendencies that you discover, and try to remain mindful of them by, for example, brainstorming a rule or a reminder such as: "I will not do X in the future" or "I will do Y in the future." Being conscious of these rules will help you overcome any bad habits that you may have acquired and can also reinforce your reliance on the strategies that have served you well.

Remember: Being humble and learning from your past mistakes is the best way to become a smarter, better, and more successful investor!

14

Information Processing Bias #6: Outcome Bias

Insanity is doing the same thing in the same way and expecting a different outcome.
—**Albert Einstein**

Bias Description

Bias Name: Outcome bias
Bias Type: Cognitive
Subtype: Information processing

General Description

Outcome bias refers to the tendency of individuals to decide to do something—such as make an investment in a mutual fund—based on the outcome of past events (such as returns of the past five years) rather than by observing the process by which the outcome came about (the investment process used by the mutual fund manager over the past five years). An investor might think, "This manager had a fantastic five years, I am going to invest with her," rather than understanding how such great returns were generated or why the returns generated by other managers might not have had good results over the past five years.

Example of Outcome Bias

Jonathan Baron and John C. Hershey of the University of Pennsylvania administered several experiments on outcome bias.[1] Subjects were given descriptions of decisions made by others under conditions of uncertainty, together with outcomes of those decisions. Some decisions were medical decisions made by a physician or a patient, and others were decisions about monetary gambles. Subjects rated the quality of thinking that went into the decisions, the competence of the decision maker, or their willingness to let the decision maker act on their behalf. Subjects understood that all relevant information was available to the decision maker. Subjects rated the thinking as better (i.e., rated the decision maker as more competent, or indicated greater willingness to yield the decision) when the outcome was favorable than when it was unfavorable. In monetary gambles, subjects rated the thinking as better when the outcome of the option *not* chosen turned out poorly than when it turned out positively. When asked, subjects felt that they should not take outcomes into account in making these evaluations. However, they did exactly that. In part, the effect of outcome knowledge on evaluation may be explained in terms of its effect on the salience of arguments for each side of the choice.

Baron and Hershey's results suggest that subjects suffer from outcome bias. Investors are not immune to this behavior. For example, when investors who are susceptible to outcome bias make mutual fund investments, they may be doing so because they are focused on the outcome of a past investment experience related to this decision—such as their manager's track record or the asset class performance of that particular investment—and are not focused on *how* the returns were generated or why they should be investing in that asset class. On the contrary, when investors who are not susceptible to outcome bias make investments, they may not make an investment with that manager or asset class (well, they might, but for different reasons) because they may see that the manager took too much risk to obtain a given set of returns or the asset class is overvalued and should be avoided. Investors subject to outcome bias are not focusing on the process, but rather the result—and this can be dangerous.

---

[1] Jonathan Baron and John C. Hershey, "Outcome Bias in Decision Evaluation," *Journal of Personality and Social Psychology* 54 (2008): 569–579.

Implications for Investors

Irrationally attributing successes and failures can impair investors in two primary ways. First, people who aren't able to perceive the mistakes that they have made are, consequently, unable to learn from those mistakes. Secondly, investors who disproportionately credit themselves when desirable outcomes do arise can become detrimentally overconfident in their own market savvy. The following points describe the pitfalls of self-serving behavior that can often lead to financial losses:

BOX 14.1 Outcome Bias: Behaviors That Can Cause Investment Mistakes

1. Investors may invest in funds that they should not because they are focused on the outcome of a prior action, such as the performance record of the manager, rather than on the process by which the manager achieved the results. This may cause investors to subject themselves to excessive risk if the source of the performance was a risky strategy.
2. Investors may avoid investing in funds that they should not because they are focused on the outcome of a prior action, such as the performance record of the manager, rather than on the process by which the manager achieved the results. Investors may avoid a manager based on a bad outcome while ignoring the potentially sound process by which the manager made the decision.
3. Investors may invest in overvalued asset classes based on recent outcomes, such as strong performance in gold or housing prices, and not pay heed to valuations or past price history of the asset class in question, thereby exposing them to the risk that the asset class may be peaking, which can be "hazardous to one's wealth."

Am I Subject to Recency Bias?

This section contains a diagnostic quiz that can help to detect susceptibility to outcome bias. In the Advice section that follows, you will find guidelines for scoring responses to this quiz, along with corresponding suggestions for managing outcome bias.

Question 1: You are contemplating making an investment in small-cap U.S. equities. Before proceeding with an investment, you decide to research the track record of a mutual fund manager that has outperformed her index, the Russell 2000, by 600 basis points per annum over the past five years. How likely would you be to then seek information to understand what strategy was used and what kinds of risks were taken to achieve this result before investing (i.e., you might not invest if you think the manager might be taking too much risk)?

a. Very unlikely

b. Unlikely

c. Likely

d. Very likely

Question 2: You are contemplating making an investment in emerging markets equities. Before making an investment, you decide to research the track record of a mutual fund manager that has underperformed his index, the MSCI EM Index, by 300 basis points per annum over the past five years. How likely would you be to then seek information to understand what strategy was used and what kinds of risks were taken to achieve this result (i.e., you might actually invest if you understand why the manager underperformed)?

a. Very unlikely

b. Unlikely

c. Likely

d. Very likely

Diagnostic Quiz: Review

Let's begin by reviewing the logic employed in the preceding diagnostic quiz. First, here are a few scoring and assessment guidelines, broken down by question/item. Afterwards, we will discuss some overall tactics that can help to prevent people from sustaining financial harm as a result of self-attribution bias.

Question 1: Often, investors examine the track record of a mutual fund, see terrific performance over three or five years, and decide to invest. This can be a mistake if returns were achieved by taking too much risk or in a single strategy. For example, the Russell 2000 manager might have achieved her returns by concentrating the portfolio in 15 names and hit two grand slam home runs and picked four substantially losing investments. This might have been a case of luck versus skill, but the track record doesn't show that. Also, what was the annualized standard deviation? If it was markedly higher than the index, this is a red flag. Investors need to focus not only on the outcome but also the process.

Question 2: Similarly, in Question 2, the emerging markets manager may have made a conscious decision to avoid a certain country or a group of countries that performed exceptionally well but unexpectedly so. (By the way, this is the case for indexing—you never need to worry about sub-strategies that you do not own performing well because you own them all.) Suppose your thesis now is that China and India will out-perform and this manager is well positioned in these markets. You may want to invest after all, even though this manager has underperformed. You need to look not only at the outcome, but also at the process that drove the outcome.

Investment Advice

One of the most basic mistakes in investing is focusing on the invest-ment outcome without regard to the process used to create the out-come. A closely related concept is when a great amount of risk is used to create the returns. It is not a positive thing when inordinate amounts of risk are used to generate returns. When analyzing investment managers, it is critical to understand how the managers are creating returns, espe-cially if they are above their stated benchmarks. How many positions are in the fund, and how does this compare to the benchmark? How many names in the portfolio created returns? What is the tracking error and R-squared to the benchmark? Sometimes you will find that a manager with a solid strategy has simply been unlucky and underperformed even though his strategy is quite sound. Numerous studies have shown that managers who have strong 10-year track records will underperform for one, two, or even three years in a row only to have the manager revert back to strong outperformance. One of the best things investors can do is dig deep into the details of the contemplated strategies and learn how returns were generated. Ex-post analysis is one of the best learning tools at any investor's disposal.

15

Information Processing Bias #7: Recency Bias

The present is never our goal; the past and present are our means, the future alone is our goal.

—**Blaise Pascal (1623–1662), French mathematician and philosopher**

Bias Description

Bias Name: Recency Bias
Bias Type: Cognitive
Subtype: Information processing

General Description

Recency bias is a cognitive predisposition that causes people to more prominently recall and emphasize recent events and observations than those that occurred in the near or distant past. Suppose, for example, that a cruise passenger peering off the observation deck of a ship spots precisely equal numbers of green boats and blue boats over the duration of the trip. However, if the green boats pass by more frequently toward the end of the cruise, with the passing of blue boats dispersed evenly or concentrated toward the beginning, then recency bias would influence the passenger to recall, following the cruise, that more green than blue boats sailed by.

Example of Recency Bias

One of the most obvious and most pernicious manifestations of recency bias among investors pertains to their misuse of investment performance records for mutual funds and other types of funds. Investors track managers who produce temporary outsized returns during a one-, two-, or three-year period and then make investment decisions based only on such recent experiences. These investors do not pay heed to the cyclical nature of asset class returns, and so, for them, funds that have performed spectacularly in the very recent past appear unduly attractive. To counteract the effects of this bias, many practitioners wisely use what has become known as the "periodic table of investment returns," an adaptation of scientists' periodic table of chemical elements.

As the periodic table of investment returns in Table 15.1 demonstrates, asset class returns are highly variable. Many investors fail to heed the advice offered by the chart—namely, that it is nearly impossible to accurately predict which asset class will be the best performer from one year to the next. Thus, diversification is prudent (note how the diversified portfolio consistently appears near the center of each column). Investors would be wise to use this chart when establishing asset allocations.

Implications for Investors

Recency bias ran rampant during the bull market period between 2004 and 2007. Many investors implicitly presumed, as they have during other cyclical peaks, that the market would continue its enormous gains forever. They all but forgot the fact that bear markets can and do occur. Investors who based decisions on their own subjective short-term memories, hoped that near-term history would continue to repeat itself. Intuitively, they insisted that evidence gathered from recent experience narrowed the range of potential outcomes and thus enabled them to project future returns. All too often, this behavior creates misguided confidence and becomes a catalyst for error.

Table 15.1 Sample of a Periodic Table of Investment Returns

Highest	2006	2007	2008	2009	2010	2011	2012	2013	2014	2015	2016	2017	2018	2019	YTD	Q320
	REITS 35.06%	MSCI EME 39.78%	Barclays Agg 5.24%	MSCI EME 79.02%	REITS 27.96%	REITS 8.28%	REITS 19.70%	Russell 2000 38.82%	REITS 28.03%	REITS 2.83%	Russell 2000 21.31%	MSCI EME 37.75%	Barclays Agg 0.01%	S&P 500 31.49%	Barclays Agg 6.79%	MSCI EME 9.70%
	MSCI EME 32.58%	EM Debt 18.11%	EM Debt −5.22%	High Yield 58.21%	Russell 2000 26.85%	Barclays Agg 7.84%	MSCI EME 18.63%	Russell 3000 33.55%	S&P 500 13.69%	S&P 500 1.38%	High Yield 17.13%	MSCI EAFE 25.62%	High Yield −2.08%	Russell 3000 31.02%	S&P 500 5.57%	Russell 3000 9.21%
	MSCI EAFE 26.86%	Blmbrg Cmdty 16.23%	AA Portfolio −23.17%	MSCI EAFE 32.46%	MSCI EME 19.20%	High Yield 4.98%	MSCI EAFE 17.90%	S&P 500 32.39%	Russell 3000 12.56%	Barclays Agg 0.55%	Russell 3000 12.74%	S&P 500 21.83%	REITS −4.04%	REITS 28.66%	Russell 3000 5.41%	Blmbrg Cmdty 9.07%
	Russell 2000 18.37%	MSCI EAFE 11.63%	High Yield −26.15%	Russell 3000 28.34%	Russell 3000 16.93%	S&P 500 2.11%	EM Debt 16.76%	MSCI EAFE 23.29%	Barclays Agg 5.97%	Russell 3000 0.48%	S&P 500 11.96%	Russell 3000 21.13%	S&P 500 −4.38%	Russell 2000 25.52%	Equity Hedge 2.24%	S&P 500 8.93%
	S&P 500 15.79%	Equity Hedge 10.48%	Equity Hedge −26.65%	REITS 27.99%	Blmbrg Cmdty 16.83%	Russell 3000 1.03%	Russell 3000 16.42%	Equity Hedge 14.28%	AA Portfolio 5.64%	MSCI EAFE −0.39%	Blmbrg Cmdty 11.77%	AA Portfolio 15.22%	Russell 3000 −5.24%	MSCI EAFE 22.66%	High Yield 0.62%	Equity Hedge 5.78%
	Russell 3000 15.72%	AA Portfolio 8.01%	Russell 2000 −33.79%	Russell 2000 27.17%	EM Debt 15.68%	AA Portfolio −0.76%	Russell 2000 16.35%	AA Portfolio 14.19%	Russell 2000 4.89%	Equity Hedge −0.96%	MSCI EME 11.60%	EM Debt 15.2%	AA Portfolio −5.85%	AA Portfolio 19.36%	AA Portfolio 0.59%	Russell 2000 4.93%
	AA Portfolio 15.61%	Barclays Agg 6.97%	Blmbrg Cmdty −35.65%	S&P 500 26.46%	High Yield 15.12%	EM Debt −1.75%	S&P 500 16.00%	High Yield 7.44%	High Yield 2.45%	AA Portfolio −1.43%	EM Debt 9.94%	Russell 2000 14.65%	EM Debt −6.21%	MSCI EME 18.90%	MSCI EME −0.91%	MSCI EAFE 4.88%
	EM Debt 15.22%	S&P 500 5.49%	S&P 500 −37.00%	Equity Hedge 24.57%	S&P 500 15.06%	Russell 2000 −4.18%	High Yield 15.81%	REITS 2.86%	Equity Hedge 1.81%	Russell 2000 −4.41%	REITS 8.63%	Equity Hedge 13.29%	Equity Hedge −7.13%	High Yield 14.32%	EM Debt −6.32%	High Yield 4.60%
	High Yield 11.85%	Russell 3000 5.14%	Russell 3000 −37.31%	AA Portfolio 23.56%	AA Portfolio 12.96%	Equity Hedge −8.38%	AA Portfolio 12.28%	Barclays Agg −2.02%	MSCI EME −1.82%	High Yield −4.47%	AA Portfolio 7.51%	REITS 8.67%	Russell 2000 −11.01%	Equity Hedge 13.69%	MSCI EAFE −6.73%	AA Portfolio 4.40%

(Continued)

131

Table 15.1 (Continued)

Highest	2006	2007	2008	2009	2010	2011	2012	2013	2014	2015	2016	2017	2018	2019	YTD	Q320
	Equity Hedge 11.71%	High Yield 1.87%	REITS −37.73%	EM Debt 21.98%	Equity Hedge 10.45%	MSCI EAFE −11.73%	Equity Hedge 7.41%	MSCI EME −2.27%	MSCI EAFE −4.48%	MSCI EME −14.60%	Equity Hedge 5.47%	High Yield 7.50%	Blmbrg Cmdty −11.25%	EM Debt −13.47%	Russell 2000 −8.69%	REITS 1.42%
	Barclays Agg 4.33%	Russell 2000 −1.57%	MSCI EAFE −43.06%	Blmbrg Cmdty 18.91%	MSCI EAFE 8.21%	Blmbrg Cmdty −13.32%	Barclays Agg 4.22%	EM Debt −8.98%	EM Debt −5.72%	EM Debt −14.92%	Barclays Agg 2.65%	Barclays Agg 3.54%	MSCI EAFE −13.36%	Barclays Agg 8.72%	REITS −13.71%	Barclays Agg 0.62%
Lowest	Blmbrg Cmdty 2.07%	REITS −15.69%	MSCI EME −53.18	Barclays Agg 5.93%	Barclays Agg 6.54%	MSCI EME −18.17%	Blmbrg Cmdty −1.06%	Blmbrg Cmdty −9.52%	Blmbrg Cmdty −17.01%	Blmbrg Cmdty −24.66%	MSCI EAFE 1.51%	Blmbrg Cmdty 1.70%	MSCI EME −14.25%	Blmbrg Cmdty 7.69%	Blmbrg Cmdty −12.08%	EM Debt 0.61%

Source: Sunpointe Investments

When studying the market, good investors analyze large data samples to determine probabilities. By doing so, solid conclusions can be scientifically obtained. Recency bias causes investors to place too much emphasis on data recently gathered, rather than examining entire, relevant bodies of information, which often span much more extensive intervals of time. Investors need to be advised to look at underlying value and not just recent performance. If prices have just risen strongly, for example, then assets may be approaching or may have exceeded their fair value. This should imply that there are, perhaps, better investment opportunities elsewhere. Box 15.1 summarizes investment mistakes that can stem from recency bias.

BOX 15.1 Recency Bias: Behaviors That Can Cause Investment Mistakes

1. Recency bias can cause investors to extrapolate patterns and make projections based on historical data samples that are too small to ensure accuracy. Investors who forecast future returns based too extensively on only a recent sample of prior returns are vulnerable to purchasing at price peaks. These investors tend to enter asset classes at the wrong times and end up experiencing losses.

2. Recency bias can cause investors to ignore fundamental *value* and to focus only on recent upward price performance. When a return cycle peaks and recent performance figures are most attractive, human nature is to chase promise of a profit. Asset classes can and do become overvalued. By focusing only on price performance and not on valuation, investors risk principal loss when these investments revert to their mean or long-term averages.

3. Recency bias can cause investors to utter the words that many market veterans consider the most deceptive and damning of all: "It's different this time." In 1998 and 1999, for example, the short-term memory of recent gains influenced some investors so strongly as to overrule, in their minds, historical facts regarding rational valuations and the bubbles, peaks, and valleys that naturally occur.

4. Recency bias can cause investors to ignore proper asset allocation. Professional investors know the value of proper asset allocation, and they rebalance when necessary in order to maintain proper allocations. Recency bias can cause investors to become infatuated with a given asset class that, for example, appears in vogue. They often concentrate their holdings accordingly. Proper asset allocation is crucial to long-term investment success.

Am I Subject to Recency Bias?

These questions are designed to detect cognitive errors stemming from recency bias. To complete the test, select the answer choice that best characterizes your response to each item.

Recency Bias Test

Note that this test requires that someone other than the respondent administer the test (i.e., it contains free recall memory exercises, etc.).

Question 1: Suppose you are asked to select a mutual fund for your portfolio based only on the fund's performance record. What is your most likely course of action?

a. I will look at the one to three-year record of the fund to see how the fund has done recently.

b. I will look at the five-year track record of the fund, as this time period showcases some elements of recent performance, but also historical performance.

c. I will look at the 10-year track record, even though it doesn't focus on the fund's most recent performance.

Question 2: Read the following list of names to the respondent. Then ask: Did the list contain more male or female names?

1. Sally

2. Mark

3. Amy

4. Annette

5. Jim

6. Barbara

7. Steven

8. David

9. Michael

10. Donna

Test Results Analysis

Question 1: People who select response "a" or "b" are likely subject to recency bias.

Question 2: This list actually contains an equal number of male and female names. The male names, however, are concentrated toward the end of the list. Therefore, people who suffer from recency bias are more likely to recall that the list was dominated by male names.

Investment Advice

Box 15.1 listed some errors that investors often commit when they are subject to recency bias. These corresponding strategies can be employed by investors who want to moderate recency bias.

Sample size and extrapolating trends. Investors afflicted with recency bias often make projections based only on recent data—based on a data sample too narrowly drawn to be accurately informative with regard to future market trends. This behavior is relatively easy to overcome, as investors can often be persuaded by data when it is presented to them. Often, investors simply don't have immediate access to the data they need in order to make good decisions; other times, they lack the patience for undertaking a careful analysis. Education is critical to overcoming this aspect of recency bias.

Price versus value. Human nature is to chase "hot money," and investors subject to recency bias often fixate on price performance while neglecting value indicators. Advisors need to demonstrate that out-of-favor, undervalued asset classes can make for very wise investments. The periodic table of investment returns is often a very persuasive visual aid and can help sway the recency-biased investor toward a balanced allocation.

"It's different this time." Investors sometimes utter the words "it's different this time." This is a phrase that should be taken with a grain of salt. Investment cycles often repeat. Rarely is it "different this time." Stay invested and don't let your emotions get in the way of sound decision making.

Unbalanced portfolio. Proper asset allocation and diversification are crucial to long-term investment success. Investors should not let themselves become enamored with one certain stock and let that stock dominate a portfolio. The stock could tumble, and you could lose money. Education is critical to demonstrating why recency bias can be so dangerous. It might, perhaps, go without saying that, in these situations, nothing can replace the benefit of objective advice.

PART IV
EMOTIONAL BIASES DEFINED
AND ILLUSTRATED

In Chapters 3 through 22, 20 behavioral biases, both cognitive and emotional, will be discussed. There are two types of cognitive biases that are reviewed in Chapters 3 through 15. The first type, belief perseverance biases, were covered in Chapters 3 through 8. The second type, information processing cognitive biases, will now be covered in Chapters 9 through 15. Emotional biases, the focus of Part Four of the book, are covered in Chapters 16 through 22.

In these chapters, the same basic format is used to discuss each bias, in order to promote greater accessibility. First, each bias is named, categorized as emotional or cognitive including subtype (belief perseverance or information processing), and then generally described. This is followed by the all-important concrete practical application, in which it is demonstrated how each bias has been used, or can be used, in a practical situation. The practical application portion varies in content, consisting of either an intensive review of applied research or a case study. Implications for investors are then delineated. A diagnostic test and test-result analysis follow, providing a tool to indicate the potential susceptibility to certain biases. Finally, advice on managing the effects of each bias, in order to minimize its effects, is offered.

16

Emotional Bias #1: Loss Aversion Bias

Win as if you were used to it, lose as if you enjoyed it for a change.
—**Ralph Waldo Emerson**

Bias Description

Bias Name: Loss aversion bias
Bias type: Emotional

General Description

Loss aversion bias was developed by Daniel Kahneman and Amos Tversky in 1979, as part of the original prospect theory,[1] specifically in response to prospect theory's observation that people generally feel a stronger impulse to avoid losses than to acquire gains. A number of studies on loss aversion have given birth to a common rule of thumb: psychologically, the possibility of a loss is on average twice as powerful a motivator as the possibility of making a gain of equal magnitude; that is, a loss–averse person might demand, at minimum, a \$2 gain for every \$1 placed at risk. In this scenario, risks that don't "pay double" are unacceptable.

---

[1] Daniel Kahneman and Amos Tversky, "Prospect Theory: An Analysis of Decision under Risk," *Econometrica* 47 (1979): 263–291.

Loss aversion can prevent people from unloading unprofitable investments, even when they see little to no prospect of a turnaround. Some industry veterans have coined a diagnosis of "get-even-itis" to describe this widespread affliction, whereby a person waits too long for an investment to rebound following a loss. Get-even-itis can be dangerous because, often, the best response to a loss is to sell the offending security and to redeploy those assets. Similarly, loss aversion bias can make investors dwell excessively on risk avoidance when evaluating possible gains, since dodging a loss is a more urgent concern than seeking a profit. When their investments do begin to succeed, loss-averse individuals hasten to lock in profits, fearing that, otherwise, the market might reverse itself and rescind their returns. The problem here is that divesting prematurely to protect gains limits upside potential. In sum, loss aversion causes investors to hold their losing investments and to sell their winning ones, leading to suboptimal portfolio returns.

Example of Loss Aversion Bias

Loss aversion bias is one of the most common behavioral biases. Investors open up the monthly statements prepared by their advisors, skim columns of numbers, and usually notice both winners and losers. In classic cases of loss aversion, investors dread selling the securities that haven't performed well. Get-even-itis takes hold, and the instinct is to hold onto a losing investment until, at the very least, it rebounds enough for the investor to break even. Often, however, research into a losing investment would reveal a company whose prospects don't forecast a rebound. Continuing to hold stock in that company actually adds risk to an investor's portfolio (hence, the investor's behavior is risk seeking, which accords with the path of the value function in Figure 16.1).

Conversely, when the monthly statement indicates that profits are being made, the loss-averse investor is gripped by a powerful urge to "take the money and run," rather than to assume continued risk. Of course, frequently, holding on to a winning stock isn't a risky proposition if the company is performing well; that is, profitable investments that the loss-averse investor wants to sell might actually be improving the portfolio's risk–return profile. Therefore, selling deteriorates that risk–return profile and eliminates the potential for further gains. When the increased risks associated with holding on to losing investments are considered in combination with the prospect of losing future gains that occur when

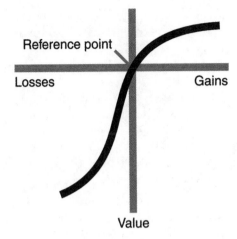

Reference point

Losses   **Gains**

Value

Figure 16.1 The Value Function—A Key Tenet of Prospect Theory
Source: The Econometric Society

selling winners, the degree of overall harm that a loss-averse investor can suffer begins to become clear.

A final thought on taking losses: Some investors, remarking on losing investments that haven't yet been sold, rationalize that "It's only a paper loss." In one sense, yes, this is true. Inasmuch as the investment is still held, a loss has technically not been triggered for tax purposes.

In reality, though, this kind of rationale covers up the fact that a loss has taken place. If you went to the market to sell, having just incurred a "paper loss," the price you would obtain for your investment would be lower than the price you paid—effecting a very "real" loss indeed. Thus, if holding on to a losing investment does not objectively enhance the likelihood of recouping a loss, then it is better to simply realize the loss, get the tax benefit, and move on.

Implications for Investors

Loss aversion is a bias that simply cannot be tolerated in financial decision making. It instigates the exact opposite of what investors want: increased risk, with lower returns. Investors should take risk to increase gains, not to mitigate losses. Holding losers and selling winners will wreak havoc on a portfolio. Box 16.1 summarizes some common investment mistakes linked to loss aversion bias.

BOX 16.1 Loss Aversion Bias: Behaviors That Can Cause Investment Mistakes

1. Loss aversion causes investors to hold losing investments too long. This behavior is sometimes described in the context of a debilitating disease: *get-even-itis*. This is the affliction in which investors hold losing investments in the hope that they will get back what they lost. This behavior has seriously negative consequences by depressing portfolio returns.
2. Loss aversion can cause investors to sell winners too early in the fear that their profit will evaporate unless they sell. This behavior limits the upside potential of a portfolio, and can lead to too much trading, which has been shown to lower investment returns.
3. Loss aversion can cause investors to unknowingly take on more risk in their portfolio than they would if they simply eliminated the investment and moved into a better one (or stayed in cash).
4. Loss aversion can cause investors to hold unbalanced portfolios. If, for example, several positions fall in value and the investor is unwilling to sell due to loss aversion, an imbalance can occur. Without proper rebalancing, the allocation is not suited to the long-term goals of the investor, leading to suboptimal returns.

Am I Subject to Loss Aversion Bias?

These questions are designed to detect signs of emotional bias stemming from loss aversion. To complete the test, select the answer choice that best characterizes your response to each item.

Loss Aversion Bias Test

Question 1: Suppose you make a plan to invest $50,000. You are presented with two alternatives. Which scenario would you rather have?

a. Be assured that I'll get back my $50,000, at the very least—even if I don't make any more money.

b. Have a 50 percent chance of getting $70,000 and a 50 percent chance of getting $35,000.

Question 2: Suppose you make a plan to invest $70,000. You are presented with two alternatives. Which scenario would you rather have?

a. Know that I'll be repaid only $60,000, for sure.

b. Take a 50–50 gamble, knowing that I'll get back either $75,000 or $50,000.

Question 3: Choose one of these two outcomes:

a. An assured gain of $475.

b. A 25 percent chance of gaining $2,000 and a 75 percent chance of gaining nothing.

Question 4: Choose one of these two outcomes:

a. An assured loss of $725.

b. A 75 percent chance of losing $1,000 and a 25 percent chance of losing nothing.

Test Results Analysis

Question 1: People who are loss averse are most likely to select "a," even though "b" offers a larger potential return on the upside.

Question 2: Increased initial endowment aside, this is basically the same question as Question 1. Most people, however, would probably select "b," because most people tend to be loss averse. Loss-averse investors are willing to gamble and risk an even greater loss rather than to admit a loss ("a"). However, this isn't simply a matter of an unconditional penchant for gambling. Most investors (that is, loss-averse investors) prefer the assurance of breaking even over the opportunity to gain a profit in Question 1.

Question 3: The rational response is "b," but loss-averse investors are likely to opt for the assurance of a profit in "a."

Question 4: The rational response is "a." Loss-averse investors are more likely to select "b."

Investment Advice

Box 16.1 listed some errors that investors often commit when they are subject to loss-aversion bias. These corresponding strategies can be employed by investors who want to attempt to moderate loss aversion.

Get-even-itis. Beware: Holding losing stocks for too long is harmful to your investment health. One symptom of get-even-itis is that an investor's decision making regarding some investments seems to be dependent on the original price paid for that investment. One effective remedy is a stop-loss rule. You may, for example, agree to sell a security immediately if it ever incurs a 10 percent loss. However, it's best to consider an investment's normal, expected levels of volatility when devising a stop-loss rule. You don't want to be forced to sell if an investment's price is just exhibiting its customary ups and downs.

Take the money and run. Loss aversion can cause investors to sell winning positions too early, fearing that that their profits will evaporate otherwise. This behavior limits the upside potential of a portfolio and can lead to overtrading (which also reduces returns). Just as stop-loss rules can help to combat get-even-itis, it is often helpful to institute rules for selling appreciating investments. As with stop-loss rules, price-appreciation rules work best when tailored to reflect details related to fundamentals and valuation. The goal is to let gains run. Remember too that, in a taxable account, you should avoid paying taxes on appreciations as long as possible.

Taking on excessive risk. Loss aversion can cause investors to hold onto losing investments even in companies that are in serious trouble. In such a case, it may be helpful to educate investors about an investment's risk profile—taking time to evaluate items such as standard deviation, credit rating, buy/sell/hold ratings, and so on. The investor will then, hopefully, make the right decision to protect the overall portfolio and jettison the risky, poorly performing investment.

Unbalanced portfolios. Loss aversion can cause investors to hold unbalanced portfolios. Education about the benefits of asset allocation and diversification is critical, yet it may be insufficient if an investor holds a concentrated stock position with emotional strings attached. A useful question in this situation is: "If you didn't own any XYZ stock today, would you still want to pick up as many shares as you own right now?" If and when the answer is "no," some leeway for maneuvering emerges. Tax considerations, such as low-cost basis, sometimes factor in, but certain strategies can be employed to manage this cost.

17

Emotional Bias #2: Overconfidence Bias

Too many people overvalue what they are not and undervalue what they are.
                                                    —Malcolm S. Forbes

Bias Description

Bias Name: Overconfidence
Bias Type: Emotional

General Description

In its most basic form, *overconfidence* can be summarized as unwarranted faith in one's intuitive reasoning, judgments, and cognitive abilities. Although the concept of overconfidence derives from psychological experiments and surveys in which subjects overestimate both their own predictive abilities and the precision of the information they've been given (essentially cognitive weaknesses), these faulty cognitions lead to emotionally charged behavior, such as excessive risk-taking, and therefore overconfidence is classified as an emotional rather than cognitive bias. In short, people think they are smarter than they actually are and have better information than they actually do. For example, they may get a tip from a financial advisor or read something on the Internet, and then they're ready to take action, such as making an investment decision, based on their perceived knowledge advantage.

Examples of Overconfidence Bias

Prediction Overconfidence

Roger Clarke and Meir Statman demonstrated a classic example of prediction overconfidence when they surveyed investors on the following question: "In 1896, the Dow Jones Average, which is a price index that does not include dividend reinvestment, was at 40. In 1998, it crossed 9,000. If dividends had been reinvested, what do you think the value of the DJIA would be in 1998? In addition to that guess, also predict a high and low range so that you feel 90 percent confident that your answer is between your high and low guesses."[1] In the survey, few responses reasonably approximated the potential 1998 value of the Dow, and no one estimated a correct confidence interval. (If you are curious, the 1998 value of the Dow Jones Industrial Average [DJIA], under the conditions postulated in the survey, would have been 652,230!)

A classic example of investor prediction overconfidence is the case of the former executive or family legacy stockholder of a publicly traded company such as Johnson & Johnson, ExxonMobil, or DuPont. These investors often refuse to diversify their holdings because they claim "insider knowledge" of, or emotional attachment to, the company. They cannot contextualize these stalwart stocks as risky investments. However, dozens of once-iconic names in U.S. business have declined or vanished.

Certainty Overconfidence

People display certainty overconfidence in everyday life situations, and that overconfidence carries over into the investment arena. People tend to have too much confidence in the accuracy of their own judgments. As people find out more about a situation, the accuracy of their judgments is not likely to increase, but their confidence does increase, as they fallaciously equate the quantity of information with its quality. In a pertinent study,

---

[1] Roger G. Clarke and Meir Statman, "The DJIA Crossed 652,230," *Journal of Portfolio Management* 26, no. 2 (Winter 2000): 89–92.

Baruch Fischhoff, Paul Slovic, and Sarah Lichtenstein gave subjects a general knowledge test and then asked them how sure they were of their answer. Subjects reported being 100 percent sure when they were actually only 70 percent to 80 percent correct.[2] A classic example of certainty overconfidence occurred during the technology boom of the late 1990s. Many investors simply loaded up on technology stocks, holding highly concentrated positions, only to see these gains vanish during the meltdown.

Implications for Investors

Both prediction and certainty overconfidence can lead to making investment mistakes. Box 17.1 lists four behaviors, resulting from overconfidence bias, that can cause harm to an investor's portfolio. Advice on overcoming these behaviors follows the diagnostic test later in the chapter.

BOX 17.1 Overconfidence Bias: Behaviors That Can Cause Investment Mistakes

1. Overconfident investors overestimate their ability to evaluate a company as a potential investment. As a result, they can become blind to any negative information that might normally indicate a warning sign that either a stock purchase should not take place or a stock that was already purchased should be sold.
2. Overconfident investors can trade excessively as a result of believing that they possess special knowledge that others don't have. Excessive trading behavior has proven to lead to poor returns over time.
3. Because they either don't know, don't understand, or don't heed historical investment performance statistics, overconfident investors can underestimate their downside risks. As a result, they can unexpectedly suffer poor portfolio performance.
4. Overconfident investors hold under-diversified portfolios, thereby taking on more risk without a commensurate change in risk tolerance. Often, overconfident investors don't even know that they are accepting more risk than they would normally tolerate.

---

[2] Sarah Lichtenstein, Baruch Fischhoff, and L. D. Phillips, "Calibration of Probabilities: The State of the Art to 1980," in David Kahneman, Paul Slovic, and Amos Tversky, eds., *Judgment under Uncertainty: Heuristics and Biases* (New York: Cambridge University Press, 1982), 306–334.

Am I Subject to Overconfidence Bias?

This is a diagnostic test for both prediction overconfidence and certainty overconfidence. After analyzing the test results in the next section, we will offer advice on how to overcome the detrimental effects of over-confidence.

Prediction Overconfidence Bias Test

Question 1: Give high and low estimates for the average weight of an adult male sperm whale (the largest of the toothed whales) in tons. Choose numbers far enough apart to be 90 percent certain that the true answer lies somewhere in between.

Question 2: Give high and low estimates for the distance to the moon in miles. Choose numbers far enough apart to be 90 percent certain that the true answer lies somewhere in between.

Question 3: How easy do you think it was to predict the collapse of the housing and credit bubbles of 2008–2009?

a. Easy

b. Somewhat easy

c. Somewhat difficult

d. Difficult

Question 4: From 1926 through 2010, the compound annual return for equities was approximately 9 percent. In any given year, what returns do you expect on *your* equity investments to produce?

a. Below 9 percent

b. About 9 percent

c. Above 9 percent

d. Well above 9 percent

Certainty Overconfidence Bias Test

Question 5: How much control do you believe you have in picking investments that will outperform the market?

a. Absolutely no control

b. Little if any control

c. Some control

d. A fair amount of control

Question 6: Relative to other drivers on the road, how good a driver are you?

a. Below average

b. Average

c. Above average

d. Well above average

Question 7: Suppose you are asked to read this statement: "Capetown is the capital of South Africa." Do you agree or disagree?

Now, how confident are you that you are correct?

a. 100 percent

b. 80 percent

c. 60 percent

d. 40 percent

e. 20 percent

Question 8: How would you characterize your personal level of investment sophistication?

a. Unsophisticated

b. Somewhat sophisticated

c. Sophisticated

d. Very sophisticated

Prediction Overconfidence Bias Test Results Analysis

Question 1: In actuality, the average weight of a male sperm whale is approximately 40 tons. Respondents specifying too restrictive a weight interval (say, "10 to 20 tons") are likely susceptible to prediction overconfidence. A more inclusive response (say, "20 to 100 tons") is less symptomatic of prediction overconfidence.

Question 2: The actual distance to the moon is 240,000 miles. Again, respondents estimating too narrow a range (say, "100,000 to 200,000 miles") are likely to be susceptible to prediction overconfidence. Respondents naming wider ranges (say, "200,000 to 500,000 miles") may not be susceptible to prediction overconfidence.

Question 3: If the respondent recalled that predicting the rupture of the credit and housing bubbles in 2008–2009 seemed easy, then this is likely to indicate prediction overconfidence. Respondents describing the collapse as less predictable are probably less susceptible to prediction overconfidence.

Question 4: Respondents expecting to significantly outperform the long-term market average are likely to be susceptible to prediction over-confidence. Respondents forecasting returns at or below the market average are probably less subject to prediction overconfidence.

Certainty Overconfidence Bias Test Results Analysis

Question 5: Respondents professing greater degrees of control over their investments are likely to be susceptible to certainty overconfidence. Responses claiming little or no control are less symptomatic of certainty overconfidence.

Question 6: The belief that one is an above-average driver correlates positively with certainty overconfidence susceptibility. Respondents describing themselves as average or below-average drivers are less likely to exhibit certainty overconfidence.

Question 7: If the respondent agreed with the statement and reported a high degree of confidence in the response, then susceptibility to certainty overconfidence is likely. If the respondent disagreed with the statement, and did so with 50 to 100 percent confidence, then susceptibility to certainty overconfidence is less likely. If respondents agree but with low degrees of confidence, then they are unlikely to be susceptible to cer-tainty overconfidence. Confidence in one's knowledge can be assessed, in general, with questions of the following kind:

Which Australian city has more inhabitants—Sydney or Melbourne?

How confident are you that your answer is correct? Choose one: 50 percent, 60 percent, 70 percent, 80 percent, 90 percent, 100 percent.

If you answer 50 percent, then you are guessing. If you answer 100 percent, then you are absolutely sure of your answer.

Two decades of research into this topic have demonstrated that in all cases wherein subjects have reported 100 percent certainty when answering a question like the Australia one, the relative frequency of correct answers has been about 80 percent. Where subjects have reported, on average, that they feel 90 percent certain of their answers, the relative frequency of correct answers has averaged 75 percent. Subjects reporting 80 percent confidence in their answers have been correct about 65 percent of the time, and so on.

Question 8: Respondents describing themselves sophisticated or highly sophisticated investors are likelier than others to exhibit certainty overconfidence. If the respondent chose "somewhat sophisticated" or "unsophisticated," susceptibility is less likely.

Investment Advice

Overconfidence is one of the most detrimental biases that an investor can exhibit. This is because underestimating downside risk, trading too frequently and/or trading in pursuit of the "next hot stock," and holding an under-diversified portfolio all pose serious "hazards to your wealth" (to borrow from Barber and Odean's phrasing). Prediction and certainty overconfidence have been discussed and diagnosed separately, but the advice presented here deals with overconfidence in an across-the-board, undifferentiated manner. Investors susceptible to either brand of overconfidence should be mindful of all four of the detrimental behaviors identified in Box 17.1. None of these tendencies, of course, is unavoidable, but each occurs with high relative frequency in overconfident investors.

This advice is organized according to the specific behavior it addresses. All four behaviors are "wealth hazards" resulting frequently from overconfidence.

1. An unfounded belief in one's own ability to identify companies as potential investments. Many overconfident investors claim above-average aptitudes for selecting stocks, but little evidence supports this belief. The Odean study showed that, after trading costs (but before taxes), the average investor underperformed the market by approximately 2 percent per year.[3] Many overconfident investors also believe they can pick mutual funds that will deliver superior future performance, yet many tend to trade in and out of mutual funds at the worst possible times because they chase unrealistic expectations. The facts speak for themselves: from 1984 through 1995, the average stock mutual fund posted a yearly return of 12.3 percent, whereas the average investor in a stock mutual fund earned 6.3 percent.[4]

2. Excessive trading. In Odean and Barber's landmark study, "Boys Will Be Boys," the average subject's annual portfolio turnover was 80 percent (slightly less than the 84 percent averaged by mutual funds).[5] The least active quintile of participants, with an average annual turnover of 1 percent, earned 17.5 percent annual returns, outperforming the 16.9 percent garnered by the Standard & Poor's index during this period. The most active 20 percent of investors, however, averaged a monthly turnover of over 9 percent, and yet realized pretax returns of only 10 percent annually. The authors of the study do indeed seem justified in labeling trading as hazardous.

   When an investor's account shows too much trading activity, the best advice is to ask the investor to keep track of each and every investment trade and then to calculate returns. This exercise will demonstrate the detrimental effects of excessive trading. Since overconfidence is a cognitive bias, updated information can often help investors to understand the error of their ways.

3. Underestimating downside risks. Overconfident investors, especially those who are prone to prediction overconfidence, tend to

[3] Terrance Odean, "Do Investors Trade Too Much?" *American Economic Review* 89(5) (December 1999): 1279–1298.

[4] Brad M. Barber and Terrance Odean, "Boys Will Be Boys: Gender, Overconfidence, and Common Stock Investment," *Quarterly Journal of Economics* 116(1) (February 2001): 261–292.

[5] Terrance Odean, "Do Investors Trade Too Much?" *American Economic Review* 89(5) (December 1999): 1279–1298.

underestimate downside risks. They are so confident in their predictions that they do not fully consider the likelihood of incurring losses in their portfolios. For an investor who exhibits this behavior, the best course of action is twofold. First, review trading or other investment holdings for potentially poor performance and use this evidence to illustrate the hazards of overconfidence. Second, point to academic and practitioner studies that show how volatile the markets are. The investor often will get the picture at this point, acquiring more cautious respect for the vagaries of the markets.

4. Portfolio under-diversification. As in the case of the retired executive who can't relinquish a former company's stock, many overconfident investors retain under-diversified portfolios because they do not believe that the securities they traditionally favored will ever perform poorly. The reminder that numerous, once-great companies have fallen is, oftentimes, not enough of a reality check. In this situation, the advisor can recommend various hedging strategies, such as costless collars, puts, and so on. Another useful question at this point is: "If you didn't own any XYZ stock today, would you buy as much as you own today?" When the answer is "No," room for maneuvering emerges. Tax considerations, such as low-cost basis, sometimes factor in; but certain strategies can be employed to manage this cost.

A Final Word on Overconfidence

One general implication of overconfidence bias in any form is that overconfident investors may not be well prepared for the future. For example, most parents of children who are high school-aged or younger claim to adhere to some kind of long-term financial plan and thereby express confidence regarding their long-term financial well-being. However, a vast majority of households do not actually save adequately for educational expenses, and an even smaller percentage actually possess any "real" financial plan that addresses such basics as investment, budgeting, insurance, savings, and wills. This is an ominous sign, and these families are likely to feel unhappy and discouraged when they do not meet their financial goals. Overconfidence can breed this type of behavior and invite this type of outcome. Investors need to guard against it, and financial advisors need to be in tune with the problem. Recognizing and curtailing overconfidence is a key step in establishing the basics of a real financial plan.

18

Emotional Bias #3: Self-Control Bias

Self-reverence, self-knowledge, self-control: these three alone lead to power.
                                                        —**Alfred, Lord Tennyson (1880)**

Bias Description

Bias Name: Self-control bias
Bias Type: Emotional

General Description

Simply put, *self-control bias* is a human behavioral tendency that causes people to fail to act in pursuit of their long-term, overarching goals because of a lack of self-discipline. Money is an area in which people are notorious for displaying a lack of self-control. Attitudes toward paying taxes provide a common example. Imagine that you, a taxpayer, estimate that your income this year will cause your income tax to increase by $3,600, which will be due one year from now. In the interest of conservatism, you decide to set money aside. You contemplate two choices: Would you rather contribute $300 per month over the course of the next 12 months to some savings account earmarked for tax season? Or would you rather increase your federal income tax withholding by $300 each month, sparing you the responsibility of writing out one large check at the end of the year? Rational economic thinking suggests that you would prefer the savings account approach because your money would accrue interest and you would actually net more than $3,600. However, many taxpayers choose the withholding option because they realize that the savings account plan might be complicated in practice by a lack of self-control (i.e., one might overspend and then the tax money might not be there when one needs it.)

Self-control bias can also be described as a conflict between people's overarching desires and their inability, stemming from a lack of self-discipline, to act concretely in pursuit of those desires. For example, a college student desiring an "A" in history class might theoretically forgo a lively party to study at the library. An overweight person desperate to shed unwanted pounds might decline a tempting triple fudge sundae. Reality demonstrates, however, that plenty of people do sabotage their own long-term objectives for temporary satisfaction in situations like the ones described.

Investing is no different. The primary challenge in investing is saving enough money for retirement. Most of this chapter will focus on the savings behaviors of investors and how best to promote self-control in this often-problematic realm.

Example of Self-Control Bias

Encouraging people to save more is a task that constantly challenges financial advisors. The "Save More Tomorrow Program,"[1] developed by Professors Richard H. Thaler of the University of Chicago and Shlomo Benartzi of the Anderson School of Business at UCLA, aims to help corporate employees who would like to save more but lack the willpower to act on this desire. The program offers many useful insights into saving behavior and examining it will serve as our practical application discussion in this chapter.

---

[1] Richard H. Thaler and Shlomo Benartzi, "Save More Tomorrow: Using Behavioral Economics to Increase Employee Saving," *Journal of Political Economy* 112(1): 5164–5187.

The "Save More Tomorrow Program" has four primary aspects:

1. Employees are approached about increasing their contribution rates a considerable time before their scheduled pay increases occur.
2. The contributions of employees who join the plan are automatically increased beginning with the first paycheck following a raise.
3. Participating employees' contribution rates continue to increase automatically with each scheduled raise, until rates reach a preset maximum.
4. Employees can opt out of the plan at any time.

Let's examine the results of a trial of the Save More Tomorrow Program (SMTP) by a midsize manufacturing company in 1988. Prior to the adoption of the SMTP, the company suffered from a low participation rate as well as low saving rates. In an effort to increase the saving rates of the employees, the company hired an investment consultant and offered this service to every employee eligible for its retirement savings plan. Of the 315 eligible participants, all but 29 agreed to meet with the consultant and get his advice. Based on information that the employee provided, the consultant used commercial software to compute a desired saving rate. The consultant also discussed with each employee how much of an increase in saving would be considered economically feasible. If the employee seemed very reluctant to increase his or her saving rate substantially, the consultant would constrain the program to increase the saving contribution by no more than 5 percent.

Of the 286 employees who talked to the investment consultant, only 79 (28 percent) were willing to accept the consultant's advice, even with the adjustment to constrain some of the saving rate increases to 5 percent. For the rest of the participants, the planner offered a version of the SMTP, proposing that they increase their saving rate by 3 percentage points a year, starting with the next pay increase. Even with the aggressive strategy of increasing saving rates, the SMTP proved to be extremely popular with the participants. Of the 207 participants who were unwilling to accept the saving rate proposed by the investment consultant, 162 (78 percent) agreed to join the SMTP.

The majority of these participants did not change their minds once the saving increases took place. Only four participants (2 percent) dropped out of the plan prior to the second pay raise, with 29 more (18 percent) dropping out between the second and third pay raises. Hence, the vast majority of the participants (80 percent) remained in the plan through three pay raises. Furthermore, even those who withdrew from the plan did not reduce their contribution rates to the original levels; they merely stopped the future increases from taking place. So, even these workers are saving significantly more than they were before joining the plan.

The key lesson here is that people are generally poor at planning and saving for retirement. They need to have self-discipline imposed on them consistently in order to achieve savings.

Implications for Investors

As previously noted, the primary issue with regard to self-control is the lack of ability to save for retirement. In addition, there are several other self-control behaviors that can cause investment mistakes. Box 18.1 summarizes some of these.

BOX 18.1 Self-Control Bias: Behaviors That Can Cause Investment Mistakes

1. Self-control bias can cause investors to spend more today at the expense of saving for tomorrow. This behavior can be hazardous to one's wealth, because retirement can arrive too quickly for investors to have saved enough. Frequently, then, people incur inappropriate degrees of risk in their portfolios in an effort to make up for lost time. This can, of course, aggravate the problem.

2. Self-control bias may cause investors to fail to plan for retirement. Studies have shown that people who do not plan for retirement are far less likely to retire securely than those who do plan. Studies have shown that people who do not plan for retirement are also less likely to invest in equity securities.

3. Self-control bias can cause asset-allocation imbalance problems. For example, some investors may prefer income-producing assets, due to a "spend today" mentality. This behavior can be hazardous to long-term wealth because too many income-producing assets can inhibit a portfolio to keep up with inflation. Other investors might favor different asset classes, such as equities over bonds, simply because they like to take risks and can't control their behavior.

4. Self-control bias can cause investors to lose sight of basic financial principles, such as compounding of interest, dollar cost averaging, and similar discipline behaviors that, if adhered to, can help create significant long-term wealth.

Am I Subject to Self-Control Bias?

This section contains a brief diagnostic quiz that deals with issues of self-control.

Question 1: Suppose that you are in need of a new automobile. You have been driving your current car for seven years, and it's time for a change. Assume that you do face some constraints in your purchase as "money doesn't grow on trees." Which of the following approaches are you most likely to take?

a. I would typically underspend on a car because I view a car as transportation, and I don't need anything fancy. Besides, I can save the extra money I might have spent on a fancy car and put it away in my savings accounts.

b. I would typically purchase a medium-priced model, with some fancy options, simply because I enjoy a nice car. I may forgo other purchases in order to afford a nice car. I don't imagine that I'd go crazy and purchase anything extravagant, but a nice car is something that I value to an extent and am willing to spend money to obtain this.

c. When it comes to cars, I like to indulge myself. I'd probably splurge on a top-of-the-line model and select most or all available luxury options. Even if I must purchase this car at the expense of saving money for the long term, I believe that it's vital to live in the moment. This car is simply my way of living in the moment.

Question 2: How would you characterize your retirement savings patterns?

a. I consult my advisors and make sure that every tax-favored investment vehicle is maxed out (401(k), IRA, etc.), and I will often save additional funds in taxable accounts.

b. I will usually take advantage of most tax-favored investment vehicles, though in some cases I'm sure that details may have escaped my attention. I may or may not save something in taxable investment accounts.

c. I hardly ever save for retirement. I spend most of my disposable income, so very little remains available for savings.

Question 3: How well would you rate your own self-discipline?

a. I always achieve a goal if it is important to me. If I want to lose 10 pounds, for example, I will diet and exercise relentlessly until I am satisfied.

b. I can often attain my goals, but sometimes I have trouble sticking to certain difficult things that I have resolved to accomplish.

c. I have a tremendous amount of difficulty keeping promises to myself. I have little or no self-discipline, and I often find myself reaching out to others for help in attaining key goals.

Test Results Analysis

Questions 1, 2, and 3: People answering "b" or "c" to any of these questions may be susceptible to self-control bias. Please note that self-control is a very common bias!

Investment Advice

When a practitioner encounters self-control bias, there are four primary topics on which advice can generally be given: (1) spending control, (2) lack of planning, (3) portfolio allocation, and (4) the benefits of discipline.

Spending control. Self-control bias can cause investors to spend more today rather than saving for tomorrow. People have a strong desire to consume freely in the present. This behavior can be counter-productive to attaining long-term financial goals because retirement often arrives before investors have managed to save enough money. This may spur people into accepting, at the last minute, inordinate amounts of risk in their portfolios to make up for lost time—a tendency that actually places one's retirement security at increased risk. Investors should pay themselves first, setting aside consistent quantities of money to ensure their comfort later in life, especially if retirement is still a long way off. If investors are past age 60 and have not saved enough for retirement, then a more difficult situation emerges. A careful balance must be struck between saving, investing, and risk-taking in order to increase the pot of money for retirement. Often, these investors might benefit from examining additional options, such as part-time work (cycling in and out of retirement) or cutting back on consumption. In either case, emphasizing paying oneself first—assigning a sufficient level of priority to future rather than present-day consumption—is critical.

Lack of planning. Self-control bias may cause investors to not plan adequately for retirement. Studies have shown that people who do not plan for retirement are much less likely not to retire securely than those who do plan. People who do not plan for retirement are also less likely to invest in equity securities. Advisors must emphasize that investing without planning is like building without a blueprint. Planning is the absolute key to attaining long-term financial goals. Furthermore, plans need to be written down so that they can be reviewed on a regular basis. Without planning, investors may not be apt to invest in equities, potentially causing a problem with keeping up with inflation. In sum, people don't plan to fail—they simply fail to plan.

Portfolio allocation. Self-control bias can cause asset allocation imbalance problems. Investors subject to this bias may prefer income-producing assets, due to a "spend today" mentality. This behavior can be counter-productive to attaining long-term financial goals because an excess of income-producing assets can prevent a portfolio from keeping up with inflation. Self-control bias can also cause people to unduly favor certain asset classes, such as equities over bonds, due to an inability to reign in impulses toward risk. Whether they prefer bonds or equities, investors exhibiting a lack of self-control need to be counseled on maintaining properly balanced portfolios so that they can attain their long-term financial goals.

Benefits of discipline. Self-control bias can cause investors to lose sight of very basic financial principles, such as compounding of interest or dollar cost averaging. By failing to reap these discipline profits over time, investors can miss opportunities for accruing significant long-term wealth. Investors should focus on the benefits of compounding. There are a number of very effective software programs that can demonstrate that even a minimal, 1 to 2 percent disparity in returns, if compounded over decades, can mean the difference between a comfortable and a subpar retirement. To return to an example that arises frequently in discussions of willpower—the matter of exercising—the benefits of self-discipline in investing, as in physical fitness, are difficult to obtain. The results, however, are well worth it.

19

Emotional Bias #4: Status Quo Bias

Whosoever desires constant success must change his conduct with the times.
—Niccolo Machiavelli (1532)

Bias Description

Bias Name: Status quo bias
Bias Type: Emotional

General Description

Status quo bias, a term coined by William Samuelson and Richard Zeckhauser in 1988,[1] is an emotional bias that predisposes people facing an array of choice options to elect whatever option ratifies or extends the existing condition (i.e., the "status quo") in lieu of alternative options that might bring about change. In other words, status quo bias operates in people who prefer things to stay relatively the same. The scientific principle of inertia bears a lot of intuitive similarity to status quo bias; it

---

[1] William Samuelson and Richard J. Zeckhauser, "Status Quo Bias in Decision Making," *Journal of Risk and Uncertainty* 1(1) (1988): 7–59.

states that a body at rest shall remain at rest unless acted on by an outside force. A simple real-world example illustrates. In the early 1990s, the states of New Jersey and Pennsylvania reformed their insurance laws and offered new programs. Residents had the opportunity to select one of two automotive insurance packages: (1) a slightly more expensive option that granted policyholders extensive rights to sue one another following an accident, and (2) a less expensive option with more restricted litigation rights. Each insurance plan had a roughly equivalent expected monetary value. In New Jersey, however, the more expensive plan was instituted as the default, and 70 percent of citizens "selected" it. In Pennsylvania, the opposite was true—residents would have to opt out of the default, less-expensive option in order to opt into the more expensive option. In the end, 80 percent of the residents "chose" to pay less.

Example of Status Quo Bias

Investors with inherited, concentrated stock positions often exhibit classic status quo bias. Take the case of a hypothetical grandson who hesitates to sell the bank stock he's inherited from his grandfather. Even though his portfolio is under-diversified and could benefit from such an adjustment, the grandson favors the status quo. A number of motives could be at work here. First, the investor may be unaware of the risk associated with holding an excessively concentrated equity position. He may not foresee that if the stock tumbles, he will suffer a significant decrease in wealth. Second, the grandson may experience a personal attachment to the stock, which carries an emotional connection to a previous generation. Third, he may hesitate to sell because of his aversion to the tax consequences, fees/commissions, or other transaction costs associated with unloading the stock.

    The advice section of this chapter reviews some strategies for dealing with each of these potential objections—all of which could contribute to status quo–biased behavior.

Implications for Investors

Box 19.1 reviews four investment mistakes that can stem from status quo bias.

> ## BOX 19.1 Status Quo Bias: Behaviors That Can Cause Investment Mistakes
>
> 1. Status quo bias can cause investors, by taking no action, to hold investments inappropriate to their own risk/return profiles. This can mean that investors take excessive risks or invest too conservatively.
> 2. Status quo bias can combine with loss aversion bias. In this scenario, an investor facing an opportunity to reallocate or alter an investment position may choose, instead, to maintain the status quo because the status quo offers the investor a lower probability of realizing a loss. This will be true even if, in the long run, the investor could achieve a higher return by electing an alternative path.
> 3. Status quo bias causes investors to hold securities with which they feel familiar or of which they are emotionally fond. This behavior can compromise financial goals, however, because a subjective comfort level with a security may not justify holding onto it despite poor performance.
> 4. Status quo bias can cause investors to hold securities, either inherited or purchased, because of an aversion to transaction costs associated with selling. This behavior can be hazardous to one's wealth because a commission or a tax is frequently a small price to pay for exiting a poorly performing investment or for properly allocating a portfolio.

Am I Subject to Status Quo Bias?

These questions are designed to detect signs of cognitive errors stemming from status quo bias. To complete the test, select the answer choice that best characterizes your response to each item.

Status Quo Bias Test

Question 1: Your financial advisor presents you with a plan to rebalance your portfolio. This rebalancing would require you to make a number of substantial changes in your portfolio, which may even involve triggering taxable events that are not pleasant but are quite necessary to get your portfolio where it needs to be. Which of the following is most likely?

a. You take action on the recommendation immediately.

b. You say you'll "think about it" to do an honest review and get back to your advisor in a week—and you actually will get back to your advisor in that time.

c. You say you'll "think about it" and get back to your advisor in a week—and you probably won't get back to your advisor and may not for three to six months because you tend to agonize over making substantial changes like this.

Question 2: Your investment portfolio contains a certain high-quality corporate bond. The bond has been providing income for you, and you are happy with it. Your financial advisor analyzes your bond holdings and recommends that you replace the corporate bond with a municipal bond of comparable quality, estimating that you will obtain a better return after taxes and fees. You aren't familiar with this municipal bond. What is your most likely response?

a. I will sell the corporate and purchase the municipal bond.

b. I will keep things as they are.

Question 3: Suppose that you have inherited a fully liquid investment in a South African gold mine from your eccentric Uncle Jim. You discuss the asset with your financial advisor, and she concludes that your portfolio already contains enough gold and commodities. More important, Uncle Jim's bequest isn't a diversified asset. Your advisor recommends selling it. What is your most likely course of action?

a. I will sell, as recommended by my financial advisor.

b. I will hold on to the gold mine interest, because I don't like to sell or modify things that people pass away and leave to me.

Test Results Analysis

Question 1: Answering "c" demonstrates a classic example of status quo bias.

Question 2: People who select "b" are likelier to suffer from status quo bias than people who select "a." Option "a" probably offers higher returns, but option "b" is, alas, the status quo.

Question 3: In this situation, most people would behave as depicted in "b," even when lacking any cogent rationale for holding the asset. Option "b" suggests status quo bias; "a" does not.

Investment Advice

This section offers advice on each of the specific investor errors outlined in Box 19.1.

Holding inappropriate assets. Education is essential to overcoming this aspect of status quo bias. As previously noted, status quo bias is exceptionally strong and difficult to overcome. Demonstrating the downside risks associated with holding inappropriate assets is often an effective tactic and may motivate people to change their behavior. Another persuasive approach is to demonstrate, based on a single stock position, what could happen to overall wealth levels if the market goes south and then to explicitly link wealth changes with probable lifestyle changes.

Status quo bias and loss aversion bias. Doing nothing is much easier than making a decision. This is especially true when a decision might bring about emotional pain; for example, the decision to sell a losing investment may register the impact of a loss. Sometimes, however, inaction can compromise long-run returns.

Status quo bias and emotional attachment. Emotions are perhaps the least legitimate concerns in asset management. When financial goals are in jeopardy, it can be too risky to sit back and adhere to an affective whim. Advisors need to demonstrate how emotions need to be managed. "Emotional intelligence," a well-publicized topic in popular psychology, offers many insights to this end.

Status quo bias and fear of transaction costs. Taxes and fees are legitimate concerns when it comes to altering an allocation status quo. However, more often than not, these concerns pale in comparison to the other potential implications of holding, or exiting, a poorly performing security. It is critical to keep in mind the crucial advantages of diversification and proper asset allocation.

20

Emotional Bias #5: Endowment Bias

A wise man should have money in his head, but not in his heart.

—Jonathan Swift

Bias Description

Bias Name: Endowment bias
Bias Type: Emotional

General Description

People who exhibit *endowment bias* value an asset more when they hold property rights to it than when they don't. Endowment bias is inconsistent with standard economic theory, which asserts that a person's *willingness to pay* for a good or an object should always equal the person's *willingness to accept dispossession* of the good or the object, when the dispossession is quantified in the form of compensation. Psychologists have found, however, that the minimum selling prices that people state tend to exceed the maximum purchase prices that they are willing to pay for the same good. Effectively, then, ownership of an asset instantaneously "endows" the asset with some added value. Endowment bias can affect

169

attitudes toward items owned over long periods of time or can crop up immediately as the item is acquired.

Example of Endowment Bias

Investors prove resistant to change once they become endowed with (take ownership of) securities. We will examine endowment bias as it relates to inherited securities.

William Samuelson and Richard Zeckhauser[1] performed an enlightening study on endowment bias that aptly illustrates investor susceptibility to this bias. Samuelson and Zeckhauser conducted an experiment in which investors were told to imagine that they had to newly acquire one of four investment options:

1. A moderately risky stock
2. A riskier stock
3. A Treasury security
4. A municipal security

Another group of investors was given the same list of options. However, they were instructed to imagine that they had already inherited one specified item on the list. If desired, the investors were told, they could cede their hypothetical inheritance in favor of a different option and could do so without penalty. In every case, however, the investors in the second group showed a tendency to retain whatever was "inherited." This is a classic case of endowment bias. Some investors are reluctant to sell securities bequeathed by previous generations. Often, in these situations, investors cite feelings of disloyalty associated with the prospect of selling inherited securities, general uncertainty in determining "the right thing to do," and tax issues.

Implications for Investors

There are some practical explanations as to why investors are susceptible to endowment bias. Understanding the origins of endowment bias

[1] William Samuelson and Richard J. Zeckhauser, "Status Quo Bias in Decision Making," *Journal of Risk and Uncertainty* 1(1) (1988): 7–59.

can help to provide intuition that guards against the mistakes that the bias can cause. First, investors may hold onto securities that they already own in order to avoid the tax costs associated with unloading securities. Make sure you don't "let the tax tail wag the investment dog." Such a rationale can be hazardous to one's wealth, because failure to take action and sell off certain assets can sometimes invite otherwise avoidable losses, while forcing investors to forgo the purchase of potentially more profitable, alternative assets. Second, investors hold onto securities because of familiarity. If investors know from experience the characteristics of the instruments that they already own (the behavior of particular government bonds, for example), then they may feel reluctant to transition into instruments that seem relatively unknown. Familiarity, effectively, has value. This value adds to the actual, market value of a security that an investor possesses, causing WTA to exceed WTP.

Box 20.1 contains a summary of investment mistakes that arise from endowment bias.

BOX 20.1 Endowment Bias: Behaviors That Can Cause Investment Mistakes

1. Endowment bias influences investors to hold onto securities that they have inherited, regardless of whether retaining those securities is financially wise. This behavior is often the result of the heirs' fear that selling will demonstrate disloyalty to prior generations.
2. Endowment bias causes investors to hold securities they have purchased (already own). This behavior is often the result of decision paralysis, which places an irrational premium on the compensation price demanded in exchange for the disposal of an endowed asset.
3. Endowment bias causes investors to hold securities that they have either inherited or purchased because they do not want to incur the tax costs associated with selling the securities. These costs, however, can be a very small price to pay when evacuating an unwise investment.
4. Endowment bias causes investors to hold securities that they have either inherited or purchased because they are familiar with the behavioral characteristics of these endowed investments. Familiarity, though, does not rationally justify retaining a poorly performing stock or bond.

Am I Subject to Endowment Bias?

The following is a brief diagnostic test that can help to detect endowment bias.

Endowment Bias Test

Question 1: Assume that your dearly departed Aunt Sally has bequeathed to you 100 shares of Netflix. Your financial advisor tells you that you are too "tech heavy" and recommends that you sell Aunt Sally's shares. What is your most likely course of action?

a. I will likely hold the Netflix shares because Aunt Sally bequeathed them to me.

b. I will likely listen to my financial advisor and sell the shares.

Question 2: Assume that you have purchased a high-quality municipal bond for your portfolio. It has been providing income for you, and you are happy with it. Your financial advisor analyzes your bond holdings and recommends switching to a corporate bond, of comparable quality, with which you are unfamiliar. Your advisor explains that, after taxes and fees, the corporate bond can be expected to provide a slightly better return than your current municipal bond. What is your most likely response?

a. I will stick with the municipal bond because I am familiar with it.

b. I will sell the municipal bond and purchase the corporate bond, even though I am unfamiliar with the corporate bond.

Test Results Analysis

Question 1: A reluctance to unload Aunt Sally's Netflix shares can signal susceptibility to endowment bias.

Question 2: People who decide that they would probably hold on to the municipal bond, due to familiarity with it, are likelier to exhibit endowment bias than people who would be willing to reallocate, even into unfamiliar territory, at a financial advisor's request.

Investment Advice

Generally, endowment bias tends to impact investors in two main contexts: (1) inherited securities, and (2) desire for familiarity.

Inherited securities. In the case of an inherited security, for example, you might ask: "If you had received, as cash, the current value of this security, what portion of that inheritance would you allocate into this specific security?" Often, the answer is none or very little. It can also be useful to explore the deceased's intent in owning the security. "Do you think that Uncle John's primary intent was to leave you this specific number of shares of this specific security? Is it possible that he was concerned about your general financial security?" Again, investors usually affirm the latter conclusion, paving the way to a more sensible allocation. If the investor does believe that his or her deceased relative valued, specifically, the opportunity to bequeath holdings in this exact security, then you might need to try a different line of questioning: "Okay, Uncle John wanted you to have these shares. But, if he really didn't want you to sell them, then . . . what did he want you to do with them?" Keeping in mind your long-term goals is essential in this situation.

Desire for familiarity. Familiarity can be a difficult craving to overcome. Comfort is crucial to an investor, and it may not be wise to take a portfolio in any direction with which you might be significantly uncomfortable. The best way to address an investor's desire for familiarity is to review the historical performance of the unfamiliar securities. This way, you can develop familiarity with the new investment instrument and achieve a corresponding comfort level.

21

Emotional Bias #6: Regret Aversion Bias

I visualized my grief if the stock market went way up and I wasn't in it—or if it went way down and I was completely in it. My intention was to minimize my future regret, so I split my retirement plan contributions 50/50 between bonds and equities.
—Harry Markowitz, father of *Modern Portfolio Theory*

Bias Description

Bias Name: Regret aversion bias
Bias Type: Emotional

General Description

People exhibiting *regret aversion* avoid taking decisive actions because they fear that, in hindsight, whatever course they select will prove less than optimal. Basically, this bias seeks to avoid the emotional pain of regret associated with poor decision making. Regret aversion makes investors, for example, unduly apprehensive about breaking into financial markets that have recently generated losses. When they experience negative investment outcomes, they feel instinctually driven to conserve, to retreat, and to lick their wounds—not to press on and snap up potentially undervalued stocks. However, periods of depressed prices often present the greatest buying opportunities. People suffering from regret aversion bias hesitate most at moments that actually merit aggressive behavior.

Regret aversion does not come into play only when following a loss; it can also affect a person's response to investment gains. People exhibiting regret aversion can be reluctant, for example, to sell a stock whose value has climbed recently—even if objective indicators attest that it's time to pull out. Instead, regret-averse investors may cling to positions that they ought to sell, pained by the prospect that a stock, once unloaded, might soar even higher.

Example of Regret Bias

The following case study illustrates both aspects of regret bias: *error of commission* and *error of omission*. The case shows a regret-averse investor under two sets of circumstances: (1) an investor experienced a loss and regrets his decision to invest; and (2) an investor missed an opportunity to invest in something that later appreciated in value and regrets his failure to reap profits.

Suppose that Jim has a chance to invest in Schmoogle, Inc., an initial public offering (IPO) that has generated a great buzz following its recent market debut. Jim thinks that Schmoogle has high potential and contemplates buying in because Schmoogle's price has recently declined by 10 percent due to some recent market weakness. If Jim invests in Schmoogle, one of two things will happen: (1) Schmoogle will drop further (Jim made the wrong decision), or (2) Schmoogle will rebound (Jim made the right decision). If Jim doesn't invest, one of two things will happen: (1) Schmoogle will rebound (Jim made the right decision), or (2) Schmoogle will drop further (Jim made the wrong decision).

Suppose that Jim does invest and Schmoogle goes down. Jim will have committed an error of commission because he actually committed the act of investing and will likely feel regret strongly because he actually lost money.

Now suppose that Jim does not invest and Schmoogle goes up. Jim will have committed an error of omission because he omitted the purchase of Schmoogle and lost out. This regret may not be as strong as the regret associated with the error of commission. Why? First, as we learned in Chapters 16 through 18, investors dislike losing money more than they like gaining money. Second, in the first possibility, the investor actually committed the act of investing and lost money; in the second possibility, the investor merely did not act and only lost out on the opportunity to gain.

Implications for Investors

Regret aversion causes investors to anticipate and fear the pain of regret that comes with incurring a loss or forfeiting a profit. The potential for financial injury isn't the only disincentive that these investors face; they also dread feeling responsible for their own misfortunes (because regret implies culpability, whereas simple disappointment does not). The anxiety surrounding the prospect of an error of commission, or a "wrong move," can make investors timid and can cause them to subjectively and perhaps irrationally favor investments that seem trustworthy (e.g., "good companies"). Suppose that regret-averse Jim is now considering two investments, both with equal projected risk and return. One stock belongs to Large Company, Inc., while the other confers a share in Medium-Size Company, Inc. Even though, mathematically, the expected payoffs of investing in these two companies are identical, Jim will probably feel more comfortable with Large Company. If an investment in Large Company, Inc., fails to pay off, Jim can rationalize that his decision making could not have been too egregiously flawed, because Large Company, Inc. must have had lots of savvy investors. Jim doesn't feel uniquely foolish, and so the culpability component of Jim's regret is reduced. Jim can't rely on the same excuse, however, if an investment in Medium-Size Company fails. Instead of exonerating himself ("Lots of high-profile people made the same mistake that I did—perhaps some market anomaly is at fault?"), Jim may condemn himself ("Why did I do that? I shouldn't have invested in Medium-Size. Only small-time players invested in Medium-Size, Inc. I feel stupid!"), adding to his feelings of regret. It's important to recall here that Large Company and Medium-Size Company stocks were, objectively, equally risky. This underscores the fact that aversion to regret is different from aversion to risk. Box 21.1 reviews five investor mistakes that can stem from regret aversion bias. Remedies for these biases will be reviewed in the Advice section.

BOX 21.1 Regret Aversion Bias: Behaviors That Can Cause Investment Mistakes

1. Regret aversion can cause investors to be too conservative in their investment choices. Having suffered losses in the past (i.e., having felt the pain of a poor decision regarding a risky investment), many people shy away from making new bold investment decisions and accept only low-risk positions. This behavior can lead to long-term underperformance and can jeopardize investment goals.

2. Regret aversion can cause investors to shy away, unduly, from markets that have recently gone down. Regret-averse individuals fear that, if they invest, such a market might subsequently continue its downward trend, prompting them to regret the decision to buy in. Often, however, depressed markets offer bargains, and people can benefit from seizing, decisively, these undervalued investments.

3. Regret aversion can cause investors to hold on to losing positions too long. People don't like to admit when they're wrong, and they will go to great lengths to avoid selling (i.e., confronting the reality of) a losing investment. This behavior, similar to loss aversion, is hazardous to one's wealth.

4. Regret aversion can cause "herding behavior" because, for some investors, buying into an apparent mass consensus can limit the potential for future regret. The demise of the real estate bubble of the late 2000s among other recent examples demonstrated that even the most massive herd can stampede in the wrong direction.

5. Regret aversion leads investors to prefer stocks of subjectively designated good companies, even when an alternative stock has an equal or a higher expected return. Regret-averse investors may feel that "riskier" companies require bolder decision making; hence, if the investment fails, the consequences reflect more dramatically on an individual's judgment than do the consequences of investing in a "routine," "safe," or "reliable" stock. With increased perception of personal responsibility, of course, comes increased potential for regret. Investing in good companies may not permit investors any more return or less return than those companies perceived to be risky.

Am I Subject to Regret Bias?

These questions are designed to detect signs of emotional bias stemming from regret aversion. To complete the test, select the answer choice that best characterizes your response to each item.

Regret Aversion Bias Test

Question 1: Suppose that you make an investment in mutual fund ABC and that over the next 12 months ABC appreciates by 10 percent. You contemplate selling ABC for normal portfolio rebalancing purposes, but then come across an item in the *Wall Street Journal* that sparks new optimism: Could ABC climb even higher? Which answer describes your likeliest response, given ABC's recent performance and this new information?

a. I think I'll hold off and sell later. I'd really kick myself if I sold now and ABC continued to go up.

b. I'll probably sell. But I'll still kick myself if ABC appreciates later on.

c. I'll probably sell the stock without any second thoughts because rebalancing is important—regardless of what happens to ABC's price after the transaction.

Question 2: Suppose that you've decided to acquire 200 shares of LMN mutual fund. You purchase 100 shares now at $30 apiece and strategize to wait a few days before picking up the additional 100. Further suppose that soon after your initial buy, the market takes a comprehensive dip. LMN is now trading at $28, with no change in fundamentals. Which answer most closely matches your thought process in this situation?

a. I will probably wait until the stock begins to go back up before buying the remaining 100 shares. I really don't want to see LMN fall below $28 because I'd regret my initial decision to buy in.

b. I will probably buy the remaining 100 shares. If LMN ends up going below $28, though, I will probably regret my decision.

c. I will probably buy the remaining 100 shares. Even if LMN falls below $28, I don't think I'll experience a lot of regret.

Question 3: Suppose you have decided to invest $5,000 in the stock market. You have narrowed your choices down to two mutual funds: one run by Big Company, Inc, and one run by Small Company, Inc. According to your calculations, both funds have equal risk and return characteristics. Big Company is a well-followed, eminently established company, whose investors include many large pension funds. Small company has performed well but has not garnered the same kind of public profile as Big Company. It has few well-known investors. Which answer most closely matches your thought process in this situation?

a. I will most likely invest in Big Company because I feel safe taking the same course as so many respected institutional investors. If Big City does decline in value, I know I won't be the only one caught by surprise—and with so many savvy professionals sharing my predicament, I could hardly blame myself for excessively poor judgment.

b. I will most likely invest in Big Company because if I invested in Small Company and my investment failed, I would feel like a fool. Few well-known investors backed Small Company, and I would really regret going against their informed consensus only to discover that I was dead wrong.

c. I would basically feel indifferent between the two investments, since both generated the same expected parameters for risk and return.

Test Result Analysis

Questions 1, 2, and 3: People answering "a" or "b" to any question may harbor susceptibility to regret aversion bias.

Advice

This section is organized to address each of the pitfalls of regret aversion bias that are enumerated in Box 21.1.

    Investing too conservatively. No matter how many times an investor has been "burned" by an ultimately unprofitable investment, risk (in the context of proper diversification) is still a healthy ingredient in any portfolio. Efficient frontier research can be very helpful here. Investing too conservatively doesn't place an investor's assets in any acute danger—by definition, an excess of conservatism denotes a relative absence of risk. However, refusing to assume a risk often means forgoing a potential reward. Investors who swear off risky assets due to regret aversion may see less growth in their portfolios than they could otherwise achieve, and they might not reach their investment goals.

Staying out of the market after a loss. There is no principle more fundamental in securities trading than "buy low, sell high." Nonetheless, many investors' behavior completely ignores this directive. Again, human nature is to chase returns, following "hot" money. Of course, it is possible to profit from following market trends . . . the problem is, you never know when the balloon is going to pop and cause, for example, yesterday's coveted security to plummet 40 percent in an afternoon. Disciplined portfolio management is crucial to long-term success. This means buying at times when the market is low and selling at the times when the market is up.

Holding losing positions too long. An adage on Wall Street is "The first loss is the best loss." While realizing losses is never enjoyable, the wisdom here is that following an unprofitable decision, it is best to cut those losses and move on. Everyone missteps occasionally—even the world's savviest traders. Investors shouldn't regret realizing their losses. If people can learn to feel less grief when realizing that they have incurred losses, then the pain of owning up to a loss can be reduced and the effects of regret aversion in such instances can be lessened.

Herding behavior. Often, investors subject to pack mentalities have a hard time explaining the rationale for a new investment if it does not fit into their long-term plan. Disconcerted by their own hesitation, many investors at this point will step back and reconsider the consensus of the herd. Others, though, may rationalize: "This is my time to take a risk." This is not, in and of itself, a dangerous statement. Investors are permitted, on occasion, to gamble. They must, however, understand the stakes and the magnitudes of the gambles they undertake.

Preference for good companies. Investors often prefer buying stock in "good" companies like Coca-Cola. Such household names have seen their ups and downs, however, just like competitor firms. Investors sometimes limit themselves to good companies simply because they fear the regret they might experience if an investment in a lesser-known company doesn't work out. Remember that high-profile brands don't necessarily deliver returns either. Coke is certainly recognizable, but that doesn't mean that either company's stock constitutes a sure thing.

Remember that you may also experience regret when a stock begins to decline after you've held it for too long. Moreover, a helpful approach is to attempt to set aside any emotions that might be impacting the sell decision. Once you feel certain, make a choice—and stick to it. You can always buy in again later on if the stock does indeed represent a good investment opportunity.

22

Emotional Bias #7: Affinity Bias

My yachts were, I suppose, outstanding status symbols.

—**Paul Getty**

Bias Description

Bias Name: Affinity bias
Bias Type: Emotional

General Description

Affinity bias refers to an individual's tendency to make irrationally uneconomical consumer choices or investment decisions based on how they believe a certain product or service will reflect their values. This idea focuses on the *expressive benefits* of a product rather than on what the product or service actually does for someone (the utilitarian benefits). A common example of this behavior in the consumer product realm is when one purchases wine. A consumer may purchase a fine bottle of well-known wine in a restaurant or wine shop for hundreds of dollars to impress their dinner guests, while a bottle that costs much less could be equally delicious but would not convey the same status. Automobiles are another example. A person may purchase a Range Rover or similar sport utility vehicle because they want to be viewed by others as someone who is "outdoorsy" (sometimes regardless of the extent to which the person actually engages in outdoor activities) when a much more affordable vehicle would easily transport them from point A to point B. Similarly, in the investment realm, individuals may invest in certain companies, such as those that produce Range Rovers, because they feel that this company reflects their values or self-image. This behavior may lead to sub-optimal investment results if the company producing the product or service is poorly managed or has financial or business-related problems.

Example of Affinity Bias

A useful application of affinity bias in the investment realm is *patriotism*. Investors who concentrate their holdings in their home country or state gain the expressive benefit of patriotism but may potentially lose the utilitarian benefits of high returns and low risk that come to those who invest elsewhere. Adair Morse and Sophie Shive[1] of the University of Chicago Booth School of Business and the University of Notre Dame, respectively, found that patriotism continuously affects investment behavior in their study, "Patriotism in Your Portfolio." They explored the role of devotion and loyalty to one's country in explaining an "equity home bias" and found that investors in more patriotic countries and regions within the United States discriminate more in favor of domestic stocks. Much like betting on the home team despite unfavorable odds or allocating retirement savings only to one's own company stock, patriotic investors choose to invest more of their stocks in firms based in their homeland. For example, the study found that U.S. investors hold 92 percent of their equity portfolio in domestic stock, although portfolio theory suggests that the optimally diversified portfolio should consist of only one third invested in domestic stocks.

Using data on 33 countries from the U-M World Values Survey, the researchers found that more patriotic countries and regions within the United States hold smaller foreign equity positions—in other words, investors discriminate in favor of domestic stocks. For example,

---

[1] Adair Morse and Sophie Shive, "Patriotism in Your Portfolio," *Journal of Financial Markets* 14 (2011): 411–440.

Americans and South Africans invest less in foreign stocks than do several European investors, while investors in the very patriotic regions of Texas, Oklahoma, Louisiana, and Arkansas invest less in international equities than do investors in the less patriotic New England states.

Morse and Shive found that patriotism accounts for an additional 7 percent of the cross-country variation in foreign equity holdings. Further, a 10 percent decrease in patriotism is associated with a 29 to 48 percent increase in foreign equity in the home country portfolio. The study also presented evidence that U.S. demand for French stocks traded in the United States declined in reaction to French opposition to the recent war in Iraq. The proportion of American Depositary Receipts (ADRs) sold increased by 15 to 18 percent during the prewar period of anti-French sentiment and the average U.S. price of the ADR decreased relative to the French price (ADRs are certificates issued by a U.S. depository bank, representing foreign shares held by the bank).

Overall, Morse and Shive say their research has two implications: patriotic behavior explains a part of the mysterious equity home bias and policies aimed at increasing investors' portfolio diversification may need to account for "irrational" investor behavior.

Implications for Investors

One of the previously referenced implications for affinity bias is that investors decide to invest in weak or otherwise unsound companies that reflect expressive characteristics rather than utilitarian characteristics in a misguided attempt to achieve investment success. A classic example of this can be found in individuals who invest in retail chain stores that produce popular products such as blue jeans, watches, or other products that reflect expressive benefits, only to discover that the company is a disaster from an investment standpoint. Other investors may also wish to invest in companies that they feel reflect their environmental, social, or governance values (ESG), which may or may not prove to be a successful strategy. Some studies have shown that ESG-type (socially responsible) investing is a successful strategy, while others have shown that ESG is not a winning investment strategy. Regardless, investors need to be aware that they may wish to invest in companies that reflect their social values and that this behavior has investment implications. Another implication of affinity bias is that some investors may wish to invest in things that convey status but that they know little about or that may involve risks, such as investing in hedge funds or other alternative investments that their social acquaintances are investing in, in order to demonstrate status or be part of an investment club—only to find that they made a bad decision in doing so. Finally, patriotic behavior may cause investors to have home country bias, which can limit the success of any portfolio, especially in the globally diverse world we now live in.

Affinity bias behaviors that can cause poor investment outcomes include the following in Box 22.1.

BOX 22.1 Affinity Bias: Behaviors That Can Cause Investment Mistakes

1. Investors subject to affinity bias can make investments in companies that make products or deliver services that they like but don't examine carefully enough the soundness of the investment characteristics of those companies.
2. Investors subject to affinity bias can invest in companies that reflect their ESG values but don't carefully examine the soundness of the investment characteristics of those companies.
3. Investors subject to affinity bias can invest in their home countries at the expense of investing in foreign countries due to home country bias.
4. Investors subject to affinity bias can sometimes invest in "sophisticated" investment products that convey status only to find they have invested in something they don't understand, which can be "hazardous to your wealth."

Am I Subject to Affinity Bias?

This section contains a diagnostic quiz that can help to detect susceptibility to Affinity bias. In the Advice section that follows, you will find guidelines for scoring responses to this quiz, along with corresponding suggestions for managing outcome bias.

Question 1:

	Strongly Disagree	Disagree	Neutral	Agree	Strongly Agree
I invest in companies that make products I like, such as cars, watches, or clothing.	☐	☐	☐	☐	☐

Question 2:

	Strongly Disagree	Disagree	Neutral	Agree	Strongly Agree
I invest in companies that reflect my personal values, such as environmental, social, or governance values.	☐	☐	☐	☐	☐

Question 3:

	Strongly Disagree	Disagree	Neutral	Agree	Strongly Agree
My investment portfolio does not contain much in the way of international investments.	☐	☐	☐	☐	☐

Question 4:

	Strongly Disagree	Disagree	Neutral	Agree	Strongly Agree
I have made investments in "sophisticated" investment products because it made me feel like a better investor or because my associates were doing it and I wanted to invest like them.	☐	☐	☐	☐	☐

Investment Advice

If you agreed or strongly agreed with any of these questions, you may be susceptible to affinity bias.

Question 1: Investors who are susceptible to affinity bias may decide to invest in weak or otherwise unsound companies that reflect expressive characteristics rather than utilitarian characteristics in a misguided attempt to find investment success. As noted earlier, a classic example of this is retail chain stores that have a popular product such as blue jeans, watches, or other products that reflect expressive benefits but turn out not to be a sound investment. Investors and advisors need to ask themselves first why they are making the investment—not just based on the product that is manufactured or promoted.

Question 2: Some investors may invest in companies that they feel reflect their ESG values, which may or may not prove to be a successful strategy. Some studies have shown that ESG-type (socially responsible) investing is a successful strategy, while others have shown that ESG is not a winning investment strategy. Regardless, investors need to be aware that they may wish to invest in companies that reflect their social values, and this may have investment implications.

Question 3: Another implication of affinity bias is that some investors may wish to invest in things that convey status but that they know nothing about or are unaware of the risks of, such as investing in hedge funds or other alternative investments that their social acquaintances are investing in, in order to demonstrate status or be part of an investment club—only to find that they made a bad decision by doing so. This is something that investors need to carefully monitor because capital can be lost if unwise investments are made in the name of status.

Question 4: Finally, patriotic behavior may cause investors to have home country bias, which can limit the success of any portfolio, especially in the globally diverse world we live in now. A simple analysis identifying how much international investments one wants can begin a conversation about this bias. I would encourage investors to take advantage of the diversification and currency benefits of international investing.

PART V
BEHAVIORAL
INVESTOR TYPES

U p to this point in the book, we have been laying the foundation for "putting it all together" in learning what type of investor each person is. The foundational elements of each Behavioral Investor Type (BIT) are the behavioral biases that each investor exhibits. You have done the hard part of understanding the origins of the biases and how to use them; we will now move to learning each BIT. Part Five starts with a discussion of why attaining financial goals is so difficult for so many people around the world. Chapter 24 then discusses the BIT framework. Then Chapters 25–28 review each of the four BITs—Preserver, Follower, Independent, and Accumulator. Which one are you?

23

Staying on Target to Reach Financial Goals Is Hard

I'd like to live as a poor man, with lots of money.

—**Pablo Picasso**

When people have a big overarching financial goal that they are working towards there is no chance for immediate gratification. A long-term financial plan is something that's not going to be completed for a long time. That time is probably measured in years, or even in decades. And humans are not exactly patient. With the ups and downs of life and the volatility of the markets, the scale of years or decades is difficult to process and it's pretty easy to lose touch with your long-term financial goal. And if things don't get off to a great start, it may be very easy to just lose faith and potentially walk away or completely give up. Like reaching most goals, it's a one step at a time, one day at a time, one week at a time, etc. process. You can do it!

Intuitively most people know that saving money is a good thing but the desire for material goods and spending on services often overrides otherwise good instincts. Understanding why behavior is so difficult to control is actually quite simple—a lack of self-discipline driven by psychological and/or environmental factors—but solutions are often

191

complex and illusory. In this chapter we start by examining some simple examples of self-defeating behavior, two of which are non-financial and three of which are financial examples. By doing so we can get a common understanding of the challenges of controlling behavior and emphasize the importance of why behavior must be carefully managed.

Non-Financial Examples of Self-Defeating Behavior

In order to get a clearer understanding of self-defeating behavior in the financial realm, it can be helpful to see examples of non-financial self-defeating behavior. The following examples are intended to be generic and purposefully not meant to bring negative light to anyone matching this description.

Example 1: The Yo-Yo Dieter

Everyone knows someone who is overweight and has tried on numerous occasions to lose weight but has not been successful. I'm not talking about the rare individual with such a severe problem that gastric bypass surgery or other drastic measure is needed, but rather the person who is 30 to 50 to 100 pounds overweight and systematically fails at weight loss. And I'm also not talking about the uneducated person who does not know the number of calories contained in food or the unhealthy effects of carrying around extra kilos. The people I am considering know that what they are putting into their bodies is what is making them overweight.

These unfortunate folks have often been traveling on a "yo-yo" or riding on a rollercoaster of diets—losing pounds then gaining pounds, gaining then losing, and back again. Through the dieting process, these people get educated on the calorie count of food and, by doing so, consciously know how much extra food is going into their bodies in terms of calories they eat per day. They also know that they don't eat enough fruits and vegetables (or none at all) or exercise enough (or not at all). Attempts at a "quick fix" are therefore attractive, however unsustainable these types of diet may be. We've all heard about diets such as all meat or no meat, or a host of others that work for a while but eventually fail as the "old behaviors" and the accompanying pounds come back. At some point these people just "give up" and say to themselves that they "can't do it" and go on with life with the extra pounds. There are a number of psychological and physiological reasons for overeating. Although the following list[1] is targeted at women, and may not be completely exhaustive, it contains some key reasons why people overeat (and much of the information is applicable to men as well):

- Boredom—You eat when you're bored or do not have anything interesting to do or to look forward to. TV is a favorite pastime especially when you are alone at home and bored. When food commercials are running 200 images per hour into our cerebral cortex it is difficult not to be drawn toward the refrigerator. If food commercials are a trigger, watch nature shows or commercial-free TV.
- Feeling Deprived—You feel deprived of the foods you enjoy, which leaves you craving for them even more. Media's attitude toward emphasizing thinness as the ideal has led to restrictive dieting and avoidance of entire groups of foods. Unfortunately, because the foods we are urged to avoid are abundantly available, and food visibility and availability are powerful eating stimuli, restrictors often break the "plan" and eat forbidden foods. Once this happens, overwhelming guilt, followed by feelings of low self-esteem, motivate the individual to go on over-consuming the avoided food in an attempt to numb these negative feelings.
- Glucose intolerance—This is a physiological trigger. In a healthy body, carbohydrates are converted to glucose and a blood glucose level of ~60–120 mg/dl is maintained without thought to the dietary consumption of carbohydrate. In the glucose-intolerant population, carbohydrates are readily converted to glucose and the pancreas responds to this shift in blood sugar by secreting an excessive amount of the hormone, insulin. Insulin's job is to remove the glucose from the blood stream and help it to enter the body cells. If done properly, the blood glucose level returns to the normal range regardless of the amount of carbohydrates consumed. If this system is not working correctly, a quick rise in blood glucose occurs, followed by an overproduction of insulin. The excessive insulin is not recognized by the body cells so it is unable to remove the glucose from the blood stream. The result is an increase in blood insulin levels, which has an appetite-stimulating effect. The person is driven to eat and, if simple carbohydrates are chosen, the cycle continues.

---

[1] Source: http://www.womenfitness.net/over-eating.htm

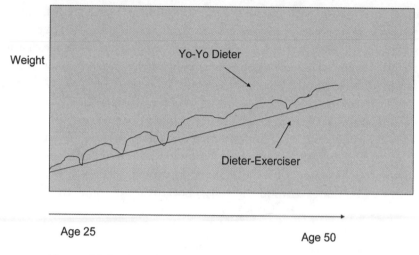

Figure 23.1 The Dieter-Exerciser versus the Yo-Yo Dieter

Other factors include a lifestyle that is constantly draining your energy, a desire for comfort, feelings of being overwhelmed, upset or hurt, and the big one—a lack of will power. Whatever the case, the basic facts are that there are too many people out there who know what they need to do to cut weight but cannot find the behavioral tools to succeed. This, naturally, is in contrast to the "dieter-exerciser" who eats right and exercises regularly and manages to get weight under control. It should be simple, right? For the record, I am a few pounds overweight myself and am guilty of several of the behaviors mentioned here . . . but the difference is that I am doing something about it. Because I realize *I* am in control of my diet and exercise and not the other way round. The following figure illustrates that as we age our weight is destined to go up (there are those who manage to keep it off their whole lives but not that many!) but if we can keep to a healthy diet and exercise, we will likely keep a more even weight gain and, if we do, we will likely weigh less than those who are on the roller coaster. Easier said than done! Figure 23.1 compares the Yo-Yo dieter to the Dieter-Exerciser.

Example 2: The Educated Smoker

Have you ever met a doctor or other health professional who is also a smoker? This one sort of astounds me. How can it be that a person who has devoted their lives to the health and well-being of others can treat their own body so carelessly? I can remember as a teenager, I would play sports with my friends in my backyard and witness my next-door neighbor, a doctor, chain-smoking on her porch. I knew even at that age the health risks of smoking and could not understand for the life of me why she smoked (I knew she had to know the risks involved.) Later, in her forties, I heard she died of lung cancer. This shocked me, but when I thought about it, I realized it shouldn't have come as a surprise. To this day, I still remember a poster in the hall of my middle school of an elderly, wrinkled, lifeless person holding a cigarette with the caption "Smoking is very debonair" across the bottom—which was meant to deter youngsters from smoking; it was shock treatment at an early age—and it worked. So how is it that a well-trained doctor, with full knowledge of the health risks of smoking, chain-smokes him- or herself to an almost certain death? As with the yo-yo dieter, there are psychological, as well as physiological, reasons why people who know smoking is bad still engage in the act. To name a few:[2]

For many people, smoking is a reliable lifestyle coping tool. Although every person's specific reasons to smoke are unique, they all share a common theme. Smoking is used as a way to suppress uncomfortable feelings, and smoking is used to alleviate stress, calm nerves, and relax. No wonder that when you are deprived of smoking, your mind and body are unsettled for a little while. Below is a list of some positive intentions often associated with smoking.

- Coping with anger, stress, anxiety, tiredness, or sadness
- Smoking is pleasant and relaxing
- Smoking is stimulating
- Acceptance—being part of a group
- As a way to socialize
- Provides support when things go wrong
- A way to look confident and in control
- Keeps weight down
- Rebellion—defining self as different or unique from a group
- A reminder to breathe
- Something to do with your mouth and hands
- Shutting out stimuli from the outside world

---

[2] "Top 10 Triggers for Over-eating." Women Fitness—A Complete Online Guide To Achieve Healthy Weight Loss and Optimum Fitness. Web. 05 July 2011. http://www.womenfitness.net/over-eating.htm.

- Shutting out emotions from the inside world
- Something to do just for you and nobody else
- A way to shift gears or change states
- A way to feel confident
- A way to shut off distressing feelings
- A way to deal with stress or anxiety
- A way to get attention
- Marking the beginning or the end of something

The National Institute on Drug Abuse (NIDA) reports that people suffering from nicotine withdrawal have increased aggression, anxiety, hostility, and anger. However, perhaps these emotional responses are due not to withdrawal, but due to an increased awareness of unresolved emotions. If smoking dulls emotions, logically quitting smoking allows awareness of those emotions to bubble up to the surface. If emotional issues aren't resolved, a smoker may feel overwhelmed and eventually turn back to cigarettes to deal with the uncomfortable feelings.

Instead, when you smoke, the carbon monoxide in the smoke bonds to your red blood cells, taking up the spaces where oxygen needs to bond. This makes you less able to take in the deep, oxygen-filled breaths needed to bring you life, to activate new energy, to allow health and healing, or bring creative insight into your problems and issues. The bottom line here is that, once again, even though it is well known and documented that smoking is an entirely unhealthy activity, there are a myriad of reasons why people smoke. Self-defeating behavior is the culprit; intellectually, we know that smoking is bad. But somehow the will to stop just isn't there.

Financial Examples of Self-Defeating Behavior

Now that we have reviewed some non-financial examples of self-defeating behavior, we can now turn to behaviors that should be equated with poor investment performance but are repeated by investors month after month, year after year, cycle after cycle.

Number 1: The Return Chaser

One of the most basic of human investment instincts is to be "in the know" regarding the latest investment trend. How silly we feel when we are at a cocktail party or barbeque in our community and we join a conversation in progress about how your neighbor just made a killing on XYZ stock that participates in ABC hot industry. Why am I not participating in this money-making opportunity, you ask yourself? This occurred with Internet stocks in the late 1990s and then with real estate during the subsequent decade and now potentially with some social media companies.

At one time or another we have all seen someone who epitomizes this type of investor—or maybe this is our own behavior! These folks follow the latest trend, paying no attention to valuation and/or have no rational basis for making an investment and "jump in" without an exit strategy or plan to get out when a profit has been made—if one is ever made. The investment may go up but since no plan is in place, the investment ultimately turns sour and losses ensue.

As investors we must resist the urge to participate in such schemes and steer clear of these money-losing opportunities. Our own behavior is often the culprit and we need to overcome our natural instincts to participate in less-than-rational investment schemes—or at least have an exit strategy if the decision is made to participate. Later in the book we will look at individual behaviors that account for chasing returns as has been described here and devise strategies for overcoming these behaviors.

Number 2: The Overconfident Gambler

It is not uncommon to come across the type of investor who thinks they are smarter than the average market participant, who enjoys the thrill of trading in and out of the market (i.e., like the thrill associated with gambling) and is more often than not on the losing end of the trade (with the occasional win to keep them in the game). And, being on the losing end of the trade often causes even more of the gambling behaviors to kick in, so that they engage in the same risky trading behavior in an attempt to get back to even. This example is in contrast to the person who avoids such behavior (or keeps it to such a modest amount that it does not affect long-term wealth creation) and manages to save and invest over long periods of time to build wealth gradually. Notice a pattern here? This example is, of course, nearly identical to the yo-yo dieter in the non-financial examples presented in the last section. The dieter attempts to lose weight quickly on a regular basis only to gain it back. (In this case, it's the opposite—the person attempts to gain wealth

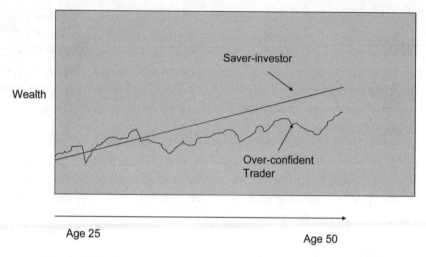

Figure 23.2 Saver–investor versus the Over–Confident Trader

quickly only to "lose it back.") Figure 23.2 illustrates the overconfident gambler versus the opposite type of investor, who I will call the saver/investor. Both started at 25 and are currently 50 years old. Figure 23.3 extends out in time to show that there are still opportunities to change behavior even at mid-life.

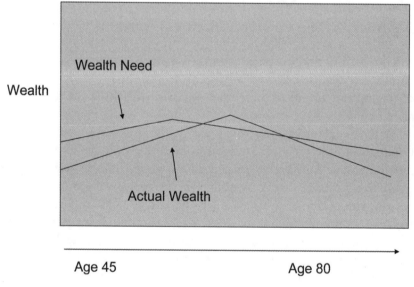

Figure 23.3 The Risk–Averse Investor

Naturally, this chart does not represent reality perfectly but you get the point: it's not hard to tell which kind of person you want to be. So, why can't we do it? The answer is we can, but we first need to identify the key factors that are rendering us incapable of engaging in good behavior.

Number 3: The "Too Conservative" Investor

Although not as common, there exists a class of investor that is too conservative in their thinking. They are afraid of losing money to a down stock market, whether through previous personal experience or not, that they simply won't accept any amount of risk. The failure with this approach is that people who cannot accept some amount of risk also risk outliving their money. The following diagram illustrates. Early into one's career, earning may not keep pace with the demand for funds, due to expenses like college and housing. At some point during mid-career, these expenses are hopefully surpassed by earnings and debt is reduced. The later in life, one's working career can end either voluntarily or not, and cash needs are surpassed by income. If one does not accumulate enough of a nest egg and invest it wisely, there can be a situation where one may outlive one's assets. This is demonstrated in Figure 23.3. Certain people in this situation intuitively know that they need to increase risk, but simply cannot take action to do it. They know concepts such as inflation and low yields on bonds but will not do what it takes to take the risk to build wealth.

Similarly, this chart does not represent reality perfectly but you get the point: You don't want to be in a situation where you don't have enough money as age increases. Taking risk in this case is advisable. In other cases, advisors spend a good deal of time talking people out of taking risk.

We have reviewed three very basic situations in which we have identified a type of investor. The intent was not to go into great detail but to provide situations in which it is difficult to control one's impulses toward a certain action or behavior. As we saw with the non-financial situations, people know they are taking actions that are not in their best interest. Similarly, in the financial examples, we saw that people can make financial decisions that are not in their best interest even when they know they should take a different path. In many other cases, people may not be aware of their irrational behavior and they need their advisors or other close relations to help them understand they are making mistakes.

24

Introduction to Behavioral Investor Types

Someone is sitting in the shade today because someone planted a tree a long time ago.
                                                                —**Warren Buffett**

Introduction

As we will learn in the next four chapters, there are four behavioral investor types (BITs): The Preserver, the Follower, the Independent, and the Accumulator. The first section in the chapter will be to provide background on how BITs were devised, including background on personality type theory. By understanding the framework for how each BIT was identified, you will have knowledge to more deeply understand the case studies in Chapter 29. The chapter then moves to explaining how to identify BITs and manage your behavioral tendencies, which includes a three-step process:

1. Taking a BIT orientation quiz
2. Taking a bias quiz

3. Contemplating advice on dealing with your individual type including understanding the upside and downside aspects of each BIT.

Introduction: Personality Type Theories

We will now introduce personality type theories. While there are many different theories of personality, it is important to understand exactly what is meant by the term personality. A brief definition is that personality is made up of the characteristic patterns of thoughts, feelings, and behaviors that make a person unique. In addition to this, personality arises from within the individual and remains fairly consistent throughout life. To gain an appreciation for the foundation of the concept of a behavioral investor type, it is essential that we take some time to explore some background on how personality types were developed. In this article we will discuss some existing personality identification schemes; this will help put into perspective the behavioral investor type framework I will discuss in subsequent articles. This section is intended to bridge the gap between mainstream personality theories and introduce the theory behind "financial personality types" or behavioral investor types, which combine elements of a number of personality theories. BITs are most strongly influenced by the Type Theories; they're a classification scheme similar to Hippocrates's four original types, the Kiersey Types, and the Myers-Briggs Types.

Type theories take us all the way back to Ancient Greece, around 400 BC, to the work of Hippocrates. The great physician believed that people could be "typed" into four distinct categories, named Melancholic, Sanguine, Choleric, and Phlegmatic, after the various bodily fluids that were then thought to influence personality. Each category was also linked to one of the four elements: fire, air, water, and earth, collectively referred to as the "humors." Today, Hippocrates's personality types are called Guardians, Artisans, Idealists, and Rationalists.

- Guardians: Fact-oriented
- Artisans: Action-oriented
- Idealists: Ideal-oriented
- Rationalists: Theory-oriented

As you can see, these humors encompass the most basic, underlying characteristics of what we today refer to as "personality," but it is clear that no one's actions are entirely "rational" or "theory-based," and that no one is solely "action-oriented," but rather that most people are a combination of many of these humors, but in varying proportions. For example, your wife may be a "rationalist" and you may be more "action-oriented," but obviously neither of these characteristics comprises your entire personality. This is also true of financial personalities. Personality-type schemes tend to overgeneralize about personality traits (since people are rarely only one type of person), but they are a useful tool for organizing one's thoughts about how to compare one type of person to another.

The Behavioral Investor Type (BIT) Framework

Similar to the psychological typing theories that we just read about, BITs are models for various types of investor. This framework has four behavioral investor types: the Preserver, the Follower, the Independent, and the Accumulator. Each of these types will be reviewed in detail in the next four chapters. In preparation for these chapters, it is important for readers to understand the background of how BITs are identified through a process called Behavioral Alpha. The process outlined below is a much more detailed process covered more deeply in my last book *Behavioral Finance and Investor Types.*

BITs were designed to help investors make rapid yet insightful assessments of what type of investor they are before deciding on an investment plan. The benefit of understanding what type of investor you are is that you can avoid behavioral surprises that may result in a desire to change your portfolio as result of market turmoil. If you can limit the number of traumatic episodes that inevitably occur throughout the investment process by delivering smoother (read here: expected) investment results because you have created an investment plan that is customized to your behavioral make-up, a stronger portfolio is the result. BITs, however, are not intended to be "absolutes" but rather "guide-posts" to use when making the journey with your portfolio; dealing with irrational investor behavior is not an exact science. For example, you may find that you correctly identified your BIT, but that you have traits (biases) of another.

The next four chapters will provide descriptions of the four behavioral investor types. Each chapter will also include a list of behavioral biases for each type, and advice for dealing with each BIT. Each BIT is characterized by a certain risk tolerance level and a primary type of bias—either cognitive (thinking errors) or emotional (driven by impulses and/or feelings). One of the most important concepts you need to keep in mind as you read these chapters is that the least risk tolerant BIT and the most risk tolerant BIT are driven by *emotional* biases, while the two BITs in between these extremes are mainly affected by *cognitive* biases. Emotional biases are much more ingrained in us, more difficult to change. If you can recognize the type of investor you are prior to making investment decisions, you will be much better prepared to deal with irrational behavior when it arises.

What Is My Behavioral Investor Type?

In this section there are two objective tests that are intended to do two main things. The first is to determine your orientation—that is, what basic type of investor you are. The second is the identification of individual behavioral biases. I call the first test "Step 1" and the second "Step 2."

It is important to keep in mind that just because a person is oriented toward or identified as one BIT versus another, it does not mean that they won't have attributes of other types. For example, you might have a *Preserver* orientation but also have *Independent* characteristics as well. As we will see in the next section, there are certain biases that are associated with each BIT but just because an investor has a certain overarching orientation, such as an *Accumulator*, he or she may have biases of other orientations, such as a *Follower*. For example, you might have a *Follower* orientation investor that demonstrates a strong tendency toward hindsight bias (a bias commonly associated with Followers). But another *Accumulator*-oriented investor type may also have hindsight, but not to the same degree. The point is that the type orientations that are the result of the test in this chapter are not meant to be taken as absolutes; they are meant to help diagnose key behavioral tendencies that can hopefully be corrected with information and advice for the purpose of attaining positive long-term financial results.

The second test in this chapter is the bias identification test. Once an orientation has been identified, it is advisable to investigate biases that are associated with a given orientation because they can be major inhibitors to successfully following an investment plan. Once again it is important to reiterate that biases associated with an investor with a certain orientation may also be associated with another orientation. Figure 24.1 describes the two-step process using the two tests in this chapter.

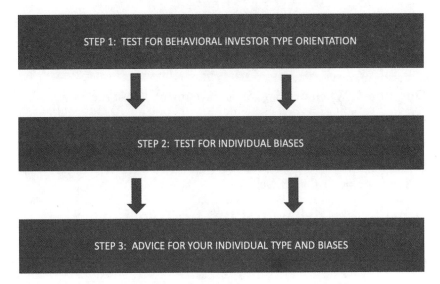

Figure 24.1 BIT Identification and Advice Process

Step 1: BIT Orientation Quiz

The first test in this chapter is an orientation of each investor type as listed in the prior section. Although the questions may seem repetitive—and even perhaps too obviously guiding the test taker in a certain direction—it is nonetheless important and relevant to make this initial identification. It should be said again that, just because someone has one orientation it doesn't mean that they won't have traits or characteristics of another orientation. It means that this is their dominant orientation and needs to be accounted for first. Here is the test:

Question 1. My main role in managing my money is:

a) To be the guardian of my wealth by not making risky investments

b) Actively trading my account to accumulate wealth

c) Doing research before investment decisions

d) Listening to others for advice on managing money

Question 2. When it comes to financial matters, I most agree with which statement?

a) Losing money is the worst possible outcome

b) I should act quickly on opportunities to make money

c) I need to be satisfied I have taken the time to understand an investment I plan to make even if I miss opportunities by doing so

d) I should not be in charge of overseeing my money

Question 3. When deciding on an investment, I trust the advice of:

a) My own self-discipline

b) My gut instincts

c) My own research

d) Someone other than myself

Question 4. When markets are going up, I am:

a) Relieved

b) Excited

c) Calm and rational

d) Glad I am following someone's advice

Question 5. In the financial realm, which word best describes you?

a) Guardian

b) Trader

c) Researcher

d) Advice-taker

Question 6. When it comes to following a plan to manage money, which best describes your thinking?

a) If following a plan will help safeguard my assets, I will do it

b) Following a plan is not that important

c) A plan is good, but investment decisions must include my thinking

d) I tend to follow others' advice; so if a plan is recommended to me I will follow it or I just listen to others' ideas

Question 7. I feel most confident about my money when:

a) I can sleep at night knowing my assets are safely invested

b) I am invested in assets that have high appreciation potential

c) I make my own investment decisions or at least have input into the process

d) I'm invested in things that many others are invested in

Question 8. When a friend suggests a "sure thing" investment idea, my response normally is:

a) I typically avoid these types of ideas

b) I love things like this and I can take action right away if needed

c) I will do my own research and then decide what to do

d) I will need to consult someone else before making a decision

Question 9. Short-term fluctuations in my portfolio make me

a) Panic, thinking about selling

b) Sense opportunity, thinking about buying

c) In control, potentially doing nothing

d) Want to call someone to see how my money is doing

Question 10. Imagine yourself at a sporting event. Which role are you most likely to play:

a) A defensive player

b) An offensive player

c) Strategist/coach

d) Fan

This 10-question test can identify the fundamental orientation of an investor. A preponderance of (a) responses indicates a *Preserver* orientation. A preponderance of (b) responses indicates an *Accumulator* orientation. A preponderance of (c) responses indicates an *Independent* orientation. A preponderance of (d) responses indicates a *Follower* orientation. What follows here is a very brief description of each type. A significantly more detailed overview of each type follows in Chapters 25–28.

BIT #1: Preserver Behavioral Investor Type

A *Preserver* Behavioral Investor Type describes an emotional investor who places a great deal of emphasis on financial security and preserving wealth rather than taking risks to grow wealth. Such investors are guardians of their assets and take losses very seriously. Preservers are often deliberate in their decisions and sometimes have difficulty taking action with their investments, out of concern that they may make the wrong decision or take too much risk. They instead may prefer to avoid decisions and stick to the status quo. Preservers often obsess over short-term performance in both up and down markets (but mostly down markets) and they also tend to worry about losing what they had previously gained. This behavior is consistent with how Preservers have approached their work and personal lives—in a deliberate and cautious way.

BIT #2: Follower Behavioral Investor Type

A *Follower* Behavioral Investor Type describes an investor who is passive and often lacks interest in and/or has little aptitude for money or investing. Furthermore, Follower investors typically do not have their own ideas about investing. Rather, they may follow the lead of their friends and colleagues, or whatever general investing fad is occurring, to make their investment decisions. Often their decision-making process is without regard to a long-term plan. They sometimes trick themselves into thinking they are smart or talented in the investment realm when an investment decision works out, which can lead to unwarranted risk-seeking behavior. Since they don't tend to have their own ideas about investing, they also may react differently when presented more than once with the same investment proposal: That is, the way something is presented (framed) can make them think and act differently. They also may regret not being in the latest investment fad and end up investing at exactly the wrong time, when valuations are the highest.

BIT #3: Independent Behavioral Investor Type

An *Independent* Behavioral Investor Type describes investors who have original ideas about investing and like to get involved in the investment process. Unlike Followers, they are not disinterested in investing and are quite engaged in the financial markets, and they may have unconventional views on investing. This "contrarian" mindset, however, may cause Independents not to believe in following a long-term investment plan. With that said, many Independents can and do stick to an investment plan to accomplish their financial goals. At their essence, Independents are analytical, critical thinkers who make many of their decisions based on logic and their own gut instinct. They are willing to take risks and act decisively when called upon to do so. Independents can accomplish tasks when they put their minds to it; they tend to be thinkers and doers as opposed to followers and dreamers.

BIT #4: Accumulator Behavioral Investor Type

The *Accumulator* behavioral investor type describes investors who are interested in accumulating wealth and are confident they can do so. These investors have typically been successful in some business pursuit and believe in themselves enough that they will be successful investors. As such, they often like to adjust their portfolio allocations and holdings to market conditions and may not wish to follow a structured plan. Moreover, they want to influence decision-making or even control the decision-making process, which potentially can diminish an advisor's role. At their core, Accumulators are risk-takers and are firm believers that whatever path they choose is the correct one. Unlike Preservers, they are in the race to win—and win big. And unlike the Followers, they rely on themselves and want to be the ones steering the ship. And unlike Individualists, they usually dig down to the details rather than forge a course with half the information that they need.

Once you have identified which type you are oriented toward, you now need to move to Step 2, which is diagnosing individual biases. Figure 24.2 illustrates at a high level which biases are associated with each BIT. As noted earlier, just because a person has biases of one BIT versus another, it does not mean that they won't have attributes of other investor types.

Biases-Typology *Mapping*

Preserver	Follower	Independent	Accumulator
Endowment	Regret	Conservatism	Over-Confidence
Loss Aversion	Hindsight	Availability	Self-Control
Status Quo	Framing	Confirmation	Outcome
Anchoring	Cognitive Dissonance	Representativeness	Illusion of Control
Mental Accounting	Recency	Self-Attribution	Affinity

Figure 24.2 Biases Associated with Each Behavioral Investor Type

Step 2: Bias Identification Quiz

The following questions identify individual biases. Make sure to answer all the questions to get a complete understanding of all biases. Keep in mind that certain biases will be linked to certain orientations. These connections will be discussed in the next four chapters. Advice as to how to handle these biases will also be discussed in those chapters. If you identify yourself as being oriented in a certain direction, such as a *Follower*, and you wish to quickly dive into biases that are associated with Followers and deal with one or two right away, you might consider answering only those bias questions that are associated with that orientation.

NOTE: Included here are the orientation types with each Answer provided in this section.

Question 1. When thinking about selling an investment, the price I paid is a big factor I consider before taking any action
a) Strongly Agree
b) Agree
c) Neutral
d) Disagree
e) Strongly Disagree
Answer: Those who Agree or Strongly Agree with this statement are likely to be susceptible to anchoring bias (*Preserver* Orientation bias)

Question 2. The pain of financial loss is at least two times stronger than the pleasure of financial gain
a) Strongly Agree
b) Agree
c) Neutral
d) Disagree
e) Strongly Disagree
Answer: Those who Agree or Strongly Agree with this statement are likely to be susceptible to loss aversion (*Preserver* Orientation bias)

Question 3. I will buy things I want even if they are not the best financial choices

a) Strongly Agree

b) Agree

c) Neutral

d) Disagree

e) Strongly Disagree

Answer: Those who Agree or Strongly Agree with this statement are likely to be susceptible to self-control bias (*Accumulator* Orientation bias)

Question 4. Poor past financial decisions have caused me to change my current investing decisions

a) Strongly Agree

b) Agree

c) Neutral

d) Disagree

e) Strongly Disagree

Answer: Those who Agree or Strongly Agree with this statement are likely to be susceptible to regret bias (Follower Orientation bias)

Question 5. I sometimes get attached to certain investments which may cause me not to take action on them

a) Strongly Agree

b) Agree

c) Neutral

d) Disagree

e) Strongly Disagree

Answer: Those who Agree or Strongly Agree with this statement are likely to be susceptible to endowment bias (Preserver Orientation bias)

Question 6. I often take action on a new investment right away, if it makes sense to me

a) Strongly Agree

b) Agree

c) Neutral

d) Disagree

e) Strongly Disagree

Answer: Those who Agree or Strongly Agree with this statement are likely to be susceptible to availability bias (*Independent* Orientation bias)

Question 7. I often find that many of my successful investments can be attributed to my decisions, while those that did not work out were based on the guidance of others

a) Strongly Agree

b) Agree

c) Neutral

d) Disagree

e) Strongly Disagree

Answer: Those who Agree or Strongly Agree with this statement are likely to be susceptible to self-attribution bias (*Independent* Orientation bias)

Question 8. When considering changing my portfolio, I spend time thinking about options but often end up changing little or sometimes nothing

a) Strongly Agree

b) Agree

c) Neutral

d) Disagree

e) Strongly Disagree

Answer: Those who Agree or Strongly Agree with this statement are likely to be susceptible to status quo bias (*Preserver* Orientation bias)

Question 9. I am confident that my investment knowledge is above average

a) Strongly Agree

b) Agree

c) Neutral

d) Disagree

e) Strongly Disagree

Answer: Those who Agree or Strongly Agree with this statement are likely to be susceptible to overconfidence (*Accumulator* Orientation bias)

Question 10. I trust the advice of national firms that do a lot of advertising compared to smaller, local firms that don't have a well-known brand name.

a) Strongly Agree

b) Agree

c) Neutral

d) Disagree

e) Strongly Disagree

Answer: Those who Agree or Strongly Agree with this statement are likely to be susceptible to framing bias (*Follower* Orientation bias)

Question 11. I don't easily change my views about investments once they are made

a) Strongly Agree

b) Agree

c) Neutral

d) Disagree

e) Strongly Disagree

Answer: Those who Agree or Strongly Agree with this statement are likely to be susceptible to conservatism bias (*Independent* Orientation bias)

Question 12. I invest in companies that make products I like or companies that reflect my personal values

a) Strongly Agree

b) Agree

c) Neutral

d) Disagree

e) Strongly Disagree

Answer: Those who Agree or Strongly Agree with this statement are likely to be susceptible to affinity bias (*Accumulator* Orientation bias)

Question 13. I tend to categorize my investments in various accounts, i.e., leisure, bill paying, college funding, etc.

a) Strongly Agree

b) Agree

c) Neutral

d) Disagree

e) Strongly Disagree

Answer: Those who Agree or Strongly Agree with this statement are likely to be susceptible to mental accounting bias (*Preserver* Orientation bias)

Question 14. When reflecting on past investment mistakes, I see that many could easily have been avoided

a) Strongly Agree

b) Agree

c) Neutral

d) Disagree

e) Strongly Disagree

Answer: Those who Agree or Strongly Agree with this statement are likely to be susceptible to hindsight bias (*Follower* Orientation bias)

Question 15. Many investment choices I make are based upon my knowledge of how similar past investments have performed

a) Strongly Agree

b) Agree

c) Neutral

d) Disagree

e) Strongly Disagree

Answer: Those who Agree or Strongly Agree with this statement are likely to be susceptible to Representativeness bias (*Independent* Orientation bias)

Question 16. What's most important is that my investments make money—I'm not that concerned with following a structured plan

a) Strongly Agree

b) Agree

c) Neutral

d) Disagree

e) Strongly Disagree

Answer: Those who Agree or Strongly Agree with this statement are likely to be susceptible to outcome bias (*Accumulator* Orientation bias)

Question 17. When making investment decisions, I tend to focus on the positive aspect of an investment rather than on what might go wrong with the investment

a) Strongly Agree

b) Agree

c) Neutral

d) Disagree

e) Strongly Disagree

Answer: Those who Agree or Strongly Agree with this statement are likely to be susceptible to cognitive dissonance bias (*Follower* Orientation bias)

Question 18. I am more likely to have a better outcome if I make my own investment choices rather than relying on others

a) Strongly Agree

b) Agree

c) Neutral

d) Disagree

e) Strongly Disagree

Answer: Those who Agree or Strongly Agree with this statement are likely to be susceptible to illusion of control bias (*Accumulator* Orientation bias)

Question 19. When an investment is not going well, I usually seek information that confirms I made the right decision about it

a) Strongly Agree

b) Agree

c) Neutral

d) Disagree

e) Strongly Disagree

Answer: Those who Agree or Strongly Agree with this statement are likely to be susceptible to confirmation bias (*Independent* Orientation bias)

Question 20. When considering the track record of an investment, I put more weight on how it has performed recently versus how it has performed historically

a) Strongly Agree

b) Agree

c) Neutral

d) Disagree

e) Strongly Disagree

Answer: Those who Agree or Strongly Agree with this statement are likely to be susceptible to recency bias (*Follower* Orientation bias)

Step 3: Advice for Each BIT

Once you have identified your BIT, you can move to understanding more detail of each BIT in the next four chapters. Advice for how best to work within each BIT framework is presented as well. If you want to get a more complete understanding of all four BITs you have the opportunity to learn those as well.

Summary

So now we have the tools to diagnose ourselves with regard to the different behavioral investor types. We have the ability to diagnose the basic orientation of an investor and then we are able to identify a number of key biases that are associated with that orientation. In essence, we have the framework for broadly understanding and identifying different types of investor. But we need to keep in mind why we are doing this. The reason, as I have said over and over, is to prevent destructive behaviors from limiting our ability to reach financial goals. For readers to better understand how to use the information that these tests provide, the next four chapters will delve into the details of each BIT and how best to deal with the impediments that arise from each type. It is important to note that each BIT also has positive elements that can and should be leveraged to help attain financial goals. These positive attributes will also be reviewed.

25

Preserver Behavioral Investor Type

Pearls don't lie on the seashore. If you want one, you must dive for it.
—**Chinese proverb**

Name of Behavioral Investor Type: Preserver
Basic Orientation: Loss averse and deliberate in decision making
Dominant Bias Types: Emotional, relating to fear of losses and inability to make decisions/take action
Impactful Biases: Loss Aversion and Status Quo
Investing Style: Wealth preservation first, growth second
Level of Risk Tolerance: Generally lower than average

A *Preserver* Behavioral Investor Type describes the investor who places a great deal of emphasis on financial security and preserving wealth rather than taking risks to grow wealth. They are guardians of their assets and take losses very seriously. Preservers are often deliberate in their decisions and sometimes have difficulty taking action with their investments, out of concern that they may make the wrong decision. They instead may prefer to avoid risk and stick to the status quo. Preservers often obsess over short-term performance (in both up and down markets—but mostly down markets), losses, and also tend to worry about losing what they had previously gained. This behavior is consistent with the way Preservers have approached their work and personal lives—in a deliberate and cautious way.

It is not uncommon to find older investors behaving in a way consistent with the above description. This is natural. As we age, behavior certainty of cash flow becomes paramount. This behavior can extend to young family members as well. As such, it is common to find Preservers focusing their wealth on taking care of their family members and future generations, especially funding life-enhancing experiences such as education and home buying. Because the focus is on financial security, Preserver biases tend to be dominated by emotion—relating to how they *feel*, rather than cognitive—relating to how they *think*. Additionally, wealth level may influence Preserver behavior. Although it's not always the case, many Preservers that have gained wealth want to preserve it and change their attitude towards risk. This is especially true when an investor has been through a crisis that threatened their wealth (as in 2008, when equities dropped 37% for the year). Preservers' behavioral biases that can affect their ability to attain financial goals mostly involve their obsession with preserving assets and (sometimes) excessively conservative behaviors as exhibited in loss aversion, status quo, and endowment biases. Preservers can also display certain cognitive biases that relate to the same orientation, namely anchoring and mental accounting biases. These biases and risk tolerance level are depicted in Figure 25.1.

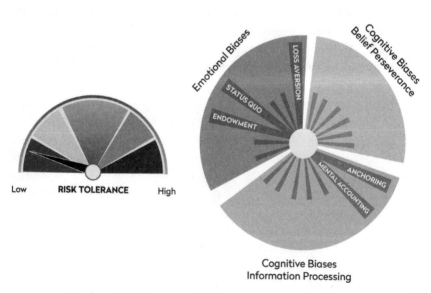

Figure 25.1 Preserver Investor Type Characteristics

What follows now is a brief analysis of the positives and negatives of the Preserver BIT (Upside/Downside analysis), a description of the biases just discussed, and how the bias relates to the Preserver BIT.

Upside/Downside Analysis

Upside: There are certain benefits that accrue to Preserver BITs. Since Preservers are focused on preserving capital and avoiding losses, they take a somewhat conservative approach to investing. This can be a benefit in terms of lowering volatility in a portfolio, which can lead to better long-term compounded returns. Additionally, Preservers who practice savings behaviors through mental accounting (i.e., saving for retirement, college funding, paying bills) can accumulate long-term wealth as long as they are careful to invest in a balanced way across these various mental accounts. Preservers are also typically less likely to engage in excessive trading activity, which has been shown to be detrimental to wealth accumulation. Taking a more deliberate approach to investing has benefits in terms of having the ability to stick to a long-term plan.

Downside: The downside to the Preserver BIT has mainly to do with excessive focus on avoiding losses. Some Preservers have been known to panic during market meltdowns, such as in 2008 and 2018, and sell out after suffering losses only to see markets rebound in the ensuing 12–24 months. It is also important to note that Preservers can sell their winning investments too quickly in an effort to protect gains, thus inhibiting long-term financial success. Additionally, excessive mental accounting can lead to sub-optimal portfolio construction if too much cash is held across various mental accounts, such as those referenced in the "upside" section above. Another caveat for the Preserver BIT is that they can take too much of a low risk approach to investment planning in general. For example, if Preserver BITs focus too many of their investments on cash and bonds, they may risk not reaching their financial goals if the goals call for a portfolio return between 5–10% or higher. Cash and bonds simply won't get you there. Additionally, Preserver BITs' biases are mainly emotional, which is hard to change, or "moderate," especially during market upheavals. During these times, investors should consider *making* risky investments, as opposed to selling them. This is counter-intuitive, especially in the heat of the moment when markets are crashing; but, in almost every case, it is the right decision to step in and buy risky assets when there is "blood on the streets."

Bias Analysis of Preservers

As previously laid out, the biases of Preservers are dominated by *emotion*. In my experience I have found that two biases have a substantial impact on Preserver behavior. These are Loss Aversion and Status Quo. We will review these now. At the end of this section we will also consider three other biases relevant to Preservers.

Loss Aversion Bias

Bias Type: Emotional

Application to the Preserver BIT

Preservers tend to feel the pain of losses more acutely than the pleasure of gains, particularly as compared to other behavioral investor types. There are two key contexts in which loss aversion can be seen and it is important to understand how loss aversion can apply in these situations. Some investors like to make investments in individual risky assets, such as a single stock. They get a tip from a friend and buy XYZ company stock. Shortly after the investment is made, XYZ drops 20% due to a problem with their production line. Some rational investors will have no problem taking the loss and getting out of XYZ because the risks associated with XYZ's production line are too great to be ignored. Preservers, or other investors who are subject to loss aversion, will hold on to XYZ mainly because it is too painful to take the loss. These investors may hold only losing investments too long—even when they see no prospect of a turnaround. This behavior is wealth-destructive.

The other context in which loss aversion can be seen is in the *asset allocation* context. Many investors wisely choose not to invest in individual stocks but instead will invest in a diversified basket of asset classes, including equities, fixed income and perhaps some alternatives. Loss aversion can occur to these investors during market meltdowns such as the one that occurred in 2008–2009. This period was tailor-made for the loss averse investor to "sell out" at the bottom. Equities started to fall in late 2008 and by the end of the year they were down about 20%. Although some loss-averse investors were scared, they could live with being down 20% on that portion of their portfolio. But then when 2009 began, and the first quarter marched on, equities continued their losses, accelerating down from a peak to a trough of 50+%. In retrospect, naturally this was the time that investors should have been considering buying equities. For some investors, this was literally a no-brainer because they kept in mind the always relevant advice of Sir John Templeton, who said "Bull markets are born on pessimism, grown on skepticism, mature on optimism and die on euphoria. The time of maximum pessimism is the best time to buy, and the time of maximum optimism is the best time to sell."

Status Quo Bias

Bias Type: Emotional

Application of Status Quo Bias to the Preserver BIT

Preservers, who as we have just learned, are loss averse, also often have difficulty when it comes to changing portfolios (status quo bias). Two examples of this bias are presented here.

Scenario #1: Suppose a Preserver investor, Jim, who is 50 years old, wakes up one day in September of 2008, after missing the latest bull market, and realizes he needs to embark upon a savings and investment program. He creates a financial plan (either with his financial advisor or on his own) and learns that he needs to invest in equities (the S&P 500 for the purposes of this example) if he is going to reach his long-term financial goals. At present he is 40% in cash, 40% in bonds, and 20% in equities. He needs to go to 50% equities, according to his plan, and as such needs to sell some of his bonds and put some of his hard-earned cash to work in the equity markets. As luck would have it, he has a difficult time pulling the trigger and doesn't act. The market tumbles in late 2008 and early 2009. He can't believe how lucky he was to avoid such carnage. But he knows he needs to start investing. But when is the right time? Earlier, we learned that the right time was March of 2009, when there was "blood in the streets" and fear was rampant. But when fear is running rampant, Preserver investors are likely to be the most fearful of all. So, there's little realistic chance that a Preserver investor like Jim—unless directed, persuaded, or otherwise told by an outside advisor—will invest during a time when markets are falling precipitously. He does not invest in March 2009.

So, let's say that it's now October of 2009, a full year after the crisis began. Markets have rebounded by 35% from the nadir in March 2009. Is this a good time to invest? Jim just missed the "easy money" from the rebound and now he could be entering right when markets might fall again. No action is taken. Now it's March of 2010. Markets are up another 25%. Jim just missed a rally of 60%. Now can't be a good time. You get the point. There is always a time for Jim *not* to invest in equities if one is afraid of losses.

Scenario #2: Suppose a Preserver investor, Jack, had an investment/asset allocation plan going into the crisis of 2008–2009 and had a fully invested portfolio of 40% equities, 40% bonds, and 20% cash. The market drops precipitously in the last quarter of 2008. Depending upon when a review might have taken place on the portfolio allocation, an investor might have been in a position to re-balance his or her portfolio. If the Preserver was in a position to rebalance in December of 2008, he may not have done for fear of buying into a declining market. Fast-forward now to the latter part of the first quarter of 2009. Many investors, including Jack, are quite happy they did not rebalance in 2008. But, certainly some kind of review of the portfolio has taken place between the end of the last quarter of 2008 (i.e. December 2008) and the latter part of the second quarter of 2009 (i.e. March 2009). The asset allocation plan calls for the investor to rebalance their portfolio. Plain and simple—when stocks go down and fixed income goes up, it's time to rebalance back to target. March 2009 was a difficult time for any investor to rebalance, let alone Jack, a Preserver. Many Preserver investors were "frozen in the headlights" in March 2009. Equity markets were tumbling. Fear was rampant. Status quo bias takes over and no action is taken. We can replay the last example for what happened to Jack after he did not rebalance in March 2009.

In conclusion, regardless of whether we have an investor who needs to put a lot of cash to work in equities, or an investor who simply needs to rebalance their portfolio, Preservers can make this a challenging process. Now that you recognize this, you should have a better idea of how to handle this situation if you are an investor or an advisor.

An additional tool that can help is a simple diagnostic for status quo bias: Ask yourself if you are more comfortable *not* taking action during times of change, or whether you can embrace change with investments or life in general. If you like to keep things the same, and take a "wait and see" approach, you are likely to be affected by status quo bias.

Additional Biases of Preserver BIT: Endowment Bias, Mental Accounting, Anchoring

As we just reviewed, Loss Aversion and Status Quo biases are two highly impactful biases for Preservers. However, there are other biases that afflict Preserver BITs with some regularity. These are endowment bias, mental accounting and anchoring: a description follows.

Endowment Bias

Bias Type: Emotional

Some Preservers, especially those who inherit wealth, tend to assign a greater value to an investment they already own (such as a piece of real estate or an inherited stock position) than if they didn't possess that investment and had the potential to acquire it. Said more simply, some investors hold onto investments that they own simply because they already own them.

Regret Aversion Bias

Bias Type: Emotional

Preservers often avoid taking decisive actions because they fear that, in hindsight, whatever course they select will prove less than optimal. Regret aversion can cause some investors to be too timid in their investment choices because of losses they have suffered in the past.

Anchoring Bias

Bias Type: Cognitive

Investors in general, and Preservers in particular, are often influenced by purchase points or arbitrary price levels, and tend to cling to these numbers when facing questions like "Should I buy or sell this investment?" Suppose that the stock is down 25% from the high that it reached five months ago ($75/share vs. $100/share). Frequently, a Preserver will resist selling until its price rebounds to the $100/share it achieved five months ago.

Mental Accounting Bias

Bias Type: Cognitive

Many investors treat sums of money differently based on where these sums are mentally categorized. For example, Preservers often segregate their assets into safe "buckets." If all of these assets are viewed as safe money, sub-optimal overall portfolio returns are usually the result.

Advice for Preservers

Preservers are driven mainly by emotion, in general, and the avoidance of loss, in particular, which is in response to fluctuations in the value of their portfolios. Statistics have shown that long-term investments in equities, which are clearly the most volatile investment one can own, have been handsomely rewarded. Therefore, it is essential that Preserver investors control their behavior in terms of not selling at the wrong time and rebalancing at the right time; this makes a difference in reaching financial goals. Preservers need to look at "big picture" advice, and oftentimes behavioral coaching, as opposed to strict financial or investing education. For example, advisor Preservers tend not to resonate with details such as standard deviations and Sharpe ratios, especially during times of market upheaval, or else they will lose focus. Preservers often need to understand how the portfolio they choose to create will address the key emotional issues that drive them, such as family members or future generations. Getting invested and staying invested at the appropriate risk level is the key to success for this investor type.

26

Follower Behavioral Investor Type

Whenever you find yourself on the side of the majority, it is time to pause and reflect.
—Mark Twain

Name of Behavioral Investor Type: Follower
Basic Orientation: General lack of interest in money and investing; typically desire direction when making financial decisions
Dominant Bias Type: Cognitive, relating to following behavior
Impactful Biases: Recency and Framing
Investing Style: Passive
Level of Risk Tolerance: Generally lower than average but often think risk tolerance level is higher than it actually is

A *Follower* behavioral investor type describes an investor who is passive and often lacks interest in and/or has little aptitude for money or investing. Furthermore, Follower investors typically do not have their own ideas about investing. Rather, they may follow the lead of their friends and colleagues, or whatever general investing fad is occurring to make their investment decisions. Often their decision-making process is without regard to a long-term plan. They sometimes trick themselves into thinking they are "smart" or talented in the investment realm when an investment decision works out which can lead to unwarranted risk-seeking behavior. Since they don't tend to have their own ideas about investing, they also may react differently when presented with the same investment proposal; that is, the way something is presented (framed) can make them think and act differently. They also may regret not being in the latest "investment fad" and end up investing at exactly the wrong time—when valuations are the highest.

One of the key aspects of Followers is that they tend to overestimate their risk tolerance. An investment may appear so compelling that they jump in without considering the risks. Advisors need to be careful not to suggest too many "hot" investment ideas—Followers will likely want to do all of them. Some don't like, or even fear, the task of investing, and many put off making investment decisions without professional advice; the result is that they maintain, often by default, high cash balances. Followers generally need professional advice and they try to educate themselves financially. However, they often don't enjoy or have an aptitude for the investment process. It is not uncommon to find 40-something, busy professional investors behaving in a way consistent with the above description. As such, it is common to find Followers doing superficial research into investing, as well as discussing investing with friends and colleagues. They might hear a stock tip from a friend and suddenly take a chance. At the same time, they may not look at their investment statement for months, simply letting them pile up, and this behavior can have disastrous results.

Followers' biases tend to be cognitive—relating well to how they *think*, rather than emotional—relating to how they *feel*. Additionally, wealth level may influence Follower behavior. Although this is not always the case, many Followers are in *wealth accumulation* mode and think that taking risks is a good thing but don't always think about the downside of taking these risks. This is especially true when an investor has been through a bull market cycle. Many Follower BITs saw what was happening in the housing bubble and regretted not being "in the game." They decided to buy houses to "flip" in 2006–2007 or bought publicly traded REITs, only to see these investments crumble in 2008–2009 when residential housing imploded. Eventually, these investments came back in value but it took a very long time. Biases of Followers are mainly cognitive: recency, hindsight, framing, cognitive dissonance, and regret (emotional). These biases and risk tolerance levels are depicted in Figure 26.1.

What follows is a brief analysis of the positives and negatives of the Follower BIT (called Upside/Downside analysis), a description of the biases just discussed (this should be a review for most of you) and how

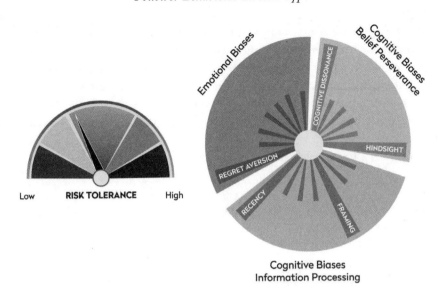

Figure 26.1 Follower Investor Type Characteristics

the bias relates to the Preserver BIT as well as a quick diagnostic for each bias.

Upside/Downside Analysis

Upside: There are certain benefits that accrue to Follower BITs. Since Followers are not overly obsessed with money, they tend to lead their lives in a somewhat more stress-free manner than those who tend to think about money on a daily basis. Also, since investing is not necessarily at the top of their minds, Followers tend not to trade their accounts excessively—which is a big positive, since trading too much has proven to be a wealth-destroying activity. This low portfolio turnover can be a benefit in terms of lowering volatility in a portfolio generally, which can lead to better long-term compounded returns. Additionally, Followers may realize that they aren't good with money and make a wise decision to hire an investment advisor to help them. Advisors can help to bring discipline to the investing process which is much needed with Follower investor types.

Downside: The downside to the Follower BIT has mainly to do with a lack of discipline during the investment process, assuming they do not hire an advisor. For example, left unadvised Followers tend to place a lot of emphasis on investing in the latest investment trends—i.e., those investments that have performed well recently. This can lead to investing in asset classes at the wrong time—when prices are peaking—which can lead to wealth destruction. Followers also can think themselves intelligent when investments go up—fooling themselves into believing they are talented investors when it was a rising tide that was raising all boats. This can increase risk-taking behavior: taking on too much risk at the wrong time can create permanent losses of capital.

Bias Analysis of Followers

As previously reviewed, the biases of Followers are mainly cognitive. In my experience I have found that two biases have a substantial impact on Follower behavior. These are Recency and Framing. We will review these now. At the end of this section we will review three other biases to be aware of for Preservers.

Recency Bias

Bias Type: Cognitive

Application to Preserver BIT

Followers tend to be dissociated from the investing process, preferring instead to take an easier route to investment decisions by either following the crowd (investing in whatever the mass audience is doing) or the advice of friends and colleagues. Recency bias occurs when investors look at the most recent performance of an investment and make a decision to invest based on that most recent performance. This is a very common behavior of the Follower BIT. The following is an illustration of the Recency bias behavior so beloved of Followers.

Example—Recency Bias

Technically speaking, recency bias is a cognitive bias that results from disproportionately weighting the prominence of recent events or observations versus those that occurred in the near or distant past. Suppose, for example, during a passenger liner cruise a guest sees an equal number of green boats as blue boats from the observation deck over the duration of the trip. However, if there happens to be an excess of green boats at the end of the cruise, recency bias will likely influence the guest to conclude that there were more green boats than blue boats during the cruise.

One of the most obvious and pernicious applications of recency bias, committed by investors, is the misuse of mutual fund (or other fund types) investment performance records which have had spectacular recent performance. Investors track managers who produce temporary outsized returns over a one-, two- or three-year period, and they make an investment decision based only on recent experience. These investors do not pay heed to the cyclical nature of asset class returns. To counteract the effects of this bias, many practitioners wisely use what has become known as the "periodic table of investment returns," an adaptation of Mendeleev's Periodic Table of The Elements, which he conceived in his book "The Principles of Chemistry," completed in 1870.

As is evident from Figure 26.2, asset class returns are highly variable. For example, if an investor is susceptible to recency bias, they might have decided to invest in a big way in emerging market stocks or real estate in 2008, after seeing these styles rise in prior years; this would obviously have been a mistake as they dropped the next year. Cash was at the bottom of the chart numerous times leading up to 2017, so investors might have left it out of their portfolio; but, as you can see, it was the best asset class in 2018. Many investors fail to heed the advice offered by the chart, namely that it is nearly impossible to successfully predict which asset class will be the best performer from one year to the next, and that diversification is the most prudent investment strategy available. Investors would be prudent to include this chart during the initial asset allocation process emphasizing diversification over return-chasing.

Framing Bias

Bias Type: Cognitive

Application of Framing Bias to Follower BIT

Framing bias describes how decision-makers may answer a question differently based on the way in which it is asked (framed). Technically, a decision frame is the decision-maker's subjective conception of the acts, outcomes, and contingencies associated with a particular choice. The frame that a decision-maker adopts is controlled partly by the formulation of the problem and by the norms, habits, and personal characteristics

The Callan Periodic Table of Investment Returns

Annual Returns for Key Indices Ranked in Order of Performance (2000–2019)

Year	Rank 1	Rank 2	Rank 3	Rank 4	Rank 5	Rank 6	Rank 7	Rank 8	Rank 9
2000	Real Estate 13.84%	U.S. Fixed Income 11.63%	Cash Equivalent 6.18%	Small Cap Equity -3.02%	Gbl ex-U.S. Fixed -3.91%	High Yield -5.86%	Large Cap Equity -9.11%	Dev ex-U.S. Equity -13.37%	
2001	U.S. Fixed Income 8.43%	High Yield 5.28%	Cash Equivalent 4.42%	Small Cap Equity 2.49%	Emerging Market Equity -2.61%	Real Estate -3.75%	Large Cap Equity -11.89%	Dev ex-U.S. Equity -21.40%	
2002	Gbl ex-U.S. Fixed 22.37%	U.S. Fixed Income 10.26%	Real Estate 2.82%	Cash Equivalent 1.78%	High Yield -1.37%	Dev ex-U.S. Equity -6.16%	Small Cap Equity -15.80%	Emerging Market Equity -20.48%	Large Cap Equity -22.10%
2003	Emerging Market Equity 55.82%	Small Cap Equity 47.25%	Real Estate 40.69%	Dev ex-U.S. Equity 39.42%	High Yield 28.97%	Large Cap Equity 28.68%	Gbl ex-U.S. Fixed 19.36%	U.S. Fixed Income 4.10%	Cash Equivalent 1.15%
2004	Real Estate 37.96%	Emerging Market Equity 25.55%	Dev ex-U.S. Equity 20.38%	Small Cap Equity 18.33%	Gbl ex-U.S. Fixed 12.54%	High Yield 11.13%	Large Cap Equity 10.88%	U.S. Fixed Income 4.34%	Cash Equivalent 1.33%
2005	Emerging Market Equity 34.00%	Real Estate 15.35%	Dev ex-U.S. Equity 14.47%	Large Cap Equity 4.91%	Small Cap Equity 4.55%	High Yield 3.07%	Cash Equivalent 2.74%	U.S. Fixed Income 2.43%	Gbl ex-U.S. Fixed -8.65%
2006	Real Estate 42.12%	Emerging Market Equity 32.17%	Dev ex-U.S. Equity 25.71%	Small Cap Equity 18.37%	Large Cap Equity 15.79%	High Yield 11.85%	Gbl ex-U.S. Fixed 8.16%	Cash Equivalent 4.85%	U.S. Fixed 4.33%
2007	Emerging Market Equity 39.38%	Dev ex-U.S. Equity 12.44%	Gbl ex-U.S. Fixed 11.03%	U.S. Fixed Income 6.97%	Large Cap Equity 5.49%	Cash Equivalent 5.00%	High Yield 1.87%	Small Cap Equity -1.57%	Real Estate -7.39%
2008	U.S. Fixed Income 5.24%	Gbl ex-U.S. Fixed 4.39%	Cash Equivalent 2.06%	High Yield -26.16%	Small Cap Equity -33.79%	Large Cap Equity -37.00%	Dev ex-U.S. Equity -43.56%	Real Estate -48.21%	Emerging Market Equity -53.33%
2009	Emerging Market Equity 78.51%	High Yield 58.21%	Real Estate 37.13%	Dev ex-U.S. Equity 33.67%	Small Cap Equity 27.17%	Large Cap Equity 26.47%	Gbl ex-U.S. Fixed 7.53%	U.S. Fixed Income 5.93%	Cash Equivalent 0.21%
2010	Small Cap Equity 26.85%	Real Estate 19.63%	Emerging Market Equity 18.88%	High Yield 15.12%	Large Cap Equity 15.06%	Dev ex-U.S. Equity 8.95%	U.S. Fixed Income 6.54%	Gbl ex-U.S. Fixed 4.95%	Cash Equivalent 0.13%
2011	U.S. Fixed Income 7.84%	High Yield 4.98%	Gbl ex-U.S. Fixed 4.36%	Large Cap Equity 2.11%	Cash Equivalent 0.10%	Small Cap Equity -4.18%	Real Estate -6.46%	Dev ex-U.S. Equity -12.21%	Emerging Market Equity -18.42%
2012	Real Estate 27.73%	Emerging Market Equity 18.23%	Dev ex-U.S. Equity 16.41%	Small Cap Equity 16.35%	Large Cap Equity 16.00%	High Yield 15.81%	U.S. Fixed Income 4.21%	Gbl ex-U.S. Fixed 4.09%	Cash Equivalent 0.11%
2013	Small Cap Equity 38.82%	Large Cap Equity 32.39%	Dev ex-U.S. Equity 21.02%	High Yield 7.44%	Real Estate 3.67%	Cash Equivalent 0.07%	U.S. Fixed Income -2.02%	Emerging Market Equity -2.60%	Gbl ex-U.S. Fixed -3.08%
2014	Real Estate 15.02%	Large Cap Equity 13.69%	U.S. Fixed Income 5.97%	Small Cap Equity 4.89%	High Yield 2.45%	Cash Equivalent 0.03%	Dev ex-U.S. Equity -2.19%	Gbl ex-U.S. Fixed -3.09%	Emerging Market Equity -4.32%
2015	Large Cap Equity 1.38%	U.S. Fixed Income 0.55%	Cash Equivalent 0.05%	Real Estate -0.79%	Dev ex-U.S. Equity -3.04%	Small Cap Equity -4.41%	High Yield -4.47%	Gbl ex-U.S. Fixed -6.02%	Emerging Market Equity -14.92%
2016	Small Cap Equity 21.31%	High Yield 17.13%	Large Cap Equity 11.96%	Emerging Market Equity 11.19%	Real Estate 4.06%	Dev ex-U.S. Equity 2.75%	U.S. Fixed Income 2.65%	Gbl ex-U.S. Fixed 1.49%	Cash Equivalent 0.33%
2017	Emerging Market Equity 37.28%	Large Cap Equity 24.21%	Small Cap Equity 21.83%	Dev ex-U.S. Equity 14.65%	Gbl ex-U.S. Fixed 10.51%	Real Estate 10.36%	High Yield 7.50%	U.S. Fixed Income 3.54%	Cash Equivalent 0.86%
2018	Cash Equivalent 1.87%	U.S. Fixed Income 0.01%	High Yield -2.08%	Gbl ex-U.S. Fixed -2.15%	Large Cap Equity -4.38%	Real Estate -5.63%	Small Cap Equity -11.01%	Dev ex-U.S. Equity -14.09%	Emerging Market Equity -14.57%
2019	Large Cap Equity 31.49%	Small Cap Equity 25.52%	Dev ex-U.S. Equity 22.49%	Real Estate 21.91%	Emerging Market Equity 18.44%	High Yield 14.32%	U.S. Fixed Income 8.72%	Gbl ex-U.S. Fixed 5.09%	Cash Equivalent 2.28%

Figure 26.2 Sample of a Periodic Table of Investment Returns
Source: Sunpointe Investments

of the decision-maker. It is often possible to frame a given decision problem in more than one way. A framing effect is a change of preferences between options as a function of the variation of frames, perhaps through variation of the formulation of the problem. For example, a problem may be presented as a gain (35% of people with a disease will be saved by a medicine) or as a loss (65% of people with a particular disease will die without the medicine). In the first case, people tend to adopt a gain frame, generally leading to risk-aversion; in the latter case, people tend to adopt a loss frame, generally leading to risk-seeking behavior.

A particularly relevant example of framing bias to follower investors involves risk tolerance questionnaires. We reviewed this in a prior chapter, but this is a crucial topic to understand so it will be presented again now.

Suppose an investor is to take a risk tolerance questionnaire for the purpose of determining which "risk category" he or she is in. The answers to these questions are highly relevant as the risk category will determine which types of investment will be selected. Consider the following two questions, focused on a hypothetical portfolio ABC. Over a 10-year period, ABC has historically averaged an annual return of 10% with an annual standard deviation of 17%. Recall that standard deviation is the average variation from the average return of an investment. Assuming a normal return distribution, in a given year there is a 67% probability that the return will fall within one standard deviation of the mean, a 95% probability that the return will fall within two standard deviations, and a 99.7% probability that the return will fall within three standard deviations. Thus, there is a 67% chance that the return earned by Portfolio ABC will be between −7% and 27%, a 95% chance that the return will be between −20% and 44%, and a 99.7% chance that the return will be between −41% and 61%.

Suppose that the test-taker could answer either Question 1 or Question 2 that follows. The questions both contain information about Portfolio ABC, but are framed differently.

Question 1: Based on the chart below, which investment portfolio fits your risk tolerance and desire for long term return?

a) Portfolio XYZ

b) Portfolio DEF

c) Portfolio ABC

Portfolio Number	95% Probability Gain/Loss Range	Long-Term Return
XYZ	2%–5%	3.5%
DEF	–6%–18%	6%
ABC	–20%–44%	10%

Question 2: Assume you own Portfolio ABC, and it lost 7% of its value over the past year, despite previous years of good performance. This loss is consistent with the performance of similar funds during the past year. What is your reaction to this situation?

a) Sell all of your Portfolio ABC shares

b) Sell some of your Portfolio ABC shares

c) Continue to hold all of your Portfolio ABC shares

d) Increase your investment in Portfolio ABC shares

Portfolio ABC may appear less attractive in the first question, where two standard deviations were used to describe the potential investments, than in the second, where only one standard deviation was used. In addition, in the second question the test-taker was reminded of previous years of good performance and that the loss was not out of line with Portfolio ABC's peers. How questions are framed can have a significant impact on how they are answered.

Other Important Follower Biases: Hindsight, Cognitive Dissonance, and Regret

As we just reviewed, Recency and Framing biases are two highly impactful biases for Followers. However, there are other biases that can be found to occur with Follower BITs with some regularity. These are hindsight bias, cognitive dissonance, and regret. In this section we will provide a description of these biases.

Hindsight Bias

Bias Type: Cognitive

Followers often lack independent thoughts about their investments and are susceptible to hindsight bias, which occurs when an investor perceives investment outcomes as if they were predictable. An example of hindsight bias is the response by investors to the financial crisis of 2008. Initially, many viewed the housing market's performance from 2003 to 2007 as "normal" (i.e., not symptomatic of a bubble), only later to say, "Wasn't it obvious?" when the market melted down in 2008. The result of hindsight bias is that it gives investors a false sense of security when making investment decisions, emboldening them to take excessive risk without recognizing it.

Cognitive Dissonance Bias

Bias Type: Cognitive

In psychology, cognitions represent attitudes, emotions, beliefs or values. When multiple cognitions intersect—for example a person believing in something only to find out it is not true—people try to alleviate their discomfort by ignoring the truth and/or rationalizing their decisions. Investors who suffer from this bias may continue to invest in a security or fund they already own after it has gone down (average down) even when they know they should be judging the new investment with objectivity. A common phrase for this concept is "throwing good money after bad."

Regret Aversion Bias

Bias Type: Emotional

Conservative investors often avoid taking decisive actions because they fear that, in hindsight, whatever course they select will prove less than optimal. Regret aversion can cause conservative investors to be too timid in their investment choices because of losses they have suffered in the past.

Advice for Followers

Followers first and foremost need to recognize that they often overestimate their risk tolerance. Risky trend-following behavior occurs in part because Followers don't like the task of investing, or the discomfort that may accompany the decision to enter an asset class when it is out of favor. They also may convince themselves that they "knew it all along" when an investment idea goes their way, which also increases future risk-taking behavior. Followers need to do due diligence on their investments because they are likely to "say yes" to investment ideas that make sense to them, regardless of whether the advice is in their best long-term interest or not. Followers need to take a hard look at behavioral tendencies that may cause them to overestimate their risk tolerance. Because Follower biases are mainly cognitive, education on the benefits of portfolio diversification and sticking to a long-term plan is usually the best course of action. Follower investors tend to be introspective and should provide themselves with data-backed substantiation for recommendations. Gaining education in clear, unambiguous ways so Followers have the chance to "get it" is a good idea.

27

Independent Behavioral Investor Type

To find yourself, think for yourself.

—Socrates

Name of Behavioral Investor Type: Independent
Basic Orientation: Engaged in the investment process and opinionated on investment decisions.
Dominant Bias Type: Cognitive, relating to the pitfalls of doing one's own research
Impactful Biases: Confirmation and Availability
Investing Style: Active
Level of Risk Tolerance: Generally above average but not as high as aggressive investors

An *Independent* behavioral investor type is someone who has original ideas about investing and likes to get involved in the investment process. Unlike Followers, they are not disinterested in investing, are quite engaged in the financial markets, and may have unconventional views on investing. This "contrarian" mindset, however, may cause Independents to not believe in following a long-term investment plan. With that said, many Independents can and do stick to an investment plan to accomplish their financial goals. At their essence, Independents are analytical, critical thinkers who make many of their decisions based on logic and their own gut instinct. They are willing to take risks and act decisively when called upon to do so. Independents can accomplish tasks when they put their minds to it; they tend to be thinkers and doers as opposed to followers and dreamers.

Unfortunately, some Independents are prone to biases that can torpedo their ability to reach goals. For example, Independents may act too quickly, without learning as much as they can about their investments before making them. For example, they may mistake reading an article in a business news publication for doing original research. In their half-ready, full-on pursuit of profit, they may leave some important stones unturned that could trip them up in the end.

Independents' risk tolerance is relatively high, and so is their ability to understand risk. Independents are realistic in understanding that risky assets can and do go down as well as up. However, when their investments fall they don't like to admit that they were wrong or that they made a mistake (sound familiar?). Independents often do their own research and don't feel comfortable with an investment until they have confirmed their decision with research or some form of corroboration. They are comfortable collaborating with advisors, though typically using those advisors as sounding boards for their own ideas. Independents

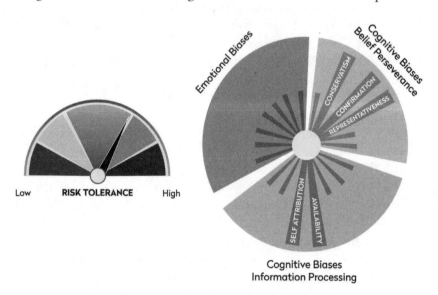

Figure 27.1 Independent Investor Type Characteristics

are often comfortable speaking the language of finance and understand financial terms, including market- and economic-related terms. They aren't afraid to delve into the details of investments, including the costs and fees of making investments.

Biases of Independents are mainly cognitive: conservatism, confirmation, self-attribution, availability, and representativeness. These biases and risk tolerance level are depicted in Figure 27.1.

What follows is a brief analysis of the positives and negatives of the Independent BIT (called Upside/Downside analysis), a description of the biases just discussed and how the biases relate to the Independent BIT.

Upside/Downside Analysis

Upside: There are certain benefits that accrue to Independent BITs. At their essence, Independents are cerebral, strong-willed, independent thinkers who aren't afraid to put their investment ideas into action by implementing them in their portfolios. Successful investing requires the fortitude to not only have original ideas but also be able to put them into action when called upon to do so; Independents can take risks and act decisively. Independents can also be contrarian investors and can be very successful as there are many investors who are herd followers and are often not happy as a result. As they are analytical by nature, they may help themselves by finding the lowest-cost service providers. They tend to be thinkers and doers as opposed to followers and dreamers.

Downside: The downside to the BIT has mainly to do with biases that can torpedo their ability to reach their financial goals. As we will see in the next section, Independents can act too quickly, without taking the time to learn as much as they can about their investments before making them. They may also seek information that confirms their decisions as opposed to finding information that may contradict their hypotheses. The Independent may also irrationally cling to self-generated ideas, rather than take on board new ideas that may prove they are wrong. Their analytical nature may work against them at times. For example, some Independents may focus too much on taxes and not enough on selecting an appropriate investing strategy. In industry parlance, this is known as letting the "tax tail wag the investment dog." The next section reviews these shortcomings in detail.

Bias Analysis of Independents

The main objective of any investor should be to stick to a plan and, much as it is with the other types, Independents can allow their biases to impede their ability to do so. Two of the most impactful biases of Independents are Confirmation and Availability. These will be reviewed now.

Confirmation Bias

Bias Type: Cognitive

Application to Independent BIT

People tend to want to stand by their decisions. It's human nature. And because it makes us feel good to believe we've made the right decision, we also tend to notice those things that support our decisions and opinions and ignore those that may contradict them. That's the essence of Confirmation Bias. It convinces us that what we want to believe is correct by mentally giving more weight to the factors that support our desired outcome. This behavior can be hazardous to one's wealth because we can be blindsided by facts that we did not consider. Confirmation Bias affects the investor by making an investment decision appear better than it actually is. An example from the last investing cycle provides a useful illustration.

Suppose an investor, Jack, who is 43 and single was an aggressive accumulator of oil and gas assets in the early 2010s. Over those years he had seen private equity and others buy up energy assets: for that reason, he believed that energy stocks would be his ticket to riches. His Confirmation Bias had been enforced year after year as fracking became popular and energy prices rose. He read article after article about the energy boom. There were economists and naysayers with differing opinions out there but he did not seek any contrary opinions. His Confirmation Bias clouded his judgment. It caused him to block out potential pitfalls and focus only on the good aspects of his investment. Like many people, he saw only the upside of the shale oil boom; he didn't see it as a bubble that could possibly burst.

Because investors with Confirmation Bias tend to seek out only information that confirms their beliefs about investments they have made or are about to make, they don't grasp the full picture, like Jack. He may have been peripherally aware that bad loans were being made, that the inventory of new energy was starting to outsize the demand—both factors that should have been as valid in informing his decisions as the others—but he was able to talk himself out of their importance, rationalizing that only certain oil patches were being affected.

Unfortunately for Jack, and so many others who got swept away by the energy boom of the last decade, Jack's portfolio, so heavily weighted as it was to energy, took a nosedive when the market crashed. Had he been aware of his Confirmation Bias, had he chosen to see outside the realm of what he wanted to be reality, he may not have lost so much.

Availability Bias

Bias Type: Cognitive

Application to Independent BIT

Another bias that weighs heavily on the investment decisions of Independents is Availability Bias. A cognitive bias, Availability makes investors believe that the facts most relevant to their own lives are the ones most relevant to the success of an investment. How "available" information is to them thus somehow determines how reliable it is. When one has this bias, the possibilities that we can easily recall, that we are most familiar with, seem more likely to be true than those that are less familiar. With all the information that comes at us every day, it's so difficult to properly process it all. For that reason, we process bits of information we can easily identify and swallow, and ignore the rest.

When it comes to investing, this behavior usually translates into judgments based on past experience and easily perceived outcomes, instead of taking in harder-to-grasp data, such as statistics. Some people put a subjective slant on information rather than look objectively at the cold, hard facts. A classic example is investing with those brokers or mutual funds that do the most advertising. These firms make information available and people buy them; but are they the best? Diligent research might prove otherwise.

The following is a simple quiz for Availability Bias.

Please answer the following:

1. Which do you believe is more likely, death by stroke or death by homicide?
2. What about death by falling airplane parts or death by shark bite?

3. Does the letter K appear more often as a first letter or a third letter in the English language?
4. Which claims more lives in the United States: lightning or tornadoes?

Evaluation

Question 1. Because death by homicide appears in the news more often than death by stroke, most believe death by homicide is more prevalent—even though death by stroke is actually 11 times more probable.

Question 2. Because shark attacks are so sensationalized, people believe they are more common, but death by falling airplane parts is actually 30 times more likely.

Question 3. The letter "K" occurs twice as often as a third than a first letter, but it's common to categorize words based on their initial letters.

Question 4. More Americans are killed every year by lightning than by tornadoes, but warnings, drills, and other publicity make tornado fatalities memorable.

Other important Independent Biases are: Self-Attribution, Conservatism, and Representativeness.

As we have just seen, Confirmation and Availability biases are two highly impactful biases for Independents. However, there are other biases that can be found to occur with Independent BITs with some regularity. These are Self-Attribution, Conservatism, and Representativeness. We will review these now.

Self-Attribution

Bias Type: Cognitive

When a decision we make works out nicely, we like to attribute the success to our own talents and foresight. And when things don't turn out as planned, we like to blame bad luck and other circumstances that are out of our control. If you score a high mark on a test, do you believe this to be a direct result of your hard work and innate intelligence—and if you do poorly, do you blame the grading system of the test? If you have a tendency to believe your successes have everything to do with your talents and abilities, and that your failures are never a result of your own shortcomings, then you probably harbor the Self-Attribution Bias.

When an Independent BIT's financial decisions pan out well, they like to congratulate themselves on their shrewdness. When things don't turn out so profitably, however, the Independent BIT consoles themselves by concluding that someone or something else is at fault. Neither is entirely correct. Oftentimes, when things work out well and people with a Self-Attribution Bias assess their portfolios, they end up having more confidence in their stock-picking abilities than is actually warranted—and, as a result, they may end up taking on more risk than they should. You've heard the phrase "a little knowledge is a dangerous thing"? In investing, it can be savage.

Winning investment outcomes are typically due to any number of factors, a bull market being the most prominent; stocks' declining in value, meanwhile, can be equally random and complex (sometimes due to fraud or mismanagement, sometimes to luck). Because they believe they have more control over these outcomes than is warranted, people with Self-Attribution Bias are consumed by the pride that surges when trades do well, and because they do not take a step back to figure out what they could have done wrong when trades fail, they tend to trade too often, resulting in a portfolio that underperforms.

Conservatism Bias

Bias Type: Cognitive

Independent BIT investors with a Conservatism Bias tend to cling to what they already know to be true at the expense of acquiring new information. The following example illustrates this. Suppose an investor named James receives some bad news regarding a company's earnings, which contradicts another earnings estimate from the month prior, which he relied on to invest in the company. Because he has a Conservatism Bias, James underreacts to the new information, holding on to the original estimate instead of acting on the new. As a result, he ends up holding on to a stock that he's going to lose money on because he refuses to see that he could. Like James, people with Conservatism Bias can make bad investment decisions because they are "stuck" in their prior beliefs.

Representative Bias

Bias Type: Cognitive

The last bias that can be attributed to Independents is Representative Bias. Like Availability Bias, Representative Bias is strongly rooted in our desire to have the information we need to process fit into a neat framework. But Representative Bias takes this tendency a step further: When someone with this bias encounters elements that don't fit into their categories, they try a "best fit" approach.

On the plus side, Representative Bias helps us quickly absorb and process new information; on the downside, it works against us as it only allows us to perceive those probabilities that fit into the framework of what we want to perceive. Think of the gambler on a "winning streak." Statistically, there is no such thing as a winning streak, but try telling the gambler that when the odds are working in his favor. The gambler sees winning hand being played after winning hand, and forces this into a framework he can understand—the winning streak. But really, it's all just chance.

Advice for Independents

Independents are firm in their views due to their independent mindset, but they are usually grounded enough to listen to sound advice when it is presented in a way that respects their independent views. As we have learned, Independents are firm in their belief in themselves and their decisions but can be blinded to contrary thinking. As with Followers, education is essential to changing the behavior of Independents; their biases are predominantly cognitive, so commitment to a long-term plan is usually the best course of action. Independent investors should try to substantiate their investment decisions with data. Using data in clear, unambiguous ways is an effective approach. Taking this approach should yield positive results.

28

Accumulator Behavioral Investor Type

Wealth is not his that has it, but his that enjoys it.

—**Benjamin Franklin**

Name of Behavioral Investor Type: Accumulator
Basic Orientation: Interested and engaged in wealth accumulation and confident in investing ability
Dominant Bias Types: Emotional, relating to overconfidence and desire for influence over investment process
Impactful Biases: Overconfidence and Illusion of Control
Investing Style: Actively engaged in decision making
Level of Risk Tolerance: High to very high

The *Accumulator* behavioral investor type describes investors who are interested in accumulating wealth and are confident they can do so. These BITs have typically been successful in some business pursuit and believe in themselves enough that they will be successful investors. As such, they often like to adjust their portfolio allocations and holdings to market conditions and may not wish to follow a structured plan. Moreover, they want to influence decision making, or even control the decision-making process, which potentially can diminish an advisor's role. At their core, Accumulators are risk takers and are firm believers that the path they choose is the correct one. Unlike Preservers, they are in the race to win—and win big. Unlike the friendly Followers, they rely on themselves and want to be the ones steering the ship. And unlike Individualists, they usually dig down to the details rather than forge a course with half the information that they need.

Unfortunately, some Accumulators are susceptible to biases that can limit their investment success. For example, Accumulators may be too confident in their abilities; since they are successful in business or other pursuits, why shouldn't they be successful investors? And overconfidence sometimes leads them to think they can control the outcome of the investing process. They may discount the fact that investing outcomes are often random and full of unknown risks. Accumulators can also let their spending get out of control at times due to the "wealth effect" of having created assets that can lead to lifestyles that are more extravagant than is prudent. Accumulators also may make investments based on how the opportunities they come across resonate with their personal affiliations or values.

Accumulators' risk tolerance is quite high, but when things go the "wrong way" (i.e., they lose money) discomfort can be very high. This discomfort may arise not only from financial loss but also the blow to their confidence and the realization that they cannot control the outcomes of investments. These investors are entrepreneurial and often the first generation to create wealth: They are even more strong-willed and confident than Individualists. Left unadvised, Accumulators often trade too much, which can be a drag on investment performance. Furthermore, they are quick decision-makers but may chase higher-risk investments than their friends. If successful, they enjoy the thrill of making a good investment. Some Accumulators can be difficult to advise because they do not believe in basic investment principles such as diversification and asset allocation. They are often "hands-on" and wish to be heavily involved in the investment decision-making process.

Biases of Accumulators are mainly emotional: overconfidence, affinity, self-control, illusion of control, and outcome. These biases and risk tolerance level are depicted in Figure 28.1.

What follows is a brief analysis of the positives and negatives of the Accumulator BIT (called Upside/Downside analysis), a description of the biases just discussed and a discussion of how the bias relates to the Accumulator BIT.

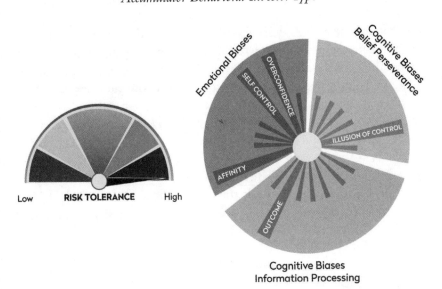

Figure 28.1 Accumulator Investor Type Characteristics

Upside/Downside Analysis

Upside: There are certain benefits that accrue to Accumulator BITs. Accumulators are confident in their abilities and as such they put their investment ideas into action. As I have said before, successful investing requires the fortitude to not only have conviction about investing ideas but also the confidence to put them into action. In short, Accumulators have the confidence to act decisively. They also understand what it takes to be successful: Hard work and the determination to succeed. Therefore, they take the time to understand investment opportunities and examine the details of what they invest in. Lastly, they understand that accumulating wealth is about accepting risk; not all investors grasp the significance of taking risk. This is not to say that Accumulators are overjoyed when things don't work out—but they typically understand that not every decision is going to work out well.

Downside: The downside to the Accumulator BIT relates mainly to biases that concern being too confident that things will go their way and believing that no matter what happens they can exert some level of control over investment outcomes. In reality, overconfidence usually leads to poor investment results—either because these BITs feel they can outsmart the markets on a regular basis or they trade too much. Similarly, believing that investing outcomes can be controlled is a fallacy; there is so much uncertainty about nearly all investing vehicles that investors who believe they can control outcomes are not accepting the reality of the situation. As we will see in the next section, Accumulators also may have trouble controlling spending, may invest based on what they relate to in other parts of their lives and be too optimistic in their investing endeavors.

Accumulator Bias Analysis

The main objective of any investor should be to stick to a plan, and much as it is with the other types, Accumulators can allow their biases to impede their ability to do so. Two of the most impactful Biases of Accumulators are Overconfidence and Illusion of Control. These will be reviewed now.

Overconfidence Bias

Bias Type: Emotional

Application of Overconfidence Bias to Accumulator BIT

Overconfidence is best described as unwarranted faith in one's own thoughts and abilities. Overconfidence manifests itself in investors' over-estimation of the quality of their judgment. Many aggressive investors believe they have an above-average aptitude for selecting investments; however, similar to other investor types, they get agitated and nervous during times of market stress and make less than optimal decisions. For example, during the fourth quarter of 2018 there were more than a few overconfident, aggressive investors who were unable to stomach the volatility of that period—selling at the wrong time as the low point was erased in a relatively short time. Those who were advised to stick with their plans—however difficult it was—and had the foresight and forti-tude to ride out the volatility saw their portfolios bounce back nicely. In retrospect, of course, this was an incredible buying opportunity.

People who have been successful in business and other pursuits tend to believe in themselves—this is how they became successful in the first place. But overconfidence can be a dangerous thing in the investing world. Markets can and do stay irrational for long periods of time. Just because the price of a security *should* be higher or lower doesn't mean it will change in the short run. A classic example of investor overconfidence is the case of the former executive or family legacy stockholder of a publicly traded company, such as Bank of America, Enron, or Lehman Brothers. These investors often refuse to diversify their holdings because they claim "insider knowledge" of, or emotional attachment to, the company. They cannot contextualize these stalwart stocks as risky investments. However, dozens of once-iconic names in U.S. business—such as those named above—have declined or vanished.

A simple diagnostic for overconfidence bias is contained in the following questions.

Question 1: How easy do you think it was to predict the collapse of the housing and credit bubbles of 2008–2009?

a. Difficult

b. Somewhat difficult

c. Somewhat easy

d. Easy

Question 2: From 1926 through 2010, the compound annual return for equities was approximately 9 percent. In any given year, what returns do you expect on your equity investments to produce?

a. Below 9 percent

b. About 9 percent

c. Above 9 percent

d. Well above 9 percent

Question 3: How much control do you believe you have in picking investments that will outperform the market?

a. Absolutely no control

b. Little if any control

c. Some control

d. A fair amount of control

The following are answers to these three questions. Answering C or D to any of these may indicate susceptibility to the bias.

Question 1: If the respondent recalled that predicting the rupture of the credit and housing bubbles in 2008–2009 seemed easy, then this is likely to indicate prediction overconfidence. Respondents describing the collapse as less predictable are probably less susceptible to prediction overconfidence.

Question 2: Respondents expecting to significantly outperform the long-term market average are likely to be susceptible to prediction over-confidence. Respondents forecasting returns at or below the market average are probably less subject to prediction overconfidence.

Question 3: Respondents professing greater degrees of control over their investments are likely to be susceptible to certainty overconfidence. Responses claiming little or no control are less symptomatic of certainty overconfidence.

Illusion of Control

Bias Type: Cognitive

Application of Illusion of Control Bias to Accumulator BIT

The illusion of control bias occurs when people believe that they can control or, at least, influence investment outcomes when, in fact, they cannot. Aggressive investors who are subject to illusion of control bias believe that the best way to manage an investment portfolio is to con-stantly adjust it. For example, trading-oriented investors, who accept high levels of risk, believe themselves to possess more "control" over the out-come of their investments than they actually do because they are "pulling the trigger" on each decision. Illusion of control bias can lead investors to trade more than is prudent. Researchers have found that traders, espe-cially online traders, believe themselves to possess more control over the outcomes of their investments than they actually do. An excess of trading results, in the end, in decreased returns. Illusions of control can lead inves-tors to maintain under-diversified portfolios because they concentrate their "bets" on only a few companies. Some investors hold concentrated positions in stocks because they gravitate toward companies over whose fate they feel some amount of control. That control proves illusory, how-ever, and the lack of diversification hurts the investors' portfolios.

Illusion of control bias contributes, in general, to investor overconfidence. Investors need to recognize that successful investing is usually a probabilistic activity. A good first step is to take a step back and realize how complex U.S. and global capitalism actually is. Even the wisest investors have absolutely no control over the outcomes of most of the investments they make. Just because you have deliberately determined to purchase a stock, do you really control the fate of that stock or the outcome of that purchase? Rationally, it becomes clear that some correlations are arbitrary rather than causal. Don't permit yourself to make financial decisions on what you can logically discern is an arbitrary basis.

Another recommended step is to seek contrary viewpoints. As you contemplate a new investment, take a moment to ponder whatever considerations might weigh against the trade. Ask yourself: Why am I making this investment? What are the downside risks? When will I sell? What might go wrong? These important questions can help you to screen the logic behind a decision before implementing that decision. Lastly, it's a good idea to keep records. Once you have decided to move forward with an investment, one of the best ways to keep illusions of control at bay is to maintain records of your transactions, including reminders spelling out the rationales that underlie each trade. Write down some of the important features of each investment that you make, and emphasize those attributes that you have determined to be in favor of the investment's success.

A simple diagnostic for illusion of control bias: The following are several questions that can test for illusion of control:

Question 1: When you participate in games of chance that involve dice—such as backgammon, Monopoly, or craps—do you feel most in control when you roll the dice yourself?

a. I feel more in control when I roll the dice.

b. I am indifferent as to who rolls the dice.

Question 2: When you are playing cards, are you usually most optimistic with respect to the outcome of a hand that you've dealt yourself?

a. A better outcome will occur when I am controlling the dealing of the cards.

b. It makes no difference to me who deals the cards.

Question 3: When and if you purchase a lottery ticket, do you feel more encouraged, regarding your odds of winning, if you choose the number yourself rather than using a computer-generated number?

a. I'm more likely to win if I control the numbers picked.

b. It makes no difference to me how the numbers are chosen.

Test Results Analysis

Question 1: People who feel more confident rolling the dice themselves, rather than allowing someone else to roll, are more likely to be susceptible to illusion of control bias.

Question 2: Question 2 parallels Question 1. People who perceive that they have more control over the outcome of a hand of cards when dealing the cards themselves are likely to be susceptible to illusion of control bias.

Question 3: Respondents selecting "a," indicating that they feel more optimistic when choosing their own lottery numbers instead of accepting randomized numbers, are likely to be susceptible to illusion of control bias.

Other important Accumulator Biases are: Affinity, Self-Control, and Outcome.

As we've seen, Overconfidence and Illusion of Control biases are two highly impactful biases for Accumulators. However, there are other biases that can be found to occur with Accumulator BITs with some regularity. These are Affinity, Self-Control, and Outcome. We will review these now.

Affinity Bias

Bias Type: Emotional

Affinity bias refers to an individual's tendency to make irrationally uneconomical consumer choices or investment decisions based on how they believe a certain product or service will reflect their beliefs or values. This idea focuses on the *expressive benefits* of a product rather than on what the product or service actually does for someone (the utilitarian benefits). A common example of this behavior in the consumer product realm is when one purchases wine. A consumer may purchase a fine bottle of well-known wine in a restaurant or wine shop for hundreds of dollars to impress their guests, while a bottle that costs much less could be equally delicious but would not convey the same status.

Self-Control Bias

Bias Type: Emotional

Self-control bias is the tendency to consume today at the expense of saving for tomorrow. The primary concern for investors with this bias is a high risk-tolerance coupled with high spending. For example, suppose an investor prefers aggressive investments and has high current spending needs and suddenly the financial markets hit severe turbulence. This investor may be forced to sell solid long-term investments that have had been priced down due to current market conditions, just to meet current expenses.

Outcome Bias

Bias Type: Emotional

Outcome bias refers to the tendency of individuals to decide to do something—such as make an investment in a mutual fund—based on the outcome of past events (such as the returns of the past five years) rather than by observing the process by which the outcome came about (the investment process used by the mutual fund manager over the past five years). An investor might think, "This manager had a fantastic five years, I am going to invest with her," rather than understanding how such great returns were generated or why the returns generated by other managers might not have had good results over the past five years.

Advice for Accumulators

Accumulators at the core can be emotional and this is often difficult to change. This investor type needs to be introspective because they like to control, or at least get deeply involved in, the details of investment decision-making. They are optimistic that their investments will do well, even if that optimism is irrational. Some Accumulators spend too much; out-of-control spending can inhibit meeting their long-term investment goals. Certain Accumulator investors make investments that align with their worldview, such as investing in stocks that relate to their lifestyle, but may not be the best investments for the long term. The best strategy for Accumulators is to create an investment policy statement and manage the portfolio without regard to emotion. A disciplined approach is key to long-term investment success.

29

Asset Allocation Case Studies for Each Behavioral Investor Type

The individual investor should act consistently as an investor and not as a speculator.
— **Ben Graham**

Congratulations! If you've gotten this far in the book, you should have developed your practical understanding of behavioral investor types (BITs) along the way. In this chapter, we'll draw on all our discussions so far regarding specific behavioral biases and examine four fictional investment case studies.

Obviously, every investor is unique, and there is no absolute, definitive way to diagnose and counteract behavioral biases. As an investor or advisor, you should read this chapter while keeping in mind how you might handle similar situations. You should focus most on applying the methodological process outlined—diagnosis, effects assessment, response determination, and best practical allocation.

The following case studies involve four hypothetical investors, three involving individual investors, Mrs. Gina Fleming, Mr. Gary Rossington, and Mr. Tony Highsmith and one high net-worth family, the Masters Family. Each case will cover one of the four behavioral investor types. The point of view of the case involves a financial advisor. Using an

253

advisory point of view can potentially help to think about your own situation more clearly.

These case studies were designed to answer the following key questions in determining an investor's modified portfolio:

- What personal biases are driving the investor's behavior and decision-making?
- What is the investor's Behavioral Investor Type?
- How might the investor's personal biases affect the investment strategy and solution decision?
- How should the investor moderate or adapt the impact of these biases?
- What is the best investment strategy and solution for this investor?

For the case study, assume a "normal" market environment. That is, the U.S. stock market is fairly valued, not over-valued or under-valued. Interest rates are holding steady at low rates. Volatility is present in the market, but not extreme. As you read the case, try to identify any biases you see based on the fact pattern. When solving for the investment strategy, for simplicity reasons, assume that all portfolio allocations will be divided between three asset classes: stocks, bonds, and cash.

When thinking about the case, it is important to keep in mind that every investor is unique, and there is no absolute way to understand and respond to behavior and biases. The cases are designed from the point of view of an advisor—but if you are an individual investor, think about how you might handle similar situations in your own way. Readers should focus most on applying methods of behavioral analysis, investment strategy and solution proposal, and tailor your investment approach in the given market situation. While reading the cases, try to evaluate which behavioral investor type each case is trying to identify.

CASE STUDY #1

Case Study: Mrs. Gina Fleming (Individual Investor)

Mrs. Fleming is a single, 70-year-old retiree living an exclusive lifestyle. Her annual living expenses are approximately $400,000 (this includes taxes). However, her only income is generated by her $5 million investment portfolio and is about 2%. Her spending rate is 8%, so she is spending down her principal. You have known her for three years. Your advisory relationship reveals that Mrs. Fleming's primary investment goal is for her assets to sufficiently support her for the rest of her life (perhaps 20 years) with a low tolerance for risk. She also has a goal of donating $2 million to a charity for animals if possible.

Although she is not that interested in the details of how her money is managed, she has told you many times that she does not, under any circumstances, want to lose money because she recalls that her relatives lost money in the crash of 1987. You have noticed that she feels the pain of losing money more acutely than the pleasure of gaining returns from her portfolio. You have also recognized that Mrs. Fleming is stubborn and inflexible in her thinking, especially when it comes to financial markets. She likes to keep things as they are, even if the world around her is changing. Although she is not an expert in financial markets, she periodically studies the markets and takes the trend of current market levels as a benchmark for predicting future market trends. When markets are falling, she says that she would be "crazy to invest now, markets are going down," and when they are up, she says, "Have we missed it?"

In your review of Mrs. Fleming's portfolio, you realize that, despite your recommendations, she has never changed her portfolio structure once. She has a big part of her portfolio (50%) in Treasury bonds and high-grade Municipal bonds. Most of Mrs. Fleming's equity (10%) is in a large concentrated position in Exxon stock. She inherited this stock from her late husband, who passed away in 2011. She holds the certificate in her safe deposit box at her local bank. The dividends are set up for automatic dividend reinvestment to buy more shares. This is how her late husband had arranged it, and she didn't want to disturb the plans that he had made for her. The rest is in cash (40%).

You are concerned that her conservative allocation will be unable to sustain her lifestyle or meet her financial goals. You suspect her discomfort at the prospect of re-allocating her portfolio is due to one or more behavioral biases.

Case Study #1: Analysis

Regardless of whether you are an investor or advisor, assume you are Mrs. Fleming's advisor. Your job is to advise her on the best allocation you believe is appropriate for her, given her unique circumstances and her behavioral profile. You are trying to ensure that she feels comfortable enough with your investment solution that she will not decide to change it in six months. To do that, answering the following questions will help you to get there. In next month's article we will review the answers to these questions and will provide a suggested solution to her investment situation.

1. What behavioral biases are driving Mrs. Fleming's behavior and decision-making? What specific evidence leads to this diagnosis?
2. What is her behavioral investor type?
3. How might Mrs. Fleming's personal biases affect the asset allocation decision?
4. How should the investor moderate or adapt the impact of these biases?
5. What is a reasonable allocation for Mrs. Fleming?

To make things easier, the key points of the case are summarized here:

- Mrs. Gina Fleming is a single, 70-year-old retiree living an exclusive lifestyle.
- Her annual living expenses are approximately $400,000 including taxes.
- Her only income is generated by her $5 million of investments and is about 2% of the portfolio.
- Her spending rate is 8%, so she is spending down her principal.
- Her goals are to sufficiently support her for the rest of her life (perhaps 20 years) with a low tolerance for risk. She also has a goal of donating $2 million to a charity for animals, if possible.
- She feels the pain of losses more than the pleasure of gains.
- She is stubborn and inflexible in her thinking, especially when it comes to financial markets.
- She likes to keep things as they are, even though the world around her is changing.
- When markets are falling, she says that she would be "crazy to invest now, markets are going down," and when they are up, she says "Have we missed it?"
- She has never changed her portfolio structure once since you began working with her three years ago.
- 50% of her portfolio is in Treasury bonds and high-grade Municipal bonds.
- 10% of her portfolio is in a large concentrated position in Exxon stock, which she wants to hold because it belonged to her husband who passed away several years ago.
- The rest is in cash (40%).

Regardless of whether you are an investor or advisor, assume you are Mrs. Fleming's advisor. As her advisor, you are concerned that given her conservative allocation, she will be unable to sustain her lifestyle or reach her financial goals. You suspect her discomfort at the prospect of re-allocating her portfolio is due to one or more behavioral biases. You are also trying to ensure that she feels comfortable enough with your investment solution that she will not decide to change it in six months.

Case Study: Answers to Questions

Mrs. Fleming's biases are very consistent with a Preserver behavioral investor type (BIT). Recall that in Chapter 25 we reviewed the characteristics of a Preserver BIT. We know that she is a Preserver because, based on the descriptions in the case study, she has the following biases:

- Loss aversion bias—the tendency to feel the pain of losses more acutely than the pleasure of gains.
- Anchoring bias—clinging to arbitrary pricing levels when considering an investment.
- Status quo bias—the desire to keep things as they are.
- Endowment—irrationally holding on to an investment regardless of possibly poor expected outcome.

The Preserver behavioral profile leads to a clear allocation preference of a conservative portfolio. Because she does not tolerate risk (loss aversion) and does not like change (status quo), she would naturally prefer the current asset allocation (90% bonds and cash, 10% stock) that she now possesses. Also, since the markets have risen significantly recently, Mrs. Fleming will likely make faulty conclusions regarding current and expected prices (anchoring) and will therefore feel wary of any exposure to equities. Mrs. Fleming has dismissed any advisor's attempts in the past (including yours) to get her to increase her exposure to equities.

Mrs. Fleming might outlive her assets if she adheres to her present allocation, and your financial planning confirms your fears. Her level of wealth, while adequate at present, isn't substantial enough to afford her the (dubious) luxury of an unbalanced allocation of funds in the long run. So, if you adapt to her biases—consent to stick with 90% bonds and cash and 10% equities—then Mrs. Fleming's only critical, financial goal becomes jeopardized. However, her biases are principally emotional (status quo, loss aversion) and typically cannot be corrected with advice and information. This will complicate things if you attempt to moderate her biases. In the end, you need to do this, but it may not be that difficult because she is so conservative now.

It is therefore your task to make a blended recommendation—one that takes into account her financial goals while at the same time accounting for her emotional (difficult to correct) biases. Therefore, you decide that a reasonable allocation is 35% equity, 20% cash, and 45% bonds. You also think that she should reduce her concentrated position in Exxon stock in a tax-efficient way.

CASE STUDY #2

Case Study: Mr. Gary Rossington (Individual Investor)

Mr. Rossington is a single (divorced) 58-year-old, hard-charging, technology executive earning $1.5 million per year. He lives extravagantly (cars, travel, art collection) by spending nearly three-fourths of his annual income but has managed to save approximately $20 million. He has accomplished this in large part because of his high income level and some stock options—together with an aggressive investment posture which has luckily produced more winners than losers. Although he has had his fair share of both. Additionally, he received some inheritance along the way. Mr. Rossington had a mild heart attack last year but now seems to have almost fully recovered. His primary financial goal is to retire comfortably at 65 and to donate $5 million over time to a healthcare foundation. The rest of his assets will be used to fund his own living expenses (including alimony) and provide a $3 million inheritance for each of his three sons; two of his sons are professional business people, and one is an artist who occasionally needs money and has a history of medical problems. Regarding his extended family, Mr. Rossington's parents are no longer living, and he has one sister who is married and financially secure.

You have been working with Mr. Rossington over the past two years. Given his health problems and financial goals, you have proposed a moderately conservative spending and investment plan. Nevertheless, Mr. Rossington refuses to agree on your plan because he prefers to spend the money today on his lifestyle instead of planning and saving for tomorrow's goals and invest in a risk-tolerant way. You have developed a good working relationship with Mr. Rossington. You realize, however, that perhaps the reason you have a good relationship is that you don't pressure him too much on following a plan. His current allocation consists of nearly 85% equities, 10% bonds, and 5% cash. Your concern is that a severe and sustained downward market fluctuation or another health scare may jeopardize Mr. Rossington's ability to meet his post-retirement daily living expenses, including health expenses, his donation, and inheritance goals, and possible support for his artist son. Your experience tells you that, with a more balanced portfolio, Mr. Rossington can keep his lifestyle and still meet his primary financial objectives. However, you are worried that Mr. Rossington may not fully buy into the idea. He told you that he sees himself as a very successful investor because he is successful in business. He knows exactly what the best investment strategy is for him: high risk. You are also worried because over the past two years he has invested in two venture capital technology deals brought to him by friends at his tennis club who are also in the technology industry. For one of these investments, he sits on the board of directors, and he has already put more money into the deal because the company needed a second cash infusion.

Case Study #2: Analysis

Regardless of whether you are an investor or advisor, assume you are Mr. Rossington's advisor. Your job is to advise him on the best allocation you believe is appropriate for him given his unique circumstances and behavioral profile. You are trying to ensure that he feels comfortable enough with your investment solution that he will not decide to change it in six months. To do that, answering the following questions will help you get there. In next month's article we will review the answers to these questions and will provide a suggested solution to her investment situation.

1. What behavioral biases are driving Mr. Rossington's behavior and decision-making? What specific evidence leads to this diagnosis?
2. What is his behavioral investor type?
3. How might Mr. Rossington's personal biases affect the asset allocation decision?
4. How should he moderate or adapt the impact of these biases?
5. What is a reasonable allocation for Mr. Rossington?

To make things easier, the key points of the case are summarized here:

- Mr. Rossington is a single (divorced) 58-year-old, hard-charging, technology executive earning $1.5 million per year.
- He lives extravagantly by spending nearly three-fourths of his annual income but has managed to save approximately $20 million. Additionally, he received some inheritance along the way.
- Mr. Rossington had a mild heart attack last year but now seems to have almost fully recovered. His primary financial goal is to retire comfortably at 65 and to donate $5 million over time to a health care foundation. He does not plan to decrease his spending in retirement.
- The other assets will be used to fund his living expenses and provide $3 million inheritance for each of his three sons; two of his sons are professional business people, and one is an artist who occasionally needs money and has a history of medical problems.
- You have proposed a moderate spending and investment plan. Nevertheless, Mr. Rossington refuses to agree on your plan because he prefers to spend the money today on his lifestyle instead of planning and saving for tomorrow's goals and invest in a risk-tolerant way.
- His current allocation consists of nearly 85% equities, 10% bonds and 5% cash. Your concern is that a severe and sustained downward market fluctuation or another health scare may jeopardize Mr. Rossington's ability to meet his financial goals.
- He has invested in two venture capital technology deals brought to him by friends at his tennis club, who are also in the technology industry. For one of these investments, he sits on the board of directors, which gives him comfort, but he has already put more money into the deal because the company needed a second cash infusion.
- You are concerned that, given his aggressive allocation combined with his high level of spending, he may sell assets when markets are down and then be unable to sustain his lifestyle or attain his financial goals. You suspect his discomfort at the prospect of re-allocating his portfolio is due to one or more behavioral biases.

Case Study: Answers to Questions

Mr. Rossington's biases are very consistent with an Accumulator behavioral investor type (BIT). Recall that in Chapter 28 we reviewed the characteristics of an Accumulator BIT. We know that he is an Accumulator because, based on the descriptions in the case study, he has the following biases:

- Overconfidence bias—the tendency to overestimate one's investment savvy.
- Affinity bias—the tendency to make an investment, not based on economic soundness, but rather because you have an affinity for the investment (friends, familiarity, etc.).
- Self-control bias—the tendency to spend today rather than save for tomorrow.
- Illusion of control—believing that one can influence events that are actually out of one's control.

The Accumulator behavioral profile leads to a clear allocation preference for risk. Because he tolerates high risk with high spending (overconfidence), invests in risky venture capital deals (affinity), and places a premium on spending today versus saving for tomorrow (self-control) he naturally prefers the current risky asset allocation. Also, Mr. Rossington believes he can control the outcome of his investments (illusion of control) and may be taking more risk than he understands; he has dismissed any advisor's attempts in the past (including yours) to decrease his exposure to risk assets.

Mrs. Rossington might outlive his assets if he adheres to his "spendy" ways and your financial planning confirms your fears. His level of wealth, while adequate at present, may not last in the long run, especially if he has to sell assets at the wrong time: during a severe market downturn. So, if you adapt to his biases—consent to stick with his risky allocation and ignore his high spending— then Mr. Rossington's financial goals may become jeopardized. His biases are principally emotional (self-control, overconfidence, affinity) and typically cannot be corrected with advice and information. This will complicate things if you attempt to moderate his biases.

It is therefore your task to make a blended recommendation— one that takes into account his financial goals while at the same time accounting for his emotional (difficult to correct) biases. Therefore, you decide that a reasonable allocation is 65% equity, 10% cash, and 25% bonds. You also think that he should reduce his spending and you plan to recommend this course of action.

CASE STUDY #3

Case Study: Mr. Tony Highsmith (Individual Investor)

Tony Highsmith is a 29-year-old successful sales executive for a real estate company. He is single, relatively well off (comes from an upper middle-class family, very well-educated), and lives a high-spending lifestyle. He owns an expensive condo in downtown Boston, enjoys a healthy social life, and, although he spends aggressively, he saves 20% of his income to invest for the long run. He recently got engaged to Chloe, aged 28, who works as a dental assistant; they plan on having a family in the next few years and Chloe will stay home to take care of the family. His investment portfolio is also aggressive—it's 100% stocks. He began investing in 2011 and has seen nothing but a bull market. Since he has never been through a market cycle, he assumes this one will continue—and continues to invest in risk stocks. He started investing in index ETFs such as the SPY (S&P 500 ETF) but has moved on to technology stocks such as Apple, Amazon, Facebook, Google and Netflix. His co-workers and friends are making a lot of money in these stocks so he figures he should do the same. He thinks that if he does not invest in these stocks he will regret it later. Tony has managed to save and invest $250,000. His near-term goal is that he wants to buy a house in the Boston suburbs with his fiancée and contribute to the cost of their wedding. Longer term he wants to raise a family and retire at age 60.

You have been working with Tony for the past two years. When you began working with Tony, he took a risk tolerance questionnaire that indicated he should have about a 65% risk, 35% bond/cash portfolio. Even though he is young, with a long time horizon, his short-term goal of saving for the wedding and a down payment for a house in the suburbs indicated to you that he should have some bonds and cash. You prepared a financial plan for him and recommended an asset allocation that was in line with this risk profile: 65% equities, 25% bonds, and 10% cash. Tony has chosen to be more aggressive with 100% equities and no bonds or cash.

This more aggressive allocation was chosen in part because Tony had trouble facing the fact that there could be a bear market in stocks. He has only seen a bull market and does not want to accept the fact that he could be wrong about it continuing indefinitely. He chose real estate as a profession because he likes the high-risk nature of it—but you note that he hasn't experienced any adversity yet; his entire working career has been during an economic boom. You also recall him mentioning that he socializes with friends and they compared notes on investing. He wants to be in the investments that all his friends are in, buying risky tech stocks. In meetings, you have pointed out that in the year 2000 tech stocks got decimated—but this has not deterred him from investing 40% of his portfolio in five technology stocks. He has FOMO—the fear of missing out. You sense he is overestimating his risk tolerance.

Tony is not receptive when you tell him you think he should diversify his portfolio. You are concerned that Tony hasn't been through any adversity in his career and is being naïve about risk. You think that he could be setting himself up for failure in his short-term goal of saving for his wedding and house and, possibly, the important years of saving for their children's college education and meeting the longer-term goal of retiring early.

Case Study #3: Analysis

Regardless of whether you are an investor or advisor, assume you are Tony's advisor. Your job is to advise him on the best allocation you believe is appropriate for him given his unique circumstances and behavioral profile. You are trying to ensure that he feels comfortable enough with your investment solution that he will not decide to change it in six months. To do that, answering the following questions will help you to get there.

1. What behavioral biases are driving Tony's behavior and decision-making? What specific evidence leads to this diagnosis?
2. What is his behavioral investor type?
3. How might Tony's personal biases affect the asset allocation decision?
4. How should the investor moderate or adapt the impact of these biases?
5. What is a reasonable allocation for Tony?

To make things easier, the key points of the case are summarized here:

- Tony Highsmith is a 29-year-old successful sales executive for a real estate company.
- He is single, relatively well off (comes from an upper middle-class family, well educated) and lives a high-spending lifestyle. He owns

an expensive condo in downtown Boston and enjoys a healthy social life.

- He saves 20% of his income to invest for the long run. His investment portfolio is 100% stocks.
- Tony recently got engaged to Chloe, aged 28, who works as a dental assistant; they plan on having a family in the next few years and Chloe will stay home to take care of the family.
- He began investing in 2011 and since he has never been through a market cycle, he assumes this one will continue—and continues to invest in risk stocks. He invests in index ETFs and risky technology stocks such as Apple, Amazon, Facebook, Google and Netflix (FAANG). He thinks that if he does not invest in these stocks he will regret it later.
- Tony has managed to save and invest $250,000. His near-term goal is that he wants to buy a house in the Boston suburbs with his fiancée and contribute to the cost of their wedding. Longer term he wants to raise a family and retire at age 60.
- You have been working with Tony for the past two years. When you began working with Tony, he took a risk tolerance questionnaire that indicated he should have about a 65% risk, 35% bond/cash portfolio.
- Even though he is young, with a long time horizon, his short-term goal of saving for the wedding and a down payment for a house in the suburbs indicated to you that he should have some bonds and cash.
- You prepared a financial plan for him and recommended an asset allocation that was in line with this risk profile: 65% equities, 30% bonds, and 10% cash. Tony has chosen to be more aggressive with 100% equities and no bonds or cash.
- He wants to be in the investments that all his friends are in, buying risky tech stocks. In meetings, you have pointed out that in the year 2000 tech stocks got decimated—but this has not deterred him from investing 40% of his portfolio in five technology stocks. He has FOMO—the fear of missing out. You sense that he is overestimating his risk tolerance.
- Tony is not receptive when you tell him you think he should diversify his portfolio. You are concerned that Tony hasn't been through any adversity in his career and is being naïve about risk. You think that he could be setting himself up for failure in his short-term goal of saving for his wedding and house and, possibly, the important years of saving for college and meeting the longer-term goal of retiring early.

Case Study: Answers to Questions

Regardless of whether you are an investor or advisor, assume you are Tony's advisor. Tony's biases are very consistent with a Follower BIT. Recall that in Chapter 26 reviewed the characteristics of a Follower BIT. We know that he is a Follower because, based on the descriptions in the case study, he has the following biases:

- Recency Bias—A predisposition to recall and emphasize recent events and/or observations and to extrapolate patterns where none exist.
- Hindsight Bias—Occurs when an investor perceives past investment outcomes as if they had been predictable.
- Framing Bias—The tendency of investors to respond to situations differently on the basis of the context in which a choice is presented (framed).
- Cognitive Dissonance Bias—Occurs when a person believes something and persists in believing it even when faced with evidence to the contrary because they don't want to acknowledge the discomfort of facing that their beliefs may be wrong.
- Regret Aversion Bias—Avoiding taking decisive actions because of the fear that an investor might, in hindsight, regret whatever course they select.

The Follower behavioral investor type profile leads an investor to move toward risk even when they don't have the risk tolerance to accept excessive risk. This is the case here because Tony wants to be in the latest fad investments (FAANG) too much; he is ignoring the risks. Tony's recency bias (thinking that prosperity will last indefinitely) coupled with regret aversion (thinking he will regret not being in FAANG stocks) have caused him to be more risk tolerant than he should be. In addition, he has cognitive dissonance bias in thinking that he won't accept the fact that there have been periods when tech stocks have done poorly.

It is now time to decide how to prepare a recommendation for Tony. You have been working with Tony for two years and your first recommendation for him was an asset allocation of 65% equities, 25% bonds, and 10% cash. He chose a more aggressive allocation of 100% equities and no bonds or cash. You decide to "meet him near the middle"—an allocation that takes into account his financial goals while at the same time accounting for his biases. Therefore, you decide that a reasonable allocation is 75% equity, 10% cash, and 15% bonds.

CASE STUDY #4

The Masters Family (Family)

NOTE: this case involves a married couple—however, while analyzing the case treat them as a single investor; try to identify biases and the behavioral investor type as if they were a single individual.

The Masters family includes a financially informed, well-educated couple, both aged 43, with two children aged four and six. The family is financially secure, but their income has suffered recently during the current business and economic environment in Mr. Masters' industry: Energy. The couple's total annual income is now $600,000, but that is down from an average of over $1 million a year for more than 10 years straight. They own and manage an Energy Services company, but capital spending in the market segment they serve has fallen. At some point this should turn around, but they are uncertain as to how long that might take. In the meantime, they have valuable service contracts that provide steady and reliable cash flow to the business.

The Masters have managed to save $4 million. Mrs. Masters wants to buy an apartment in Manhattan. She has referred several times to how much money has been made on New York real estate. She believes that New York real estate will be a great investment. Their primary financial goals are first to be able fund their children's college education, and second, to enjoy a comfortable early retirement, perhaps as early as age 55.

You have been working with the Masters for ten years, starting with them just after the financial crisis of 2008. Mr. Masters tends to lead the meetings, but Mrs. Masters also participates actively. Back then, you prepared a financial plan for them and recommend an asset allocation which was in line with their risk profile: 70% equities, 25% bonds, and 5% cash. When you first started working with them the Masters, however, chose to be more conservative, 40% equities, 40% bonds, and 20% cash.

This more conservative allocation was chosen in part because the Masters were of the opinion that there would be another financial crisis. They often brought articles to the meetings with you referencing high debt levels of companies and articles about the 2008 financial crisis. In meetings, you pointed out that Central Bank action can help to repair the global economy and that economic trends are favorable. The Masters disagreed and were more pessimistic. This behavior caused them to miss a wealth building opportunity by not investing in equities more heavily immediately after the crisis when they were undervalued. They still believe another financial crisis is coming.

This couple is typically not receptive when you advise them to "stay on course" with their plan. They believe they are correct in their assessment of the current economic environment and do not plan to invest more aggressively until they are convinced the "coast is clear." You are concerned because you think that if they do not take more risk with their portfolio, they may not be able to meet their long-term goals.

Case Study #4: Analysis

Regardless of whether you are an investor or advisor, assume you are the Masters' advisor. Your job is to advise them on the best allocation you believe is appropriate for them given their unique circumstances and behavioral profile. You are trying to ensure that they feel comfortable enough with your investment solution that they will not decide to change it in six months. To do that, answering the following questions will help you to get there.

1. What behavioral biases might drive the Masters' behavior and decision-making? What specific evidence leads to this diagnosis?
2. What is their behavioral investor type?
3. How might Mr. Masters personal biases affect the asset allocation decision?
4. How should the investor moderate or adapt the impact of these biases?
5. What is a reasonable allocation for the Masters?

To make things easier, the key points of the case are summarized here:

- The Masters family includes a financially informed, well-educated couple, both aged 43, and two children aged four and six.
- The couple's total annual income is now $600,000, but that is down from an average of over $1 million a year for more than 10 years straight.
- They own and manage an Energy Services company, but capital spending in the market segment they serve has fallen.
- The Masters have managed to save $4 million.

- In addition to Mrs. Masters' desire to buy and apartment in Manhattan, their primary financial goals are first to be able fund their children's college education, and second, to enjoy a comfortable early retirement, perhaps as early as age 55.
- You have been working with the Masters for 10 years, starting with them just after the financial crisis of 2008. Back then, you prepared a financial plan for them and recommend an asset allocation which was in line with their risk profile: 70% equities, 25% bonds, and 5% cash.
- When you first started working with them, the Masters, however, chose to be more conservative, 40% equities, 40% bonds, and 20% cash. This more conservative allocation was chosen in part because the Masters were of the opinion that there would be another financial crisis.
- They often brought articles to the meetings with you referencing high debt levels of companies and articles about the 2008 financial crisis. This behavior caused them to miss a wealth-building opportunity by not investing in equities more heavily immediately after the crisis, when they were undervalued. They still believe another financial crisis is coming.
- This couple is typically not receptive when you advise them to "stay on course" with their plan. They believe they are correct in their assessment of the current economic environment and do not plan to invest more aggressively until they are convinced the "coast is clear."
- You are concerned because you think that if they do not take more risk with their portfolio, they may not be able to meet their long-term goals.

Case Study: Answers to Questions

Regardless of whether you are an investor or advisor, assume you are the Masters' advisor. Your job is to advise them on the best allocation you believe is appropriate for them, given their unique circumstances and behavioral profile. The Masters' biases are very consistent with an Independent BIT. Recall that in Chapter 27 we reviewed the characteristics of an Independent BIT. We know that they are an Independent because, based on the descriptions in the case study, he has the following cognitive biases:

- Conservatism bias—when someone makes a forecast and clings to that forecast irrationally, even when presented with contrary information.

- Confirmation bias—seeking information that confirms a pre-existing view rather than seeking information that may contradict a pre-existing view.
- Availability bias—the tendency to believe that what is easily recalled is more likely to happen.
- Representativeness—letting pre-existing ideas unduly influence how new information is processed.
- Self-Attribution—ascribing success to innate talents and blaming failures on outside influences.

The Independent behavioral investor type profile leads to a clear allocation preference for risk; typically, Independents are risk tolerant. In the case of the Masters, their availability bias (thinking that another crisis is near) coupled with conservatism bias (making a forecast and clinging to that forecast irrationally) has caused them to be more risk averse. In addition, confirmation bias is reinforcing these views and preventing them from taking on a riskier allocation.

It is now time to decide how to prepare a recommendation for the Masters. You have been working with the Masters for a long time (10 years) and have gotten to know them well. You reflect on when you started—back then, you prepared a financial plan for them and recommended an asset allocation of 70% equities, 25% bonds, and 5% cash. They chose a more conservative allocation of 40% equities, 40% bonds, and 20% cash. They never did get to your target. You decide to "meet them near the middle"—one that takes into account their financial goals while at the same time accounting for their biases. Therefore, you decide that a reasonable allocation is 60% equity, 10% cash, and 35% bonds.

Case Study Summary and Conclusion

I hope that you can take away from these case studies an application to your investment situation. The key point to recognize is that we need to account for our behavioral biases when creating our portfolio allocations. The most important thing we can do as investors is understand the level of risk we can live with over the long term. If you can identify this risk level and manage your emotions during the ups and downs of the markets, you should be able to achieve long-term investment success. The next chapter discusses retirement. There are key issues to investing as a retiree.

PART VI
BEHAVIORAL ASPECTS
OF PORTFOLIO
IMPLEMENTATION

I n the final section of the book, we will cover implementation of your portfolio from a behavioral finance perspective. We will first cover behavioral aspects of the active/passive debate in Chapter 30, which includes the potential benefits of active management and how to create the *Best Practical Allocation* for your portfolio. Chapter 31 covers behaviorally aware portfolio construction: We discuss the benefits of mental accounting, the goals-based approach to asset allocation, and my firm's portfolio approach. In Chapter 32 the topic is behavioral finance and market corrections. We review why investors panic and explain what happens from a behavioral finance perspective.

30

Behavioral Finance Aspects of the Active versus Passive Debate

There seems to be some perverse human characteristic that likes to make easy things difficult.

—**Warren Buffett**

As many investors know, there is an ongoing debate about the efficacy of active money management compared to simply using passive index investing. Active managers make investment decisions in an effort to outperform their benchmark, while passive managers simply track an index to gain exposure to a market, country, or special segment of a market. Active managers need to have enough skill to consistently outperform the market, but many active managers do not outperform on a consistent basis. This lack of performance, plus the higher cost compared to passive management, has caused a surge of money flow into passive indexing and out of actively managed funds. However, for long-term investors it doesn't just come down to lower costs, as this discussion might suggest. Behavioral finance demonstrates that, although passive funds outperform in the long term, there are challenges of staying invested in long-only index products, especially in times of extreme market volatility. This is the behavioral gap discussed in Chapter 2.

Fundamentally, active management is the pursuit of selecting securities to take advantage of mis-pricings or creating a mix of securities to create an outcome such as lower volatility. On the other hand, passive investing makes the assumption that markets are efficient and securities are always fairly priced. Both active management and passive management have pros and cons. Much of the active versus passive argument has centered on "beating the market," with active managers making the case that they can hedge during market downturns and invest at market bottoms allows them to beat the market. On the other hand, the buy and hold investment advocates follow the mantra that "if you missed the 10 best days in the last 10 years you would have negative returns." That is, timing the market is impossible. The truth is that both arguments have merit, yet both are partially misplaced. The best strategy is to find what I call the "best practical allocation," which typically involves a blend of both active and passive investing. This concept will be explored later in the chapter.

The Logic of Passive Management

Among the most compelling evidence of the shortfall of active management comes from the SPIVA U.S. Scorecard, an annual performance analysis produced by S&P Dow Jones. The scorecard tracks the short- and long-term performance of thousands of U.S. stock funds across 13 distinct style categories.[1] The scorecard highlights the variability that exists in active manager performance over time. As per Figure 30.1, 70% of active managers underperformed their benchmark in 2019. This was the fourth worst year since 2001. With these statistics it's easy to see why passive management is so popular. So why isn't active management dead?

The Potential Benefits of Active Management

In Chapter 29 we learned about recency bias. This bias occurs when investors place undue weight on events that occurred in the recent past. In the past 10+ years, passive investing has exploded. But will this

---

[1] https://www.spglobal.com/_assets/documents/corporate/us-spiva-report-11-march-2019.pdf

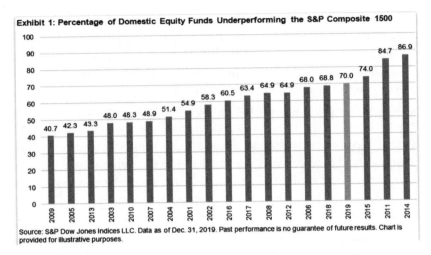

Figure 30.1 Percentage of Domestic Equity Underperforming the S&P 1500

Source: S&P Dow Jones

continue when markets get choppy such as the coronavirus period? At the time of writing, we are in the middle of the coronavirus bear market, so the jury is still out. But there is reasonable evidence that active fund managers tend to outperform during bear markets.

Consider the Following

Vanguard analyzed the six bear markets that have occurred since 1980 and concluded that active managers outperformed on average in three out of the six.[2] Research firm Morningstar analyzed rolling three-year returns for the 20-year period beginning in February 1998 and found that nearly 60% of active funds "on average" achieved outperformance during down markets.[3] Hartford Funds did a similar study and looked at 26 market corrections of 10% or more that were not greater than 20% (i.e., not full-blown bear markets) and demonstrated that active management outperformed 15 out of 26 times.[4] Although this is not 100% ironclad evidence, the results referenced here lend credence that there

---

[2] "Myth: Active Management Performs Better in Bear Markets," Vanguard, 2018.
[3] "Will Active Stock Funds Save Your Bacon in a Downturn?," Jeffrey Ptak, CFA, Morningstar, February 28, 2018.
[4] "The Cyclical Nature of Active and Passive Investing," Hartford Funds, 2019.

is at least a reasonable chance that active management can protect on the downside on average. If this helps investors stay invested, then this is good news.

While we are on the potential benefits of active management, it is always useful to point out that most index ETFs or other indexes are capitalization-weighted, which means in effect that, as a bull market approaches its peak valuation, passive investors own more and more of the most expensive stocks. Examples of this are the overweighting of the technology sector in the S&P 500 in 1999–2000, when the NASDAQ bubble peaked and crashed, and the overweighting of the financial sector in 2006, when the housing/subprime finance bubble peaked.[5] Losses for passive investors in both instances can be magnified by overweight sector allocations to overpriced sectors with high valuations. Another aspect of the question regarding active vs. passive investing is the observed tendency for active funds to do better during rising rate environments, and for passive funds to do better in a falling interest rate environment. (See Figure 30.2.) Given what is happening now, meaning rates are falling (approaching zero), passive management might hold favor for a while.

Outperformance of Active Funds vs. Interest Rates

As interest rates rise, the stock market on the whole often suffers—and that's when active managers shine. As rates fall, the average outperformance of active funds declines, and indexing looks better.

U.S. Active Fund Excess Return vs. Rate Environment

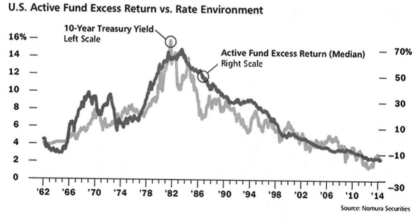

Figure 30.2 Outperformance of Active Funds vs. Interest Rates
Source: Nomura Securities

---

[5] https://seekingalpha.com/article/3972436

Limitations of Risk Tolerance Questionnaires

The proper test of an investment strategy is whether investors actually stick with their program to reach their investment goals. It takes a lot of behavioral introspection to ensure the correct portfolio approach is taken. Unfortunately, most investors use the wrong assessment tool. This section points out the limitations of risk tolerance questionnaires. In an attempt to standardize asset allocation processes, financial service firms ask and may, for compliance reasons, require their investors to administer risk tolerance questionnaires prior to drafting any asset allocation. In the absence of any other diagnostic analysis, this methodology is certainly useful and generates important information. However, there are a number of factors that restrict the usefulness of risk tolerance questionnaires.

Aside from ignoring behavioral issues, a risk tolerance questionnaire can also generate dramatically different results when administered repeatedly but in slightly varying formats to the same individual. Such imprecision arises primarily from inconsistencies in the wording of questions. Additionally, most risk tolerance questionnaires are administered once and may not be revisited. Risk tolerance can vary directly as a result of changes and events throughout life. Another critical issue with respect to risk tolerance questionnaires is that many advisors interpret their results too literally. For example, some investors might indicate that the maximum loss they would be willing to tolerate in a single year would comprise 20 percent of their total assets. Does that mean that an ideal portfolio would place investors in a position to lose 20 percent? No! Advisors should set portfolio parameters that preclude investors from incurring the maximum specified tolerable loss in any given period. For these reasons, risk tolerance questionnaires provide, at best, broad guidelines for asset allocation and should only be used in concert with other behavioral assessment tools.

Advice: Use the Best Practical Allocation for Your Portfolio

Investors interests derive from their natural psychological preferences—and these preferences may not be served best by the output of a mean-variance model optimization output, such as one derived from a risk tolerance questionnaire. Investors may be better served by moving themselves up or down the efficient frontier, adjusting risk and return levels depending on their behavioral tendencies. More simply, an investor's best practical allocation (which may also be referred to as a behaviorally modified allocation) may be a slightly underperforming long-term investment program to which the investor can comfortably adhere, warding off an impulse to "change horses" in the middle of the race. In other cases, the best practical allocation might contradict investors' natural psychological tendencies, and these investors may be well served to accept risks in excess of their individual comfort levels in order to maximize expected returns. In sum, the right allocation is the one that helps the investor to attain financial goals while simultaneously providing enough psychological security for the investor to sleep at night. The ability to create such optimal portfolios is what investors should try to gain from this book.

In most cases, investors would be best served to have a blend of active and passive investing. Both active management and passive management have pros and cons. Most investors should "meet in the middle" and see the benefits of both active and passive. In my experience, when active and passive strategies are mixed, they can provide a better overall experience for the investor. Active management strategies can add value and help control risk through their management strategy or by responding to changing market conditions. When combined with passive strategies, active strategies provide diversification benefits. Active money management, coupled with a passive core, is an excellent strategy to get investors to meet their investment objectives. In addition, there are other tools that can be used to keep investors on track such as dollar cost averaging in expensive markets, regular rebalancing, and tax loss harvesting. All of these methods are based on logical rules that take common behavioral biases of investors into account, to establish new portfolios and help investors stay invested.

31

Behaviorally Aware Portfolio Construction

The difference between successful people and really successful people is that really successful people say no to almost everything.

—**Warren Buffett**

Introduction

The Behavioral Finance Approach to Asset Allocation Based on Mental Accounting

Leveraging the power of mental accounting for the benefit of attaining financial goals can be powerful. Our biases aren't necessarily harmful! There are two main topics in this chapter. First, we are going to discuss how a behavioral finance or a "goals-based" approach to asset allocation can be helpful in order to keep financial goals in mind when creating a portfolio. I have found the following approach, outlined in Figure 31.1, and based on investors' tendency to put money in separate mental accounts, to be of tremendous value at times. Not every investor likes or needs this approach to investing but some really like it. The second will be my firm's approach to asset allocation that leverages mental accounting but in a different way which we will explore later in the chapter.

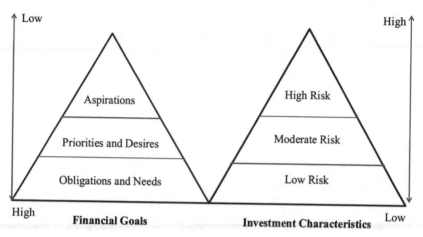

Figure 31.1 Behavioral Finance or Goals-Based Approach to Asset Allocation

Generally, what investors should aspire to do is focus on their needs and obligations, and make sure that they have enough of their portfolio carved out in capital preservation assets to meet those needs and obligations. Next, if desired, more risk can be taken to attain one's priorities and expectations, and, going further, even more risk can be taken to meet one's desires and aspirations. At the end of the process, investors usually end up with a diversified portfolio, though it will likely differ from a portfolio based on traditional mean-variance framework. However, the components of the portfolio are individually justified, based on needs and obligations versus priorities and expectations versus desires and aspirations.

Goals-Based Investing

Having specific goals for specific "buckets" of money leverages the positive aspects of mental accounting. Goals-based planning emphasizes the use of investment portfolios that allow you to reach your goals, rather than targeting a specific rate of return. Because each goal has a different return requirement and risk profile, you would in theory use different types of investments to reach each goal. Some investors are taking this approach but may not realize they are using a mental accounting or behavioral finance approach. For example, if an investor has an account geared toward saving for retirement (IRA, etc.), another for college savings (529 plan), and a third to serve as a bill-paying reserve—this is one form of goals-based investing. A typical approach is that investors have more equities (risk) in a retirement account while the emergency reserve may hold less-risky investments like bonds or cash per Figure 31.1. The power lies in the fact that if these accounts are viewed as "untouchable" (college funds or retirement funds, for example) and investors may be less inclined to disturb long-term investment plans by making changes that could cause long-term accumulation problems. For risk-averse investors, mental accounting can help investors feel more comfortable taking on the risk they may need to reach specific goals.

This "bucketing" approach is particularly helpful for people who may be approaching the actual time of their retirement. As their focus shifts from saving to spending, many retirees need to tap their "retirement bucket" to fund their lifestyle. Many people who use this approach leverage three separate pools of capital to assist during this transition. These are: (a) a cash account for safety, (b) a short-term fixed income account (i.e., short duration) so you are earning income but still reasonably safe, and (c) a third longer-term pool of capital that is intended to keep up with growth and inflation.

Consolidating Accounts into a Portfolio View

One of the main "problems" with mental accounting is that it can produce inefficiencies if too many accounts are used for "safe" assets such as cash. For example, if you have too many "rainy day" or savings accounts you can lose out on long-term appreciation by not investing the pools of cash as one portfolio. To correct this, if you recognize that this mental accounting is happening you can consolidate accounts that are focused on the same goal—retirement, for example. If you have several retirement accounts, a few IRAs or 401ks that have come about from job changes over the years, try folding them all into a single account which you can then monitor and manage as a single portfolio. If not, it can be difficult to monitor funds and allocations, and therefore risk, when investments are too spread out. Get organized!

Consolidating accounts according to their goals, to bring order to your finances, is recommended.

In sum, investors using this approach will typically first estimate how much should be invested in low-risk (capital preservation) assets to meet those needs and obligations. Next, riskier assets are considered to attain priorities and desires. Finally, even riskier assets are added to meet one's aspirational goals. Typically, investors will end up having a diversified portfolio using this approach, but the resulting portfolio may not be efficient from a traditional finance perspective. The lack of efficiency stems from the components of the portfolio being individually justified rather than based on modern portfolio theory that considers correlations between investments. However, investors may be better able to understand risk by using this methodology. As a result, investors may find it easier to adhere to investment decisions and portfolio allocations made using this approach.

Portfolio Approach

At my firm, Sunpointe Investments, we leverage mental accounting albeit in a slightly different way. Our approach categorizes assets by two broad categories—Risky Assets and Risk Mitigation Assets. And each of those categories is broken down further into four categories. Risky Assets contain "Growth Assets" and "Hybrid/Income Assets". Risk Mitigation Assets have two categories: "Defensive Assets" and "Flexible Assets." These broad categories (Risky Assets and Risk Mitigation Assets) allow investors to think about risk in a simple way—such as 60%/40% or 70%/30%. This leverages the tendency to want to "bucket" money according to mental accounts. This is a very effective way of reducing complexity and communication simplicity.

Each of these buckets can be scaled up or down based on investor objectives. Investor allocations are then built from this model based upon specific return objectives and risk tolerances. We use a concept of risk in these models that augments conventional parameters with concepts more specifically useful to portfolio management, such as the lowest likely portfolio return, the Sharpe ratio, and downside risk (an estimate of the probability of missing the stated return objective over a given time horizon). These measures provide a more complete view of the value added to (or subtracted from) a portfolio with the addition or deletion of various asset classes. If you want more information on this, visit www .sunpointeinvestments.com.

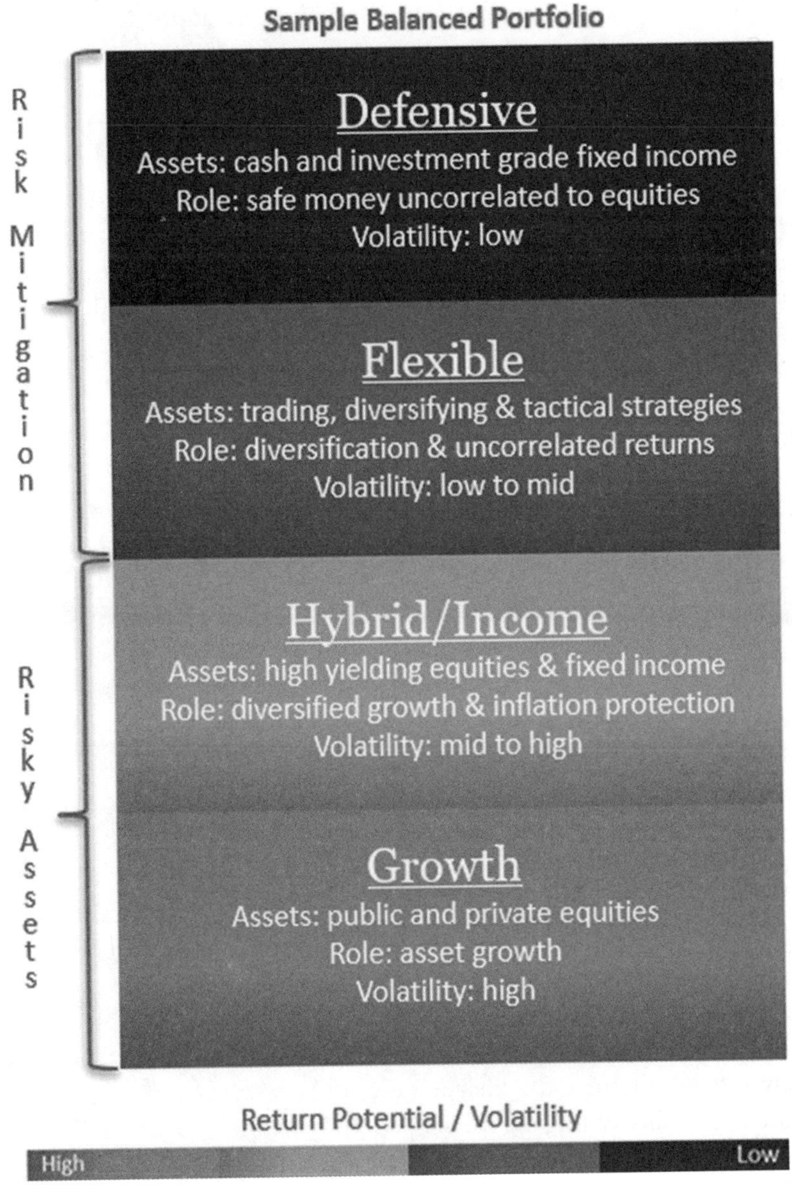

Sample Balanced Portfolio

Defensive
Assets: cash and investment grade fixed income
Role: safe money uncorrelated to equities
Volatility: low

Flexible
Assets: trading, diversifying & tactical strategies
Role: diversification & uncorrelated returns
Volatility: low to mid

Hybrid/Income
Assets: high yielding equities & fixed income
Role: diversified growth & inflation protection
Volatility: mid to high

Growth
Assets: public and private equities
Role: asset growth
Volatility: high

Risk Mitigation

Risky Assets

Return Potential / Volatility

High · Low

Figure 31.2 Sunpointe Asset Allocation Framework

32

Behavioral Finance and Market Corrections

All there is to investing is picking good stocks at good times and staying with them as long as they remain good companies.

—Warren Buffett

Market panics and the subsequent bear markets occur in a few fairly predictable steps. First, there is a trigger to the panic. Most recently we had the coronavirus panic. But there are others as we know: the crash of 1987, the Asian crisis of 1998, the collapse of Lehman Brothers during the popping of the housing bubble in 2008–2009. In these cases, stock markets fall rapidly and, often, unexpectedly. Other assets including risky credit, real estate, commodities and others also fall. Then investors want cash and sell good assets to raise cash. More market pressure on the downside. Potential buyers get spooked and decide to wait to buy. The "negative" animal spirits pattern takes over and a recession is typically the result. What happens during these times, from a behavioral finance perspective, is what will be covered in this chapter. The proper course of action is to stay invested through panics; markets can and do recover.

The Most Recent Panic

With the price action on March 20, 2020, the U.S. and global equity markets moved into a "bear market" (20% or greater loss) due to the novel coronavirus. At the time, all signals were that the U.S. would have at least one quarter of negative GDP. In just over a month, the market traded off about 35% from its peak on February 19, 2020. The headlines at this time were that Starbucks would close its cafes across the United States, Boeing said its chief executive and chairman would forgo their pay and more than $8 trillion in shareholder value had been lost. To provide some perspective, in 2019 there wasn't a single daily loss for the S&P 500 in excess of 3%. Over the past 10 trading sessions from March 20, 2020, there were losses of −3.4%, −3.0%, −4.6%, −3.4%, and −8%. This volatility wreaked havoc on the psychology of market participants. The purpose of this section is to give some behavioral finance explanations of why this angst is happening and some perspective on bear markets—so that investors can reduce panic and make sound investment decisions.

Why Investors Panic: A Macroeconomic Behavioral Perspective

Pompian's (2006) *Behavioral Finance and Wealth Management* discussed the biases that became apparent in the wake of the popping of the 2000 stock market bubble. Since that time, investors have experienced numerous bouts of volatility, including the Global Financial Crisis (GFC) in 2008 and a near–bear market in 2018. Taking a longer-term perspective, over the past 20 years there have been 10 market corrections (10% down), as can be seen in Figure 32.1. Of these corrections, only two have turned into bear markets—with the brief correction in Q4 of 2018 almost making it to 20% down.

Investor biases exist in some form or other within all investors. These biases become amplified during significant market declines like the one in March 2020. People tend to copy the behavior of others when they are faced with uncertain prospects and the stock market provides a great example. In fact, the behavior of crowds is often what causes large

Start date	Duration	High	Low	Change
7/17/1998	45 days	1186.75	957.28	−19.3%
7/16/1999	91	1418.78	1247.41	−12.1%
3/24/2000	**929**	**1527.46**	**776.76**	**−49.1%**
11/27/2002	104	938.87	800.73	−14.7%
10/9/2007	**517**	**1565.15**	**676.53**	**−56.8%**
4/23/2010	70	1217.28	1022.58	−16.0%
4/29/2011	157	1363.61	1099.23	−19.4%
5/21/2015	96	2130.82	1867.61	−12.4%
11/3/2015	100	2109.79	1829.08	−13.3%
1/26/2018	13	2872.87	2581	−10.2%
9/20/2018	95	2930.75	2351.1	−19.8%

Figure 32.1 Market Corrections

Source: Yardini Research

amounts of volatility in the stock markets—both on the upside and the downside—because everyone wants to get in or out at the same time. During times like the tech stock bubble of the late 1990s or the real estate bubble of the 2000s investors followed the behavior of other people they believed to be "industry experts" or people deemed prescient by the financial media. This effect is called *Herding*, and appears to be what happened in 2020. In these cases, herding behavior caused massive inflows and outflows into a particular asset class and in effect a tsunami was created. Herding is a reactive phenomenon (i.e., not something that people contemplate to any great degree): it just happens. When investors herd, they override their common sense and just want to "get in" or "get out" so they don't get left behind. They experience "FOMO"—fear of missing out, which is classic herding behavior. As others make money (bull market) or lose money (bear market), the investors who are *not* participating follow the crowd because they feel their economic status will fall relative to those who *are* participating. This behavior causes even more of the same behavior and bubbles begin to form causing irrational asset prices.

Explaining Individual Investor Decision Making During Market Meltdowns: Loss and Regret Aversion

Daniel Kahneman and Amos Tversky (K&T) revolutionized our understanding of individual economic decision making.[1] Importantly, K&T discovered that most people are loss averse. They estimated that avoiding loss is approximately two times as powerful as winning. More practically, it would take a win of $50 to compensate for losing $25. Therefore, most people are willing to sacrifice gain to avoid loss and this concept is known as *loss aversion*. Loss aversion compounds when stock markets are tanking. This concept explains why stocks have such a higher long-term return than bonds. Because stocks are risky, people overpay for bonds (i.e., insurance) because they fear the risk of losses in stocks. With the market down nearly 20% and the 10-year US bond below 1%, this is key evidence of this concept. In general, people prefer certainty to uncertainty even if the value of the certain choice is less than the value of the uncertain choice. K&T demonstrated that people are willing to make a much larger sacrifice for certain choices versus rational economists who believe that people are willing to make only small sacrifices in exchange for certainty.

Regret-aversion is an emotional bias in which people tend to avoid making decisions that will result in action out of fear that the decision will turn out poorly. Simply put, people try to avoid the pain of regret associated with bad decisions. Regret aversion can drive some investors to panic sell at exactly the wrong time; they fear the market will continue its slide and hit the panic sell button when markets have recently generated sharp losses. When deciding, for example, whether to sell into a market meltdown, investors' instincts indicate the potential for serious regret if the market slides further. However, in the long run, stocks have *always* recovered. Panic selling is almost *always* the wrong course of action.

Keeping Things in Perspective: Epidemics and Stock Market Performance

There are many factors that can impact stock market returns, but one concern of investors today is how the stock market will be impacted by a major epidemic or outbreak. Figure 32.2 depicts the historical

---

[1] Daniel Kahneman and Amos Tversky, "Prospect Theory: An Analysis of Decision under Risk," *Econometrica* 47 (1979): 263–291.

Figure 32.2 Market Recoveries from Epidemic Episodes
Source: Bloomberg as of 2/24/20

performance of the S&P 500 Index during several epidemics over the past 40 years. In sum, this too shall pass. Looking at the market's resiliency through numerous major epidemics gives us perspective on the benefits of investing for the long term.

Market Recovery

If history is any guide, after the market scares are over, investors should see a relatively quick recovery in the stock market (Figure 32.3). For example, at today's writing, there are numerous things the federal government is doing, such as fiscal stimulus for coronavirus. Current legislation passed injecting over $2 trillion. In addition, the FED cut rates to zero similar to the GFC aftermath. The length of the recession will determine how quickly things recover. This has become a typical response to market crises which helps tremendously to calm the markets.

Conclusion

It is easy to have a knee-jerk reaction to market losses. At Sunpointe, our team works with clients to mitigate behavioral biases during the investment process and stay invested during market upheavals, such as

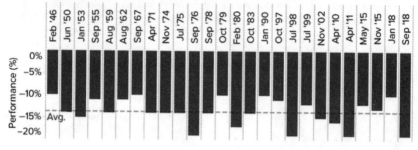

SOURCE: Goldman Sachs, CNBC research

Figure 32.3 Market Recoveries since 1946
Source: Goldman Sachs and CNBC

the upheaval of the coronavirus. In short, Sunpointe helps ensure our clients focus on rebalancing and making sure that their long-term strategic allocations always properly align with their goals and risk tolerance. While short-term volatility may be uncomfortable, it should not cause us to deviate from long-term strategic plans.

Index

NOTE: Page references in *italics* refer to boxes and figures.